W9-AZV-254

McGraw-Hill's
500
Calculus
Questions

Also in McGraw-Hill's 500 Questions Series

McGraw-Hill's

500

Calculus

Questions

Ace Your College Exams

Elliott Mendelson, PhD

New York Chicago San Francisco Lisbon London Madrid Mexico City
Milan New Delhi San Juan Seoul Singapore Sydney Toronto

ISBN   978-0-07-178963-9
MHID   0-07-178963-4

e-ISBN   978-0-07-178964-6
e-MHID   0-07-178964-2

Library of Congress Control Number 2011944579

McGraw-Hill products are available at special quantity discounts to use as premiums and sales promotions or for use in corporate training programs. To contact a representative, please e-mail us at bulksales@mcgraw-hill.com.

This book is printed on acid-free paper.

CONTENTS

INTRODUCTION

Congratulations! You've taken a big step toward college success by purchasing *McGraw-Hill's 500 Calculus Questions.* We are here to help you take the next step and prepare for your midterms, finals, and other exams so you can get the top grades you want!

This book gives you 500 questions that cover the most essential concepts in elementary and intermediate calculus and in much of advanced calculus. In the Answers section, for each problem you'll find *one way* to reach the solution. The questions and solutions will give you valuable independent practice to supplement your regular textbook and the ground you have already covered in your calculus class.

This book and the others in this series were written by expert teachers who know the subject inside and out and can indentify crucial information as well as the kinds of questions that are most likely to appear on your exams.

You might be the kind of student who spends weeks preparing for an exam. Or you might be the kind of student who puts off your exam preparation until the last minute. No matter what your preparation style, you will benefit from reviewing these 500 questions, which cover the calculus concepts you need to know to get top scores. These questions and solutions are the ideal preparation tool for any college calculus test.

If you practice with all the questions and solutions in this book, we are certain you will build the skills and confidence needed to excel on your exams. Good luck!

—The Editors of McGraw-Hill Education

McGraw-Hill's

500
Calculus
Questions

Inequalities

1. Solve $2/x < 3$.

2. Solve $\dfrac{x+4}{x-3} < 2$ (1)

3. Solve $x^2 - 6x + 5 > 0$.

4. Solve $(x - 1)^2(x + 4) < 0$.

5. Solve $(2x + 1)(x - 3)(x + 7) < 0$.

6. Solve $x > x^2$.

7. Solve $x^2 > x^3$.

8. Find all solutions of $\dfrac{1}{x} < \dfrac{1}{y}$.

Absolute Value

9. (A) Solve $|5 - 3x| < 2$.
   (B) Solve $|3x - 2| \geq 1$.
   (C) Solve $|3 - x| = x - 3$.
   (D) Solve $|2x + 3| = 4$.

10. (A) Solve $|2x - 3| = |x + 2|$.
    (B) Solve $2x - 1 = |x + 7|$.
    (C) Solve $|2x - 3| < |x + 2|$.
    (D) Solve $0 < |3x + 1| < \dfrac{1}{3}$.

11. (A) The well-known triangle inequality asserts that $|u + v| \leq |u| + |v|$. Prove by mathematical induction that, for $n \geq 2$, $|u_1 + u_2 + \cdots + u_n| \leq |u_1| + |u_2| + \cdots + |u_n|$.
    (B) Prove $|u - v| \geq ||u| - |v||$.

12. (A) Solve $\left| x + \dfrac{1}{x} \right| > 2$.

    (B) Solve $\left| x + \dfrac{1}{x} \right| < 4$.

    (C) Solve $x + 1 < |x|$.

13. Prove $|ab| = |a| \cdot |b|$.

14. (A) Solve $|3x - 2| \leq |x - 1|$.
    (B) Solve $|x - 2| + |x - 5| = 9$.
    (C) Solve $4 - x \geq |5x + 1|$.

15. Solve the inequality $|x - 1| \geq |x - 3|$.

CHAPTER 3

Lines

16. (A) Find the slope of the line through the points $(-2, 5)$ and $(7, 1)$.
    (B) Find a point-slope equation of the line through the points $(1, 3)$ and $(3, 6)$.
    (C) Write a point-slope equation of the line through the points $(1, 2)$ and $(1, 3)$.
    (D) Find a point-slope equation of the line going through the point $(1, 3)$ with slope 5.
    (E) Find the slope-intercept equation of the line through the points $(2, 4)$ and $(4, 8)$.

17. Show that every line has an equation of the form $Ax + By = C$, where A and B are not both 0, and that, conversely, every such equation is the equation of a line.

18. Find an equation of the line L through $(-1, 4)$ and parallel to the line M with the equation $3x + 4y = 2$.

19. Show that the lines parallel to a line $Ax + By = C$ are those lines having equations of the form $Ax + By = E$ for some E. (Assume that $B \neq 0$.)

20. Show that any line that is neither vertical nor horizontal and does not pass through the origin has an equation of the form $\frac{x}{a} + \frac{y}{b} = 1$, where b is the y-intercept and a is the x-intercept (Figure 3.1).

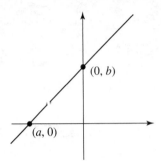

Figure 3.1

21. Find the slope-intercept equation of the line M through $(1, 4)$ that is perpendicular to the line L with the equation $2x - 6y = 5$.

22. Show that two lines, L with equation $A_1 x + B_1 y = C_1$ and M with equation $A_2 x + B_2 y = C_2$, are parallel if and only if their coefficients of x and y are proportional; that is, there is a nonzero number r such that $A_2 = rA_1$ and $B_2 = rB_1$.

23. (A) Use slopes to determine whether the points $A(4, 1)$, $B(7, 3)$, and $C(3, 9)$ are the vertices of a right triangle.
    (B) Determine k so that the points $A(7, 5)$, $B(-1, 2)$, and $C(k, 0)$ are the vertices of a right triangle with right angle at B.

24. (A) Find the midpoint of the line segment between $(2, 5)$ and $(-1, 3)$.
    (B) A triangle has vertices $A(1, 2)$, $B(8, 1)$, and $C(2, 3)$. Find the equation of the median from A to the midpoint M of the opposite side.
    (C) For the triangle of Question 24(B), find an equation of the altitude from B to the opposite side $\overleftrightarrow{AC}$.

25. If a line L has the equation $3x + 2y = 4$, prove that a point $P(x, y)$ is above L if and only if $3x + 2y > 4$.

26. (A) Describe geometrically the family of lines $y = mx + 2$.
    (B) Describe geometrically the family of lines $y = 3x + b$.

27. Prove by use of coordinates that the altitudes of any triangle meet at a common point.

28. Using coordinates, prove that the figure obtained by joining midpoints of consecutive sides of a quadrilateral $ABCD$ is a parallelogram.

29. Using coordinates, prove that, if the medians $\overline{AM_1}$ and $\overline{BM_2}$ of $\triangle ABC$ are equal, then $\overline{CA} = \overline{CB}$.

30. Find the distance from the point $(1, 2)$ to the line $3x - 4y = 10$.

31. Find the equations of the lines through $(4, -2)$ and at a perpendicular distance of 2 units from the origin.

32. Temperature is usually measured either in degrees Fahrenheit or Celsius. The relation between Fahrenheit and Celsius temperatures is given by a linear equation. The freezing point of water is $0°$ Celsius or $32°$ Fahrenheit, and the boiling point of water is $100°$ Celsius or $212°$ Fahrenheit. Find an equation giving Fahrenheit temperature y in terms of Celsius temperature x.

CHAPTER 4

Circles

33. Write the standard equation for a circle with center at (a, b) and radius r.

34. Identify the graph of the equation $x^2 + y^2 - 12x + 20y + 15 = 0$.

35. Find the standard equation of a circle with radius 13 that passes through the origin and whose center has abscissa -12.

36. Find the standard equation of the circle with center at $(1, 3)$ and tangent to the line $5x - 12y - 8 = 0$.

37. Let $x^2 + y^2 + C_1x + D_1y + E_1 = 0$ be the equation of a circle $\mathscr{C}_1$, and $x^2 + y^2 + C_2x + D_2y + E_2 = 0$ be the equation of a circle $\mathscr{C}_2$ that intersects $\mathscr{C}_1$ at two points. Show that, as k varies over all real numbers $\neq -1$, the equation $(x^2 + y^2 + C_1x + D_1y + E_1) + k(x^2 + y^2 + C_2x + D_2y + E_2) = 0$ yields all circles through the intersection points of $\mathscr{C}_1$ and $\mathscr{C}_2$ except $\mathscr{C}_2$ itself.

38. Find an equation of the circle that contains the point $(3, 1)$ and passes through the points of intersection of the two circles $x^2 + y^2 - x - y - 2 = 0$ and $x^2 + y^2 + 4x - 4y - 8 = 0$.

CHAPTER 5

Functions and Their Graphs

39. Find the domain and range of each of the functions determined by the formulas (A) through (H) and draw the graphs of those functions.

(A) $H(x) = \sqrt{4 - x^2}$.

(B) $V(x) = |x - 1|$.

(C) $h(x) = \dfrac{1}{x}$.

(D) $F(x) = \dfrac{1}{x - 1}$.

(E) $K(x) = -\tfrac{1}{2}x^3$.

(F) $G(x) = \dfrac{x^2 - 4}{x + 2}$.

(G) $H(x) = \begin{cases} x & \text{if} & x \le 2 \\ 4 & \text{if} & x > 2 \end{cases}$.

(H) $f(x) = \dfrac{|x|}{x}$.

40. (A) Is Figure 5.1 the graph of a function?

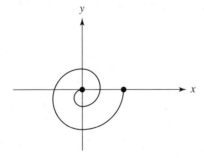

Figure 5.1

(B)   Is Figure 5.2 the graph of a function?

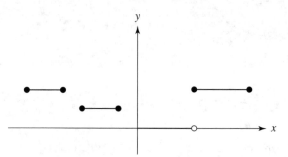

Figure 5.2

41.   Specify the domain and range of each of the functions defined in (A) through (E) below.

(A) $f(x) = \dfrac{1}{(x-2)(x-3)}$.

(B) $g(x) = \dfrac{1}{\sqrt{1-x^2}}$.

(C) $h(x) = \begin{cases} x+1 & \text{if} \quad -1 < x < 1 \\ 2 & \text{if} \quad 1 \le x \end{cases}$

(D) $F(x) = \begin{cases} x-1 & \text{if} \quad 0 \le x \le 3 \\ x-2 & \text{if} \quad 3 < x < 4 \end{cases}$.

(E) $G(x) = |x| - x$.

42.   Specify the domain and range of each of the functions defined in (A) through (C) below.

(A) $f(x) = \sqrt{x}$ for all nonnegative x.

(B) $f(x) = x^2$ for all x.

(C) $f(x) = \dfrac{1}{x}$ for all nonzero x.

43. For each of the functions $f(x)$ defined in (A) through (E) below, evaluate the expression $\dfrac{f(x+h)-f(x)}{h}$.

    (A) $f(x)=x^2-2x$.

    (B) $f(x)=x+4$.

    (C) $f(x)=x^3+1$.

    (D) $f(x)=\sqrt{x}$.

    (E) $f(x)=\dfrac{1}{x}$.

44. For each of the one-one functions $f(x)$ in (A) and (B), find a formula for the inverse function $f^{-1}(y)$.

    (A) $f(x)=2x+1$.

    (B) $f(x)=x^3$.

45. Find all real roots of each of the following polynomials.

    (A) x^4-10x^2+9.

    (B) $x^3+2x^2-16x-32$.

    (C) $x^3-9x^2+26x+24$.

    (D) x^3-5x-2.

CHAPTER 6

Limits

46. Define $\lim\limits_{x \to a} f(x) = L$.

47. (A) Find $\lim\limits_{u \to 5} \dfrac{u^2 - 25}{u - 5}$.

(B) Find $\lim\limits_{x \to 1} \dfrac{x^3 - 1}{x - 1}$.

(C) Find $\lim\limits_{u \to 0} \dfrac{5u^2 - 4}{u + 1}$.

(D) Find $\lim\limits_{x \to 4} \dfrac{x^2 - x - 12}{x - 4}$.

(E) Find $\lim\limits_{x \to 2} \dfrac{x^3 - 5x^2 + 2x - 4}{x^2 - 3x + 3}$.

(F) Find $\lim\limits_{x \to 0} \dfrac{\sqrt{x + 3} - \sqrt{3}}{x}$.

(G) Find $\lim\limits_{x \to 3} \dfrac{1}{(x - 3)^2}$.

(H) Find $\lim\limits_{x \to 2} \dfrac{3}{x - 2}$.

48. (A) Evaluate $\lim\limits_{x \to +\infty} (2x^{11} - 5x^6 + 3x^2 + 1)$.

(B) Evaluate $\lim\limits_{x \to -\infty} (2x^3 - 12x^2 + x - 7)$.

(C) Find $\lim\limits_{x \to +\infty} \dfrac{2x + 5}{x^2 - 7x + 3}$.

(D) Find $\lim\limits_{x\to+\infty} \dfrac{3x^3 - 4x + 2}{7x^3 + 5}$.

(E) Evaluate $\lim\limits_{x\to+\infty} \dfrac{4x^5 - 1}{3x^3 + 7}$.

(F) Find $\lim\limits_{x\to+\infty} \dfrac{4x - 1}{\sqrt{x^2 + 2}}$.

(G) Evaluate $\lim\limits_{x\to+\infty} \dfrac{7x - 4}{\sqrt{x^3 + 5}}$.

(H) Evaluate $\lim\limits_{x\to-\infty} \dfrac{3x^3 + 2}{\sqrt{x^4 - 2}}$.

49. (A) Find any vertical and horizontal asymptotes of the graph of the function $f(x) = (4x - 5)/(3x + 2)$.

(B) Find the vertical and horizontal asymptotes of the graph of the function $f(x) = (2x + 3)/\sqrt{x^2 - 2x - 3}$.

(C) Find the vertical and horizontal asymptotes of the graph of the function $f(x) = \sqrt{x + 1} - \sqrt{x}$.

50. Evaluate $\lim\limits_{x\to 4^+} \dfrac{3}{x - 4}$ and $\lim\limits_{x\to 4^-} \dfrac{3}{x - 4}$.

51. Evaluate $\lim\limits_{x\to 3^+} \dfrac{1}{x^2 - 7x + 12}$ and $\lim\limits_{x\to 3^-} \dfrac{1}{x^2 - 7x + 12}$.

52. Find $\lim\limits_{h\to 0} \dfrac{f(x + h) - f(x)}{h}$ when $f(x) = 4x^2 - x$.

53. Find $\lim\limits_{h\to 0} \dfrac{f(x + h) - f(x)}{h}$ when $f(x) = \sqrt{2x}$.

54. Evaluate $\lim\limits_{x\to 2} \dfrac{\sqrt{x^2 + 5} - 3}{x^2 - 2x}$.

55. (A) Let $f(x) = a_n x^n + a_{n-1} x^{n-1} + \cdots + a_1 x + a_0$ with $a_n > 0$. Prove that

$$\lim_{x \to +\infty} f(x) = +\infty.$$

(B) If $f(x) = \dfrac{a_n x^n + \cdots + a_1 x + a_0}{b_n x^n + \cdots + b_1 x + b_0}$, with $a_n \neq 0$ and $b_n \neq 0$, show that

$$\lim_{x \to \pm\infty} f(x) = \frac{a_n}{b_n}.$$

(C) If $f(x) = \dfrac{a_n x^n + \cdots + a_1 x + a_0}{b_k x^k + \cdots + b_1 x + b_0}$ with $a_n > 0$ and $b_k > 0$, prove that

$$\lim_{x \to +\infty} f(x) = +\infty \text{ if } n > k.$$

(D) If $f(x) = \dfrac{a_n x^n + \cdots + a_1 x + a_0}{b_k x^k + \cdots + b_1 x + b_0}$ with $a_n > 0$ and $b_k > 0$, and $n < k$, prove

that $\lim_{k \to \pm\infty} f(x) = 0.$

(E) Find $\lim\limits_{x \to \pm\infty} \dfrac{7x^3 + 2x^2}{4x^3 - x}$.

(F) Find $\lim\limits_{x \to +\infty} \dfrac{x^4 + 2x - 3}{x^2 + 100x}$.

(G) Find $\lim\limits_{x \to \pm\infty} \dfrac{4x^3 + 20x^2}{x^4 - 1}$.

(H) Find $\lim \dfrac{3x - 4}{\sqrt[3]{x^2 - 1}}$.

(I) Find $\lim\limits_{x \to +\infty} \dfrac{2x + 1}{\sqrt[3]{x^3 - 2}}$.

CHAPTER 7

Continuity

56. Define: $f(x)$ is continuous at $x = a$.

57. (A) Find the points of discontinuity (if any) of the function $f(x)$ whose graph is shown in Figure 7.1.

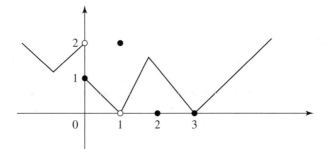

Figure 7.1

(B) Determine the points of discontinuity (if any) of the function $f(x)$ such that $f(x) = x^2$ if $x \leq 0$ and $f(x) = x$ if $x > 0$.

(C) Determine the points of discontinuity (if any) of the function $f(x)$ such that $f(x) = 1$ if $x \geq 0$ and $f(x) = -1$ if $x < 0$. (See Figure 7.2.)

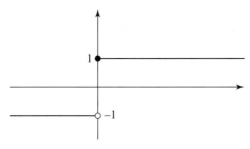

Figure 7.2

(D) Determine the points of discontinuity (if any) of the function $f(x)$ such that $f(x) = \dfrac{x^2 - 4}{x + 2}$ if $x \neq -2$ and $f(x) = 0$ if $x = -2$. (See Figure 7.3.)

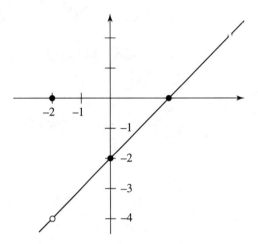

Figure 7.3

(E) Find the points of discontinuity of the function $f(x) = \dfrac{x^2 - 1}{x - 1}$.

(F) Find the points of discontinuity (if any) of the function $f(x)$ such that $f(x) = \dfrac{x^2 - 9}{x - 3}$ for $x \neq 3$ and $f(x) = 6$ for $x = 3$.

(G) Find the points of discontinuity (if any) of the function $f(x)$ such that

$$f(x) = \begin{cases} x + 1 & \text{if } x \geq 2 \\ 2x - 1 & \text{if } 1 < x < 2. \\ x - 1 & \text{if } x \leq 1 \end{cases}$$

(See Figure 7.4.)

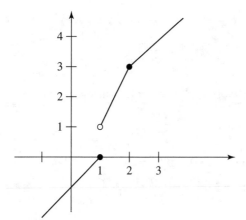

Figure 7.4

(H) Find the points of discontinuity (if any) of $f(x) = \dfrac{3x + 3}{x^2 - 3x - 4}$, and
write an equation for each vertical and horizontal asymptote of the
graph of f.

58. Define: (A) $f(x)$ is continuous on the left at $x = a$. (B) $f(x)$ is continuous
on the right at $x = a$.

59. Consider the function $f(x)$ graphed in Figure 7.5. At all points of discontinuity, determine whether $f(x)$ is continuous on the left and whether $f(x)$ is
continuous on the right.

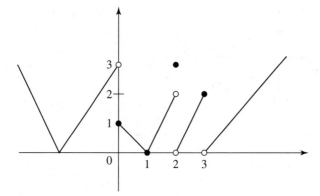

Figure 7.5

60. Show that the function $f(x) = 2x^3 - 4x^2 + 5x - 4$ has a zero between $x = 1$ and $x = 2$.

61. Verify the intermediate value theorem in the case of the function $f(x) = \sqrt{16 - x^2}$, the interval $[-4, 0]$, and the intermediate. value $\sqrt{7}$.

62. (A) Is the function f such that $f(x) = \dfrac{1}{x}$ for $x > 0$ and $f(0) = 0$ continuous over $[0, 1]$?

(B) Consider the function f such that $f(x) = 2x$ if $0 \le x \le 1$ and $f(x) = x - 1$ if $x > 1$. Is f continuous over $[0, 1]$?

(C) Is the function of part (B) continuous over $[1, 2]$?

63. Let

$$f(x) = \begin{cases} 3x^2 - 1 & \text{if } x < 0 \\ cx + d & \text{if } 0 \le x \le 1 \\ \sqrt{x+8} & \text{if } x > 1 \end{cases}$$

Determine c and d so that f is continuous everywhere (as indicated in Figure 7.6).

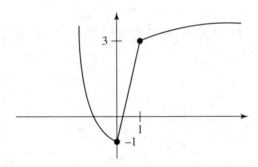

Figure 7.6

CHAPTER **8**

The Derivative

64. (A) Using the Δ-definition, show that the derivative of any linear function $f(x) = Ax + B$ is $f'(x) = A$.
    (B) Using the Δ-definition, find the derivative $f'(x)$ of the function $f(x) = 2x^2 - 3x + 5$.
    (C) Using the Δ-definition, find the derivative $f'(x)$ of the function $f(x) = x^3$.

65. (A) State the formula for the derivative of an arbitrary polynomial function $f(x) = a_n x^n + a_{n-1} x^{n-1} + \cdots + a_2 x^2 + a_1 x + a_0$.
    (B) Write the derivative of the function $f(x) = 7x^5 - 3x^4 + 6x^2 + 3x + 4$.

66. (A) Given functions $f(x)$ and $g(x)$, state the formulas for the derivatives of the sum $f(x) + g(x)$, the product $f(x) \cdot g(x)$, and the quotient $f(x)/g(x)$.
    (B) Using the product rule, find the derivative of $f(x) = (5x^3 - 20x + 13)(4x^6 + 2x^5 - 7x^2 + 2x)$.
    (C) Using the formula from Question 66(A), find the derivative of
    $$G(x) = \frac{3x - 2}{x^2 + 7}.$$
    (D) Using formulas, find the derivatives of the following functions:
    (i) $-8x^5 + \sqrt{3}x^3 + 2\pi x^2 - 12$, (ii) $2x^{51} + 3x^{12} - 14x^2 + \sqrt[3]{7}x + \sqrt{5}$.

67. (A) Find the slope-intercept equation of the tangent line to the graph of the function $f(x) = 4x^3 - 7x^2$ at the point corresponding to $x = 3$.
    (B) At what point(s) of the graph of $y = x^5 + 4x - 3$ does the tangent line to the graph also pass through the point $B(0, 1)$?

68. Find the slope-intercept equation of the normal line to the graph of $y = x^3 - x^2$ at the point where $x = 1$.

69. Evaluate $\lim\limits_{h \to 0} \dfrac{5\left(\frac{1}{3}+h\right)^4 - 5\left(\frac{1}{3}\right)^4}{h}$.

70. Find the points on the curve $y = \dfrac{1}{3}x^3 - x$ where the tangent line is parallel to the line $y = 3x$.

71. (A) Show that a differentiable function $f(x)$ is continuous.
   (B) Show that the converse of part (A) is false.

72. Let $f(x) = 3x^3 - 11x^2 - 15x + 63$. Find all points on the graph of f where the tangent line is horizontal.

73. Determine the points at which the function $f(x) = |x - 3|$ is differentiable.

CHAPTER 9

The Chain Rule

74. If $f(x) = x^2 + 2x - 5$ and $g(x) = x^3$, find formulas for the composite functions $f \circ g$ and $g \circ f$.

75. Write the function $\sqrt{3x - 5}$ as the composition of two functions.

76. If $f(x) = 2x$ and $g(x) = 1/(x - 1)$, find all solutions of the equation $(f \circ g)(x) = (g \circ f)(x)$.

77. (A) Write the chain rule formula for the derivative of $f \circ g$.

(B) If $y = F(u)$ and $u = G(x)$, then we can write $y = F(G(x))$. Write the chain rule formula for dy/dx, where we think of y as a function of x.

(C) Find the derivative of $(x^3 - 2x^2 + 7x - 3)^4$.

(D) Find the derivatives of $\dfrac{1}{(3x^2 + 5)^4}$.

(E) Find the derivative of $\sqrt{2x + 7}$.

(F) Find the derivative of $\left(\dfrac{x + 2}{x - 3}\right)^3$.

78. Find the derivative of $(4x^2 - 3)^2(x + 5)^3$.

79. Find the slope-intercept equation of the tangent line to the graph of $y = \dfrac{\sqrt{x - 1}}{x^2 + 1}$ at the point $\left(2, \dfrac{1}{5}\right)$.

80. Find the slope-intercept equation of the normal line to the curve $y = \sqrt{x^2 + 16}$ at the point $(3, 5)$.

81. If $y = x^3 - 2$ and $x = 3z^2 + 5$, then y can be considered a function of z. Express $\dfrac{dy}{dz}$ in terms of z.

82. Let F and G be differentiable functions such that $F(3) = 5$, $G(3) = 7$, $F'(3) = 13$, $G'(3) = 6$, $F'(7) = 2$, $G'(7) = 0$. If $H(x) = F(G(x))$, find $H'(3)$.

83. Find the derivations of $F(x) = \sqrt[3]{(1 + x^2)^4}$.

84. A point moves along the curve $y = x^3 - 3x + 5$ so that $x = \dfrac{1}{2}\sqrt{t} + 3$, where t is time. At what rate is y changing when $t = 4$?

CHAPTER 10

Trigonometric Functions and Their Derivatives

85. Define radian measure, that is, describe an angle of 1 radian.

86. Give the equations relating degree measure and radian measure of angles.

87. Give the radian measure of angles of 30°, 45°, 60°, 90°, 120°, 135°, 180°, 270°, and 360°.

88. Give the degree measure of angles of $3\pi/5$ radians and $5\pi/6$ radians.

89. In a circle of radius 10 inches, what arc length along the circumference is intercepted by a central angle of $\pi/5$ radians?

90. Draw a picture of the rotation determining an angle of $-\pi/3$ radians.

91. Give the definition of $\sin\theta$ and $\cos\theta$.

92. State the values of $\cos\theta$ and $\sin\theta$ for
$\theta = 0, \pi/6, \pi/4, \pi/3, \pi/2, \pi, 3\pi/2, 2\pi, 9\pi/4$.

93. Evaluate:
(A) $\cos(-\pi/6)$.
(B) $\sin(-\pi/6)$.
(C) $\cos(2\pi/3)$.
(D) $\sin(2\pi/3)$.

94. Sketch the graph of the cosine and sine functions.

95. Sketch the graph of $y = \cos 3x$.

96. Sketch the graph of $y = 1.5 \sin 4x$.

97. (A) Calculate $\lim\limits_{x \to 0} \dfrac{\sin 3x}{x}$.

(B) Calculate $\lim\limits_{x \to 0} \dfrac{\sin 2x}{\sin 3x}$.

(C) Calculate $\lim\limits_{x \to 0} \dfrac{1 - \cos x}{x}$.

98. (A) Using the Δ-definition, calculate $\dfrac{d}{dx}(\sin x)$.

(B) Calculate $\dfrac{d}{dx}(\cos x)$ from the known derivative of $\sin x$.

(C) Calculate $\dfrac{d}{dx}(\sin 3x)$.

(D) Calculate $\dfrac{d}{dx}(\cos^2 x)$.

(E) Calculate $\dfrac{d}{dx}(\sqrt{\sin x})$.

99. Find an equation of the tangent line to the graph of $y = \sin^2 x$ at the point where $x = \pi/3$.

100. (A) Derive the formula $\dfrac{d}{dx}(\tan x) = \sec^2 x$.

(B) Find an equation of the tangent line to the curve $y = \tan^2 x$ at the point $(\pi/3, 3)$.

(C) Show that $\dfrac{d}{dx}(\sec x) = \sec x \tan x$.

101. Find an equation of the normal line to the curve $y = 3 \sec^2 x$ at the point $(\pi/6, 4)$.

102. Evaluate $\lim\limits_{x \to 0} \dfrac{\tan x}{x}$.

103. At what values of x does the graph of $y = \sec x$ have a horizontal tangent?

CHAPTER 11

Rolle's Theorem, the Mean Value Theorem, and the Sign of the Derivative

104. State Rolle's theorem.

In Questions 105 through 107, determine whether the hypotheses of Rolle's theorem hold for the function $f(x)$ in the given interval, and, if they do, verify the conclusion.

105. $f(x) = x^2 - 2x - 3$ on $[-1, 3]$.

106. $f(x) = \dfrac{x^2 - x - 6}{x - 1}$ on $[-2, 3]$.

107. $f(x) = x^{2/3} - 2x^{1/3}$ on $[0, 8]$.

108. (A) State the mean value theorem.

For parts (B), (C), and (D), determine whether the hypotheses of the mean value theorem hold for the function $f(x)$ on the given interval, and, if they do, find a value c satisfying the conclusion of the theorem.

(B) $f(x) = 2x + 3$ on $[1, 4]$.
(C) $f(x) = 3x^2 - 5x + 1$ on $[2, 5]$.
(D) $f(x) = x^{3/4}$ on $[0, 16]$.

109. Prove that, if $f'(x) > 0$ for all x in the open interval (a, b), then $f(x)$ is an increasing function on (a, b).

110. For each function $f(x)$, determine where $f(x)$ is increasing and where it is decreasing.
  (A) $f(x) = 3x + 1$.
  (B) $f(x) = x^2 - 4x + 7$.
  (C) $f(x) = x^3 - 9x^2 + 15x - 3$.
  (D) $f(x) = x + 1/x$.

111. Consider the polynomial $f(x) = 5x^3 - 2x^2 + 3x - 4$. Prove that $f(x)$ has a zero between 0 and 1 that is the only zero of $f(x)$.

112. Show that $x^3 + 2x - 5 = 0$ has exactly one real root.

113. (A) If $f'(x) = 0$ throughout an interval $[a, b]$, prove that $f(x)$ is constant on that interval.
  (B) If $f'(x) = g'(x)$ for all x in an interval $[a, b]$, show that there is a constant K such that $f(x) = g(x) + K$ for all x in $[a, b]$.

CHAPTER 12

Higher-Order Derivatives and Implicit Differentiation

114. Find all derivatives $y^{(n)}$ of the function $y = \pi x^3 - 7x$.

115. Find all derivatives $y^{(n)}$ of the function $y = 1/(3 + x)$.

116. Find all derivatives $y^{(n)}$ of the function $y = \sin x$.

117. On the circle $x^2 + y^2 = a^2$, find y''.

118. If $x^2 + 2xy + 3y^2 = 2$, find y' and y'' when $y = 1$.

119. Evaluate y'' on the ellipse $b^2x^2 + a^2y^2 = a^2b^2$.

CHAPTER 13

Maxima and Minima

120. State the second-derivative test for relative extrema.

121. State the first-derivative test for relative extrema.

122. (A) Find the critical numbers of $f(x) = 5 - 2x + x^2$, and determine whether they yield relative maxima, relative minima, or inflection points.

(B) Find the critical numbers of $f(x) = x^3 - 5x^2 - 8x + 3$, and determine whether they yield relative maxima, relative minima, or inflection points.

(C) Find the critical numbers of $f(x) = x(x-1)^3$, and determine whether they yield relative maxima, relative minima, or inflection points.

(D) Find the critical numbers of $f(x) = \sin x - x$, and determine whether they yield relative maxima, relative minima, or inflection points.

123. Find the critical numbers of $f(x) = (x-1)^{2/3}$, and determine whether they yield relative maxima, relative minima, or inflection points.

124. (A) Describe a procedure for finding the absolute maximum and absolute minimum values of a continuous function $f(x)$ on a closed interval $[a, b]$.

(B) Find the absolute maximum and minimum of the function $f(x) = 4x^2 - 7x + 3$ on the interval $[-2, 3]$.

(C) Find the absolute maximum and minimum of $f(x) = 4x^3 - 8x^2 + 1$ on the closed interval $[-1, 1]$.

(D) Find the absolute maximum and minimum of $f(x) = x^4 - 2x^3 - x^2 - 4x + 3$ on the interval $[0, 4]$.

(E) Find the absolute maximum and minimum of $f(x) = x^3/(x + 2)$ on the interval $[-1, 1]$.

(F) Find the absolute extrema of $f(x) = \sin x + x$ on $[0, 2\pi]$.

125. Show that $f(x) = (x - a_1)^2 + (x - a_2)^2 + \cdots + (x - a_n)^2$ has an absolute minimum when $x = (a_1 + a_2 + \cdots + a_n)/n$. (In words: the least-squares estimate of a finite set of numbers is their arithmetic mean.)

126. (A) Find the absolute maximum and minimum (if they exist) of
$f(x) = x/(x^2 + 1)^{3/2}$ on $[0, +\infty)$.

(B) Find the absolute maximum and minimum of $f(x) = 2 \sin x + \sin 2x$ on $[0, 2\pi]$.

(C) Find the absolute maximum and minimum (if they exist) of
$f(x) = (x + 2)/(x - 1)$.

CHAPTER 14

Related Rates

127. The top of a 25-foot ladder leaning against a vertical wall is slipping down the wall at the rate of 1 foot per second. How fast is the bottom of the ladder slipping along the ground when the bottom of the ladder is 7 feet away from the base of the wall?

128. A cylindrical tank of radius 10 feet is being filled with wheat at the rate of 314 cubic feet per minute. How fast is the depth of the wheat increasing? (The volume of a cylinder is $\pi r^2 h$, where r is its radius and h is its height.)

129. A 5-foot girl is walking toward a 20-foot lamppost at the rate of 6 feet per second. How fast is the tip of her shadow (cast by the lamp) moving?

130. A rocket is shot vertically upward with an initial velocity of 400 feet per second. Its height s after t seconds is $s = 400t - 16t^2$. How fast is the distance changing from the rocket to an observer on the ground 1,800 feet away from the launching site, when the rocket is still rising and is 2,400 feet above the ground?

131. A plane flying parallel to the ground at a height of 4 kilometers passes over a radar station R (Figure 14.1). A short time later, the radar equipment reveals that the distance between the plane and the station is 5 kilometers and that the distance between the plane and the station is increasing at a rate of 300 kilometers per hour. At that moment, how fast is the plane moving horizontally?

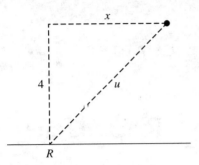

Figure 14.1

132. A boat passes a fixed buoy at 9 A.M. heading due west at 3 miles per hour. Another boat passes the same buoy at 10 A.M. heading due north at 5 miles per hour. How fast is the distance between the boats changing at 11:30 A.M.?

133. A revolving beacon is situated 3,600 feet off a straight shore. If the beacon turns at 4π radians per minute, how fast does its beam sweep along the shore at its nearest point A?

CHAPTER 15

Curve Sketching (Graphs)

When sketching a graph, show all relative extrema, inflection points, and asymptotes. Indicate concavity, and suggest the behavior at infinity.

In Questions 134 and 135, determine the intervals where the graphs of the following functions are concave upward and where they are concave downward. Find all inflection points and draw the graphs.

134. $f(x) = x^3 + 15x^2 + 6x + 1$.

135. $f(x) = x^4 + 18x^3 + 120x^2 + x + 1$.

In Questions 136 through 141, find the critical numbers and determine whether they yield relative maxima, relative minima, or inflection points, or none of these.

136. $f(x) = x^3 - 5x^2 - 8x + 3$.

137. $f(x) = x^2/(x^2 + 1)$.

138. $f(x) = x^4 + 4x^3$.

139. $f(x) = 3x^5 - 20x^3$.

140. $f(x) = x^2 + 2/x$.

141. $f(x) = (x^2 - 3)/x^3$.

142. If for all x, $f'(x) > 0$ and $f''(x) < 0$, which of the curves in Figure 15.1 could be part of the graph of f?

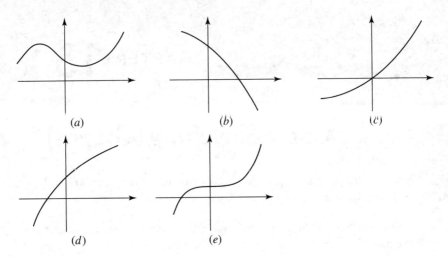

(a)   (b)   (c)

(d)   (e)

Figure 15.1

In Questions 143 through 147, sketch the graphs of the given functions.

143. $f(x) = \sin^2 x.$

144. $f(x) = \sin x + \cos x.$

145. $f(x) = \dfrac{x}{x^2 - 1}.$

146. $f(x) = \dfrac{3}{5}x^{5/3} - 3x^{2/3}.$

147. $f(x) = 3x^5 - 5x^3 + 1.$

CHAPTER 16

Applied Maximum and Minimum Problems

148. Find the point(s) on the hyperbola $x^2 - y^2 = 2$ closest to the point $(0, 1)$ (Figure 16.1).

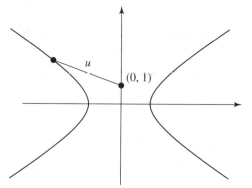

Figure 16.1

149. Find the dimensions of the closed cylindrical can that will have a capacity of k units of volume and will use the minimum amount of material. Find the ratio of the height h to the radius r of the top and bottom.

150. A man at a point P on the shore of a circular lake of radius 1 mile wants to reach the point Q on the shore diametrically opposite P (Figure 16.2). He can row 1.5 miles per hour and walk 3 miles per hour. At what angle θ $(0 \le \theta \le \pi/2)$ to the diameter PQ should he row in order to minimize the time required to reach Q?

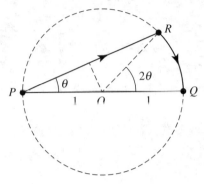

Figure 16.2

151. A wire 16 feet long has to be formed into a rectangle. What dimensions should the rectangle have to maximize the area?

152. A rectangular box with an open top is to be formed from a rectangular piece of cardboard that is 3 inches × 8 inches (Figure 16.3). What size square should be cut from each corner to form the box with maximum volume? (The cardboard is folded along the dotted lines to form the box.)

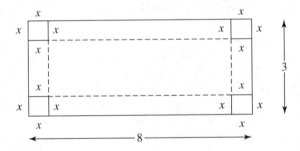

Figure 16.3

153. A telephone company has to run a line from a point A on one side of a river to another point B that is on the other side, 5 miles down from the point opposite A (Figure 16.4). The river is uniformly 12 miles wide. The company can run the line along the shoreline to a point C and then run the line under the river to B. The cost of laying the line along the shore is $1000 per mile, and the cost of laying it underwater is twice as great. Where should the point C be located to minimize the cost?

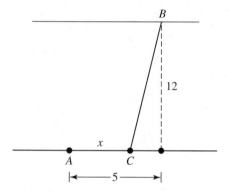

Figure 16.4

CHAPTER 17

Rectilinear Motion

154. (A) The equation of the free fall of an object (under the influence of gravity alone) is $s = s_0 + v_0 t - 16t^2$, where s_0 is the initial position and v_0 is the initial velocity at time $t = 0$. (We assume that the s-axis is directed upward away from the earth, along the vertical line on which the object moves, with $s = 0$ at the earth's surface. s is measured in feet and t in seconds.) Show that, if an object is released from rest at any given height, it will have dropped $16t^2$ feet after t seconds.

  (B) How many seconds does it take the object released from rest to fall 64 feet?

  (C) A rock is dropped down a well that is 256 feet deep. When will it hit the bottom of the well?

  (D) Assuming that one story of a building is 10 feet, with what speed, in miles per hour, does an object dropped from the top of a 40-story building hit the ground?

155. An automobile moves along a straight highway, with its position s given by $s = 12t^3 - 18t^2 + 9t - 1.5$ (s in feet, t in seconds). When is the car moving to the right, when to the left, and where and when does it change direction?

156. A particle moves along the x-axis according to the equation $x = 10t - 2t^2$. What is the total distance covered by the particle between $t = 0$ and $t = 3$?

157. A rocket was shot straight up from the ground. What must its initial velocity have been if it returned to earth in 20 seconds?

158. Two particles move along the x-axis. Their positions $f(t)$ and $g(t)$ are given by $f(t) = 6t - t^2$ and $g(t) = t^2 - 4t$.
(A) When do they have the same position?
(B) When do they have the same velocity?
(C) When they have the same position, are they moving in the same direction?

159. A particle moving on a line is at position $s = t^3 - 6t^2 + 9t - 4$ at time t. At which time(s) t, if any, does it change direction?

160. (A) A ball is thrown vertically upward. Its height s (in feet) after t seconds is given by $s = 40t - 16t^2$. Find (i) when the ball hits the ground, (ii) the instantaneous velocity at $t = 1$, and (iii) the maximum height.
(B) An object is thrown straight up from the ground with an initial velocity v_0 feet per second. Show that the time taken on the upward flight is equal to the time taken on the way down.
(C) Under the conditions of Question 160(B), show that the object hits the ground with the same speed at which it was initially thrown.

161. A stone is dropped from the roof of a building 256 feet high. Two seconds later a second stone is thrown downward from the roof of the same building with an initial velocity of v_0 feet per second. If both stones hit the ground at the same time, what is v_0?

CHAPTER 18

Approximation by Differentials

162. (A) State the approximation principle for a differentiable function $f(x)$.

In Questions 162(B) and (C), estimate the value of the given quantity.

(B) $\sqrt{51}$
(C) $\sqrt[3]{123}$

163. If the side of a cube is measured with an error of at most 3 percent, estimate the percentage error in the volume of the cube.

164. Assume, contrary to fact, that the earth is a perfect sphere, with a radius of 4,000 miles. The volume of ice at the north and south poles is estimated to be about 8,000,000 cubic miles. If this ice were melted and if the resulting water were distributed uniformly over the globe, approximately what would be the depth of the added water at any point on the earth?

165. Let $y = x^{3/2}$. When $x = 4$ and $dx = 2$, find the value of dy.

166. A cubical box is to be built so that it holds 125 cm^3. How precisely should the edge be made so that the volume will be correct to within 3 cm^3?

167. Show that the relative error in the nth power of a number is about n times the relative error in the number.

CHAPTER **19**

Antiderivatives (Indefinite Integrals)

168. (A) Evaluate $\int (g(x))^r \, g'(x) \, dx$.

(B) Evaluate $\int x^r \, dx$ for $r \neq -1$.

(C) Evaluate $\int (3 \sin x + 5 \cos x) \, dx$.

(D) Find $\int (7 \sec^2 x - \sec x \tan x) \, dx$.

(E) Evaluate $\int (\csc^2 x + 3x^2) \, dx$.

169. (A) Evaluate $\int \sqrt{7x + 4} \, dx$.

(B) Evaluate $\int \dfrac{\cos 3x}{\sin^2 3x} \, dx$.

170. A particle moves along the x-axis with acceleration $a = 2t - 3$ feet per second square. At time $t = 0$ it is at the origin and moving with a speed of 4 ft/s in the positive direction. Find formulas for its velocity v and position s, and determine where it changes direction and where it is moving to the left.

171. A motorist applies the brakes on a car moving at 45 miles per hour on a straight road, and the brakes cause a constant deceleration of 22 feet per second square. In how many seconds will the car stop, and how many feet will the car have traveled after the time the brakes were applied?

172. Suppose that a particle moves along the x-axis, and its velocity at time t is given by $v = t^2 - t - 2$ for $1 \le t \le 4$. Find the total distance traveled in the period from $t = 1$ to $t = 4$.

173. Evaluate $\int \sec^5 x \tan x \, dx$.

174. Compute $\int \cos^2 x \, dx$.

CHAPTER 20

The Definite Integral and the Fundamental Theorem of Calculus

175. Show that $\int_0^b x \, dx = \dfrac{b^2}{2}$ by the direct definition of the integral.

176. For the function f graphed in Figure 20.1, express $\int_0^5 f(x) \, dx$ in terms of the areas A_1, A_2, and A_3.

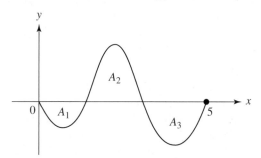

Figure 20.1

In Questions 177 and 179, evaluate the indicated definite integrals. In Question 178, find the definite integrals of the indicated functions on the given intervals.

177. (A) $\displaystyle\int_{-1}^3 (3x^2 - 2x + 1) \, dx$.

(B) $\displaystyle\int_0^{\pi/4} \cos x \, dx$.

178. (A) $f(x) = \sin x$, $a = \pi/6$, $b = \pi/3$.
 (B) $f(x) = x^2 + 4x$, $a = 0$, $b = 3$.
 (C) $f(x) = \sin^2 x \cos x$, $a = 0$, $b = \pi/2$.

179. (A) $\int_0^{\pi/2} \cos x \sin x\, dx$.

 (B) $\int_0^{\pi/4} \tan x \sec^2 x\, dx$.

 (C) $\int_{-1}^{2} \sqrt{x+2}\, x^2\, dx$.

180. Find the average value of $f(x) = \sqrt[3]{x}$ on $[0, 1]$.

181. (A) State the mean-value theorem for integrals.
 (B) Verify the mean-value theorem for integrals for the function
 $f(x) = x + 2$ on $[1, 2]$.

182. If, in a period of time T, an object moves along the x-axis from x_1 to x_2, find a formula for its average velocity.

183. (A) Prove that, if f is continuous on $[a, b]$, $D_x \left[\int_a^x f(t)\, dt \right] = f(x)$.

 (B) Find. $D_x \left[\int_x^b f(t)\, dt \right]$.

184. The region above the x-axis and under the curve $y = \sin x$, between $x = 0$ and $x = \pi$, is divided into two parts by the line $x = c$. If the area of the left part is one-third the area of the right part, find c.

185. The velocity v of an object moving on the x-axis is $\cos 3t$, and the object is at the origin at $t = 0$. Find the average value of the position x over the interval $0 \le t \le \pi/3$.

186. (A) State the trapezoidal rule for approximation of integrals.
 (B) State Simpson's rule for approximation of integrals.
 (C) Apply Simpson's rule with $n = 4$ to approximate $\int_0^1 x^4\, dx$.

 (D) Use the trapezoidal rule with $n = 10$ to approximate $\int_0^1 x^2\, dx$.

187. Use geometric reasoning to calculate $\int_{-a}^{a} \sqrt{a^2 - x^2}\, dx$.

188. Find the area inside the ellipse $x^2/a^2 + y^2/b^2 = 1$.

189. Find the volume of the solid generated when the region between the semicircle $y = 1 - \sqrt{1 - x^2}$ and the line $y = 1$ is rotated around the x-axis (see Figure 20.2).

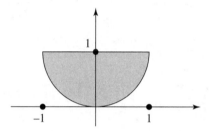

Figure 20.2

CHAPTER 21

Area and Arc Length

190. Sketch and find the area of the region to the left of the parabola $x = 2y^2$, to the right of the y-axis, and between $y = 1$ and $y = 3$.

191. Sketch and find the area of the region above the line $y = 3x - 2$ in the first quadrant, and below the line $y = 4$.

192. Find the area of the regions in parts (A) and (B).
   (A)   The bounded region between the parabola $x = -y^2$ and the line $y = x + 6$.
   (B)   The bounded region between the parabola $y = x^2 - x - 6$ and the line $y = -4$.

Find the arc lengths of the curves in Questions 193 and 194.

193. $y = \dfrac{x^4}{8} + \dfrac{1}{4x^2}$ from $x = 1$ to $x = 2$.

194. $x^{2/3} + y^{2/3} = 4$ from $x = 1$ to $x = 8$.

195. Find the area under the arch of $y = \sin x$ between $x = 0$ and $x = \pi$.

CHAPTER 22

Volume

196. Derive the formula $V = \dfrac{4}{3}\pi r^3$ for the volume of a sphere of radius r.

197. Derive the formula $V = \dfrac{1}{3}\pi r^2 h$ for the volume of a right circular cone of height h and radius of base r.

198. Find the volume generated by revolving the given region about the given axis.

(A) The region above the curve $y = x^3$, under the line $y = 1$, and between $x = 0$ and $x = 1$, about the x-axis.

(B) The region of part (A), about the y-axis.

(C) The region inside the circle $x^2 + y^2 = r^2$ with $0 \le x \le a < r$, about the y-axis. (This gives the volume cut from a sphere of radius r by a pipe of radius a whose axis is a diameter of the sphere.)

(D) The region below the quarter-circle $x^2 + y^2 = r^2$ $(x \ge 0, y \ge 0)$ and above the line $y = a$, where $0 < a < r$, about the y-axis. (This gives the volume of a polar cap of a sphere.)

(E) The region inside the circle $x^2 + (y - b)^2 = a^2$ $(0 < a < b)$, about the x-axis. (This yields the volume of a doughnut.)

199. Use the cross-section formula to find the volume of the given solid.

(A) The solid has a base which is a circle of radius r. Each cross-section perpendicular to a fixed diameter of the circle is an isosceles triangle with altitude equal to one-half of its base.

(B) The solid is a wedge, cut from a perfectly round tree of radius r by two planes, one perpendicular to the axis of the tree and the other intersecting the first plane at an angle of 30° along a diameter. (See Figure 22.1.)

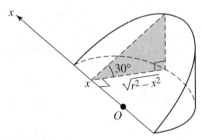

Figure 22.1

(C) A square pyramid with a height of h units and a base of side r units.

(D) The tetrahedron formed by three mutually perpendicular edges of lengths a, b, c.

200. Let $\mathcal{R}$ be the region bounded by the curves $y = x^2 - 4x + 6$ and $y = x + 2$. Find the volume of the solid generated when $\mathcal{R}$ is rotated about the x-axis.

201. Find the volume of the solid generated when the region in the first quadrant under the hyperbola $xy = 1$, between $x = 1$ and $x = b > 1$, is rotated about the x-axis.

202. Find the volume of the ellipsoid obtained when the ellipse $\dfrac{x^2}{a^2} + \dfrac{y^2}{b^2} = 1$ is rotated

(A) about the x-axis, and

(B) about the y-axis.

203. Find the volume of the solid obtained by rotating about the x-axis the region in the first quadrant under the line segment from $(0, r_1)$ to (h, r_2), where $0 < r_1 < r_2$ and $0 < h$. (See Figure 22.2. Note that this is the volume of a frustum of a cone with height h and radii r_1 and r_2 of the bases.)

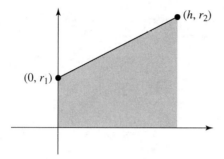

Figure 22.2

CHAPTER 23

The Natural Logarithm

204. (A) State the definition of $\ln x$, and show that $D_x(\ln x) = \dfrac{1}{x}$.

    (B) Show that $\displaystyle\int \dfrac{1}{x} dx = \ln|x| + C$ for $x \ne 0$.

205. Find the derivative of the given function.
    (A) $\ln(4x - 1)$.
    (B) $\ln(\ln x)$.
    (C) $\ln\left(\dfrac{x-1}{x+1}\right)$.

206. Find the indicated antiderivative.

    (A) $\displaystyle\int \dfrac{1}{3x} dx$.

    (B) $\displaystyle\int \dfrac{1}{7x - 2} dx$.

    (C) $\displaystyle\int \dfrac{1}{x \ln x} dx$.

    (D) $\displaystyle\int \dfrac{\ln x}{x} dx$.

207. (A) Show that $\displaystyle\int \dfrac{g'(x)}{g(x)} dx = \ln|g(x)| + C$.

    (B) Find $\displaystyle\int \dfrac{x}{3x^2 + 1} dx$.

    (C) Find $\int \tan x \, dx$.

208. Use logarithmic differentiation to find the derivative of $y = x^3\sqrt{4 - x^2}$.

209. Express the given numbers in terms of $\ln 2$ and $\ln 5$.

    (A) $\ln 10$.

    (B) $\ln \dfrac{1}{2}$.

    (C) $\ln \dfrac{1}{5}$.

    (D) $\ln 25$.

    (E) $\ln \sqrt{2}$.

    (F) $\ln \sqrt[3]{5}$.

    (G) $\ln \dfrac{1}{20}$.

    (H) $\ln 2^{12}$.

210. (A) Show that $1 - \dfrac{1}{x} \le \ln x \le x - 1$.

    (B) Show that $\dfrac{\ln x}{x} < \dfrac{2}{\sqrt{x}}$.

    (C) Prove that $\lim\limits_{x \to +\infty} \dfrac{\ln x}{x} = 0$.

    (D) Prove that $\lim\limits_{x \to 0^+} x \ln x = 0$.

    (E) Prove that $\lim\limits_{x \to +\infty} (x - \ln x) = \infty$.

211. Use the trapezoidal rule, with $n = 10$, to approximate $\ln 2 = \int_1^2 \dfrac{1}{x}\,dx$.

212. Prove that $|\ln b - \ln a| < |b - a|$ for any distinct a, b in $[1, +\infty)$.

213. Prove the basic property of logarithms: $\ln uv = \ln u + \ln v$.

CHAPTER 24

Exponential Functions

214. (A) Evaluate $e^{-\ln x}$.
   (B) Evaluate $\ln e^{-x}$.
   (C) Find $(e^2)^{\ln x}$.

In Question 215, find the derivative of the given function.

215. Find the derivative of the given function.
   (A) e^{-x}.
   (B) $e^{1/x}$.
   (C) $e^{\cos x}$.
   (D) x^{π}.
   (E) π^x.
   (F) $\ln e^{2x}$.
   (G) $e^x - e^{-x}$.

In Problem 216, evaluate the given antiderivative.

216. Evaluate the given antiderivative.
   (A) $\int e^{3x}\,dx$.
   (B) $\int e^{-x}\,dx$.
   (C) $\int e^{\cos x}\sin x\,dx$.
   (D) $\int a^x\,dx$, for $a \neq 1$.

217. Find the derivative of $y = x^{\ln x}$.

218. (A) Solve $e^{3x} = 2$ for x.
   (B) Solve $\ln x^3 = -1$ for x.
   (C) Solve $e^x - 2e^{-x} = 1$ for x.
   (D) Solve $\ln(\ln x) = 1$ for x.
   (E) Solve $\ln(x - 1) = 0$ for x.

219. (A) Let $\mathcal{R}$ be the region under the curve $y = e^x$, above the x-axis, and between $x = 0$ and $x = 1$. Find the area of $\mathcal{R}$.
   (B) Find the volume of the solid generated by rotating the region of Part (A) around the x-axis.

220. Find the absolute extrema of $y = e^{\sin x}$ on $[-\pi, \pi]$.

221. (A) Graph $y = e^{-x^2}$.
   (B) Graph $y = x \ln x$.

   (C) Graph $y = \dfrac{\ln x}{x}$.

   (D) Sketch the graph of $y = e^{-x}$.

    Question 222 refers to the function $\log_a x \equiv \dfrac{\ln x}{\ln a}$, the so-called *logarithm of x to the base a.* (Assume $a > 0$ and $a \neq 1$.)

222. (A) Show that $D_x(\log_a x) = \dfrac{1}{x \ln a}$.

   (B) Show that $a^{\log_a x} = x$.
   (C) Show that $\log_a a^x = x$.
   (D) Show that $\log_e x = \ln x$.
   (E) Show that $\log_a uv = \log_a u + \log_a v$.

   (F) Show that $\log_a \dfrac{u}{v} = \log_a u - \log_a v$.

   (G) Show that $\log_a u^r = r \log_a u$.

   (H) Prove that $\ln x = \dfrac{\log_a x}{\log_a e}$.

223. Prove that the only solutions of the differential equation $f'(x) = f(x)$ are the functions Ce^x, where C is a constant.

224. Prove $e^x = \lim\limits_{u \to +\infty} \left(1 + \dfrac{x}{u}\right)^u$.

225. Prove that, for any positive n, $\lim\limits_{x \to +\infty} \dfrac{x^n}{e^x} = 0$.

226. Evaluate $\lim\limits_{x \to 0^+} x^{\sin x}$.

227. Evaluate $\lim\limits_{x \to 0}(\sin x)^{\cos x}$.

228. Show that $e = \lim\limits_{u \to +\infty} \left(1 + \dfrac{1}{u}\right)^u$.

229. Graph $y = x^2 e^x$.

230. (A) Find $D_x(\sinh x)$ and $D_x(\cosh x)$.
   (B) Find $D_x^2(\sinh x)$ and $D_x^2(\cosh x)$.

CHAPTER 25

L'Hôpital's Rule

231. State L'Hôpital's rule.

In Questions 232–240, evaluate the given limit.

232. $\lim\limits_{x \to 0} \dfrac{\sin x}{x}$.

233. $\lim\limits_{x \to 0} \dfrac{1 - \cos x}{x}$.

234. $\lim\limits_{x \to +\infty} \dfrac{5x^3 - 4x + 3}{2x^2 - 1}$.

235. $\lim\limits_{x \to 0} \left(\dfrac{1}{x} - \dfrac{1}{\sin x} \right)$.

236. $\lim\limits_{x \to 0} \dfrac{\tan x}{x}$.

237. $\lim\limits_{x \to 0} \dfrac{3^x - 2^x}{x}$.

238. $\lim\limits_{x \to 0^+} x^{\sin x}$.

239. $\lim\limits_{x \to 0} \dfrac{e^{3x} - 1}{\tan x}$.

240. $\lim\limits_{x \to 0} \dfrac{\tan x - \sin x}{x^3}$.

CHAPTER 26

Exponential Growth and Decay

241. (A) A quantity y is said to *grow* or *decay exponentially* in time if $D_t y = Ky$ for some constant K. (K is called the *growth constant* or *decay constant*, depending on whether it is positive or negative.) Show that $y = y_0 e^{Kt}$, where y_0 is the value of y at time $t = 0$.

(B) A bacteria culture grows exponentially so that the initial number has doubled in 3 hours. How many times the initial number will be present after 9 hours?

(C) A certain chemical decomposes exponentially. Assume that 200 grams becomes 50 grams in 1 hour. How much will remain after 3 hours?

(D) If a quantity y grows exponentially with a growth constant K and if during each unit of time there is an increase in y of r percent, find the relationship between K and r.

242. If a population is increasing exponentially at the rate of 2 percent per year, what will be the percentage increase over a period of 10 years?

243. (A) If an amount of money y_0 is invested at a rate of r percent per year, compounded n times per year, what is the amount of money that will be available after k years?

(B) An amount of money y_0 earning r percent per year is compounded continuously (that is, assume that it is compounded n times per year, and then let n approach infinity). How much is available after k years?

(C) If an amount of money earning 8 percent per year is compounded quarterly, what is the equivalent yearly rate of return?

(D) If money is invested at 5 percent, compounded continuously, in how many years will it double in value?

244. (A) Assume that a quantity y decays exponentially, with a decay constant K. The *half-life* T is defined to be the time interval after which half of the original quantity remains. Find the relationship between K and T.

(B) The half-life of radium is 1,690 years. If 10 percent of an original quantity of radium remains, how long ago was the radium created?

(C) If radioactive carbon-14 has a half-life of 5,750 years, what will remain of 1 gram after 3,000 years?

(D) If 20 percent of a radioactive element disappears in 1 year, compute its half-life.

245. If y represents the amount by which the temperature of a body exceeds that of the surrounding air, then the rate at which y decreases is proportional to y (Newton's law of cooling). If y was initially 8 degrees and was 7 degrees after 1 minute, what will it be after 2 minutes?

246. A tank initially contains 400 gallons of brine in which 100 pounds of salt are dissolved. Pure water is running into the tank at the rate of 20 gallons per minute, and the mixture (which is kept uniform by stirring) is drained off at the same rate. How many pounds of salt remain in the tank after 30 minutes?

CHAPTER 27

Inverse Trigonometric Functions

247. Draw the graph of $y = \sin^{-1} x$.

248. Show that $D_x(\sin^{-1} x) = 1/\sqrt{1-x^2}$.

249. Draw the graph of $y = \tan^{-1} x$.

250. Show that $D_x(\tan^{-1} x) = 1/(1 + x^2)$.

251. Find the indicated numbers.
   (A) $\cos^{-1}(-\sqrt{3}/2)$.
   (B) $\sin^{-1}(\sqrt{2}/2)$.
   (C) $\sin^{-1}(-\sqrt{2}/2)$.
   (D) $\tan^{-1} 1$.
   (E) $\tan^{-1}(\sqrt{3}/3)$.

252. Compute the indicated functional values.
   (A) $\sin\left(\cos^{-1}\dfrac{4}{5}\right)$.

   (B) $\cos\left(\sin^{-1}\dfrac{3}{5} + \sec^{-1} 3\right)$.

   (C) $\sin^{-1}(\sin \pi)$.

253. Evaluate the indicated antiderivatives.
   (A) $\displaystyle\int \dfrac{1}{4+x^2}\, dx$.

   (B) $\displaystyle\int \dfrac{dx}{\sqrt{25-x^2}}$.

254. A person is viewing a painting hung high on a wall. The vertical dimension of the painting is 2 feet and the bottom of the painting is 2 feet above the eye level of the viewer. Find the distance x that the viewer should stand from the wall in order to maximize the angle θ subtended by the painting.

CHAPTER 28

Integration by Parts

In Questions 255 through 261, find the indicated antiderivative.

255. $\int x^2 e^{-x} dx$.

256. $\int e^x \sin x \, dx$.

257. $\int \sin^{-1} x \, dx$.

258. $\int x \sin x \, dx$.

259. $\int \sin^2 x \, dx$.

260. $\int x e^{3x} dx$.

261. Find $\int x^n \ln x \, dx$ for $n \neq -1$.

CHAPTER **29**

Trigonometric Integrands
and Substitutions

In Questions 262 through 268, find the indicated antiderivatives.

262. $\int \sin x \cos^2 x \, dx$.

263. $\int \sin^4 x \cos^5 x \, dx$.

264. $\int \sin \pi x \cos 3\pi x \, dx$.

265. $\int \sin 5x \sin 7x \, dx$.

266. $\int \dfrac{x^2}{\sqrt{4-x^2}} \, dx$.

267. $\int \dfrac{\sqrt{1+x^2}}{x} \, dx$.

268. $\int \dfrac{dx}{x^2 \sqrt{x^2-9}}$.

269. Find the arc length of the curve $y = \ln \cos x$ from $(0, 0)$ to $(\pi/3, -\ln 2)$.

CHAPTER 30

Integration of Rational Functions: The Method of Partial Fractions

In Questions 270 through 275, evaluate the indicated antiderivative.

270. $\int \dfrac{dx}{x^2 - 9}$.

271. $\int \dfrac{x-5}{x^2(x+1)}\,dx$.

272. $\int \dfrac{dx}{x(x^2+5)}$.

273. $\int \dfrac{dx}{(x^2+1)(x^2+4)}$.

274. $\int \dfrac{dx}{x(x^2+1)^2}$.

275. $\int \dfrac{dx}{1+e^x}$.

276. Find $\int \dfrac{x^2+3}{(x-1)^3(x+1)}\,dx$.

CHAPTER 31

Integrals for Surface Area, Work, Centroids

Surface Area of a Solid of Revolution

277. If the region under a curve $y = f(x)$, above the x-axis, and between $x = a$ and $x = b$, is revolved about the x-axis, state a formula for the surface area S of the resulting solid.

278. Find the surface area of a sphere of radius r.

279. Find the surface generated when the given arc is revolved about the given axis.

(A) $y = x^3$, $0 \le x < 1$; about the x-axis.

(B) $y = \dfrac{1}{4}x^4 + \dfrac{1}{8x^2}$, $1 \le x \le 2$; about the y-axis.

280. Find the surface area of a right circular cone of height h and radius of base r.

Work

281. A spring with a natural length of 10 inches is stretched $\dfrac{1}{2}$ inch by a 12-pound force. Find the work done in stretching the spring from 10 to 18 inches.

Centroid of a Planar Region

In Questions 282 and 283, find the centroid of the given planar region.

282. The region bounded by $y = x^2$, $y = 0$, and $x = 1$ (See Figure 31.1).

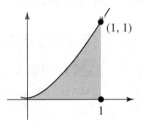

Figure 31.1

283. The region bounded by the semicircle $y = \sqrt{a^2 - x^2}$, and $y = 0$.

Improper Integrals

284. Determine whether the area in the first quadrant under the curve $y = 1/x$, for $x \geq 1$, is finite.

285. (A) Determine whether $\int_1^\infty (1/x^2)\,dx$ converges.

(B) For what values of p is $\int_1^\infty (1/x)^p\,dx$ convergent?

286. (A) For $p > 1$, is $\int_1^\infty \dfrac{\ln x}{x^p}\,dx$ convergent?

(B) For $p \leq 1$, is $\int_1^\infty \dfrac{\ln x}{x^p}\,dx$ convergent?

287. Evaluate $\int_a^\infty xe^{-x}\,dx$.

288. (A) Is $\int_e^\infty \dfrac{dx}{(\ln x)^p}$ convergent when $p \geq 1$?

(B) If $\int_a^\infty f(x)\,dx = +\infty$ and $g(x) \geq f(x)$ for all $x \geq x_0$, show that $\int_a^\infty g(x)\,dx$ is divergent.

289. Show that $\int_e^\infty \dfrac{dx}{(\ln x)^p}$ is divergent for $p < 1$.

290. Evaluate $\int_0^\infty \dfrac{dx}{x^2 + a^2}$.

291. Evaluate $\int_0^\infty e^{-x}\,dx$.

292. (A) Investigate $\int_0^1 \frac{1}{x}\, dx$.

   (B) Investigate $\int_0^1 \frac{1}{\sqrt{x}}\, dx$.

   (C) Investigate $\int_0^1 \frac{1}{x^2}\, dx$.

   (D) For what values of k, with $k \neq 1$ and $k > 0$, does $\int_0^1 \frac{1}{x^k}\, dx$ converge?

293. Evaluate $\int_1^3 \frac{dx}{x-2}$.

294. Evaluate $\int_{-1}^8 \frac{1}{x^{1/3}}\, dx$.

295. Evaluate $\int_0^1 \ln x\, dx$.

CHAPTER 33

Planar Vectors

296. Find the vector from the point $A(1, -2)$ to the point $B(3, 7)$.

297. Given $\mathbf{A} = 3\mathbf{i} + 4\mathbf{j}$ and $\mathbf{C} = 2\mathbf{i} - \mathbf{j}$, find the magnitude and direction of $\mathbf{A} + \mathbf{C}$.

298. Describe a method for resolving a vector $\mathbf{A}$ into components $\mathbf{A}_1$ and $\mathbf{A}_2$ that are, respectively, parallel and perpendicular to a given nonzero vector $\mathbf{B}$.

299. Use vector methods to find the distance from $P(2, 3)$ to the line $3x + 4y - 12 = 0$. See Figure 33.1.

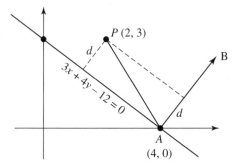

Figure 33.1

300. Generalize the method of Question 299 to find a formula for the distance from a point $P(x_1, y_1)$ to the line $ax + by + c = 0$.

301. Write the vector of length 2 and direction $150°$ in the form $a\mathbf{i} + b\mathbf{j}$.

302. Given $O(0, 0)$, $A(3, 1)$, and $B(1, 5)$ as vertices of the parallelogram $OAPB$, find the coordinates of P (see Figure 33.2).

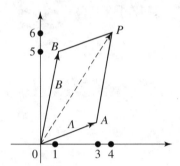

Figure 33.2

303. Find a vector perpendicular to the vector $(2, 5)$.

CHAPTER **34**

Parametric Equations, Vector Functions, Curvilinear Motion

Parametric Equations of Plane Curves

304. (A) Sketch the curve given by the parametric equations $x = a \cos \theta$, $y = a \sin \theta$.
(B) Sketch the curve with the parametric equations $x = 2 \cos \theta$, $y = 3 \sin \theta$.
(C) Sketch the curve with the parametric equations $x = t$, $y = t^2$.

305. Find the arc length of the curve $x = e^t \cos t$, $y = e^t \sin t$, from $t = 0$ to $t = \pi$.

Vector-Valued Functions

306. $\mathbf{F}(u) = (f(u), g(u))$ is a two-dimensional vector function, $\lim_{u \to a} \mathbf{F}(u) = (\lim_{u \to a} f(u), \lim_{u \to a} g(u))$, where the limit on the left exists if and only if the limits on the right exist. Taking this as the definition of vector convergence, show that $\mathbf{F}'(u) = (f'(u), g'(u))$.

307. Show that, if $\mathbf{R}(u)$ traces out a curve, then $\mathbf{R}'(u)$ is a tangent vector pointing in the direction of motion along the curve.

308. Show that, if $\mathbf{R}(t)$ traces out a curve and the parameter t represents time, then $\mathbf{R}(t)$ is the velocity vector—that is, its direction is the direction of motion and its length is the speed.

309. If $h(u) = \mathbf{F}(u) \cdot \mathbf{G}(u)$, show that $h'(u) = \mathbf{F}(u) \cdot \mathbf{G}'(u) + \mathbf{F}'(u) \cdot \mathbf{G}(u)$, another analogue of the product formula for derivatives.

310. If $|\mathbf{R}(t)|$ is a constant $c > 0$, show that the tangent vector $\mathbf{R}'(t)$ is perpendicular to the position vector $\mathbf{R}(t)$.

311. For any vector function $\mathbf{F}(u)$ and scalar function $h(u)$, prove a chain rule:

$$\frac{d}{du}\mathbf{F}(h(u)) = h'(u)\mathbf{F}'(h(u)).$$

312. Assume that an object moves on a circle of radius r with constant speed $v > 0$. Show that the acceleration vector is directed toward the center of the circle and has length v^2/r.

313. (A) Let ϕ be the angle between the velocity vector and the positive x-axis. Show that $|d\mathbf{T}/d\phi| = 1$.

  (B) Define the *curvature* κ and *radius of curvature* ρ of a curve $\mathbf{R}(t)$.

  (C) For a circle of radius a, traced out in the counterclockwise direction, show that the curvature is $1/a$, and the radius of curvature is a, the radius of the circle.

  (D) Find the curvature of a straight line $\mathbf{R}(t) = \mathbf{A} + t\mathbf{B}$.

  (E) Show that, for a curve $y = f(x)$, the curvature is given by the formula $\kappa = y''/[1 + (y')^2]^{3/2}$. (We assume that $ds/dx > 0$—that is, the arc length increases with x.)

CHAPTER 35

Polar Coordinates

314. (A) Write the relations between polar coordinates (r, θ) and rectangular coordinates (x, y).
     (B) Give all possible polar representations of the point with rectangular coordinates $(1, 0)$.

315. (A) Describe the graph of the polar equation $r = 2$.
     (B) Describe the graph of the polar equation $\theta = \pi/4$.
     (C) Describe the graph of the polar equation $\theta = 0$.

316. Write a polar equation for the y-axis.

317. Describe the graph of the polar equation $r = 2 \sin \theta$.

318. Transform the rectangular equation $x = 3$ into a polar equation.

319. (A) Sketch the graph of $r = 1 + \cos \theta$.
     (B) Sketch the graph of $r = 1 + 2 \cos \theta$.
     (C) Sketch the graph of $r^2 = \cos 2\theta$.
     (D) Sketch the graph of $r = \sin 2\theta$.

320. (A) Sketch the graph of $r = \sin 3\theta$.
     (B) Sketch the graph of $r = \sin 4\theta$.

321. Find all points of intersection of the curves $r = 1 + \sin^2 \theta$ and $r = -1 - \sin^2 \theta$.

322. Find the area enclosed by the cardioid $r = 1 + \cos \theta$.

323. (A) Find the arc length of the spiral $r = \theta$ from $\theta = 0$ to $\theta = 1$.
     (B) Find the arc length of the spiral $r = e^\theta$. from $\theta = 0$ to $\theta = \ln 2$.

CHAPTER 36

Infinite Sequences

In Questions 324 through 332, write a formula for the nth term a_n of the sequence and determine its limit (if it exists). It is understood that $n = 1, 2, 3, \ldots.$

324. $\dfrac{1}{2}, \dfrac{2}{3}, \dfrac{3}{4}, \dfrac{4}{5}, \dfrac{5}{6}, \ldots$

325. $\dfrac{2}{1}, \left(\dfrac{3}{2}\right)^2, \left(\dfrac{4}{3}\right)^3, \left(\dfrac{5}{4}\right)^4, \ldots$

326. $\ln\dfrac{2}{1}, \ln\dfrac{3}{2}, \ln\dfrac{4}{3}, \ldots$

327. $\dfrac{2}{1}, \dfrac{4}{2}, \dfrac{8}{6}, \dfrac{16}{24}, \dfrac{32}{120}, \ldots$

328. $1, \sqrt{2}, \sqrt[3]{3}, \sqrt[4]{4}, \ldots$

329. $a_n = \dfrac{4n+5}{n^3 - 2n + 3}.$

330. $a_n = \dfrac{2n^5 - 3n + 20}{5n^4 + 2}.$

331. $a_n = \sqrt{n+1} - \sqrt{n}.$

332. $a_n = 2n\sin\dfrac{\pi}{n}.$

333. Show that $a_n = 2n/(3n + 1)$ is an increasing sequence.

334. (A) Determine whether the sequence $a_n = \dfrac{1 \cdot 3 \cdot 5 \cdot \,\cdots\, \cdot (2n-1)}{2 \cdot 4 \cdot 6 \cdot \,\cdots\, \cdot (2n)}$ is increasing, decreasing, or neither.

    (B) Show that the sequence (a) of Question 334(A) is convergent.

CHAPTER 37

Infinite Series

335. Prove that, if $\sum a_n$ converges, then $\lim\limits_{n \to +\infty} a_n = 0$.

336. (A) Show that the harmonic series $\sum 1/n = 1 + \dfrac{1}{2} + \dfrac{1}{3} + \cdots$ diverges.

(B) Does $\lim\limits_{n \to +\infty} a_n = 0$ imply that $\sum a_n$ converges?

337. (A) Let $S_n = a + ar + \cdots + ar^{n-1}$, with $r \neq 1$. Show that $S_n = \dfrac{a(r^n - 1)}{r - 1}$.

(B) Let $a \neq 0$. Show that the infinite geometric series $\sum\limits_{n=0}^{\infty} ar^n = \dfrac{a}{1 - r}$ if $|r| < 1$ and diverges if $|r| \geq 1$.

(C) Evaluate $\sum\limits_{n=0}^{\infty} \dfrac{1}{2^n} = 1 + \dfrac{1}{2} + \dfrac{1}{4} + \cdots$.

(D) Evaluate the infinite repeating decimal $d = 0.215626262 \ldots$.

338. Investigate the series $\dfrac{1}{1 \cdot 2} + \dfrac{1}{2 \cdot 3} + \dfrac{1}{3 \cdot 4} + \cdots + \dfrac{1}{n(n+1)} + \cdots$.

339. Find the sum of the series $4 - 1 + \dfrac{1}{4} - \dfrac{1}{16} + \cdots$.

340. Test the convergence of $3 + \dfrac{5}{2} + \dfrac{7}{3} + \dfrac{9}{4} + \cdots$.

341. Evaluate $\sum\limits_{n=0}^{\infty} \dfrac{1}{n + 100} = \dfrac{1}{100} + \dfrac{1}{101} + \cdots$.

342. Zeno's paradox: Achilles (A) and a tortoise (T) have a race. T gets a 1000-ft head start, but A runs at 10 ft/s while the tortoise only does 0.01 ft/s. When A reaches T's starting point, T has moved a short distance ahead. When A reaches that point, T again has moved a short distance ahead, etc. Zeno claimed that A would never catch T. Show that is not so.

343. Investigate $\displaystyle\sum_{n=1}^{\infty} \frac{3}{5^n + 2}$.

344. If $0 < p \le 1$, show that the series $\displaystyle\sum_{n=1}^{\infty} \frac{1}{n^p} = 1 + \frac{1}{2^p} + \frac{1}{3^p} + \cdots$ is divergent.

345. Determine whether $\displaystyle\sum_{n=0}^{\infty} \frac{1}{n!}$ is convergent.

346. (A) State the integral test.

 (B) For $p > 1$, show that the so-called p-series $\displaystyle\sum_{n=1}^{\infty} \frac{1}{n^p}$ converges.

 (Compare with Problem 344.)

 (C) Determine whether $\displaystyle\sum_{n=2}^{\infty} \frac{1}{n \ln n}$ converges.

347. (A) State the limit comparison test.

 (B) Determine whether $\displaystyle\sum_{n=1}^{\infty} \frac{1}{\sqrt{n^3 + 3}}$ converges.

 (C) Determine whether $\displaystyle\sum_{n=1}^{\infty} \frac{n^3}{2n^4 + 1}$ is convergent.

348. Determine whether $\displaystyle\sum_{n=1}^{\infty} \frac{1}{n^n}$ is convergent.

349. Determine whether $\displaystyle\sum_{n=1}^{\infty} \frac{\ln n}{n}$ converges.

350. Give an example of a series that is conditionally convergent (that is, convergent but not absolutely convergent).

351. (A) State the ratio test for a series $\Sigma\, a_n$.

(B) Determine whether $\displaystyle\sum_{n=1}^{\infty} \frac{n^2}{e^n}$ is convergent.

352. Find the error if the sum of the first three terms is used as an approximation to the sum of the alternating series $\displaystyle\sum_{n=1}^{\infty}(-1)^{n+1}\,\frac{1}{n}$.

353. Study the convergence of $\displaystyle\sum_{n=0}^{\infty}(-1)^{n+1}\,\frac{2^n}{n!}$.

354. Determine whether $\displaystyle\sum_{n=1}^{\infty}(-1)^{n+1}\,\frac{\sin(\pi/n)}{n^2}$ converges.

355. (A) Prove the *root test*: A series of positive terms $\Sigma\, a_n$ converges if $\displaystyle\lim_{n\to+\infty} \sqrt[n]{a_n} < 1$ and diverges if $\displaystyle\lim_{n\to+\infty} \sqrt[n]{a_n} > 1$.

(B) Test $\displaystyle\sum_{n=2}^{\infty} \frac{1}{(\ln n)^n}$ for convergence.

356. Determine the nth term of and test for convergence the series

$$2 - \frac{2^3}{3!} + \frac{2^5}{5!} - \frac{2^7}{7!} + \cdots.$$

357. Show how to rearrange the terms of the conditionally convergent series $1 - \frac{1}{2} + \frac{1}{3} - \frac{1}{4} + \cdots$ so as to obtain a series whose sum is 1.

358. Show that the ratio test gives no information when $\lim |a_{n+1}/a_n| = 1$.

359. Show that, in Figure 37.1, the areas in the rectangles and above $y = 1/x$ add up to a number γ between $\dfrac{1}{2}$ and 1. (γ is called *Euler's constant*.)

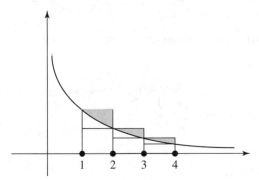

Figure 37.1

360. (A) Find the values of x for which the series $1 + x + x^2 + \cdots$ converges, and express the sum as a function of x.

(B) Find the values of x for which the series $\ln x + (\ln x)^2 + (\ln x)^3 + \cdots$ converges, and express the sum as a function of x.

Power Series

In Question 361, find the interval of convergence of the given power series. Use the ratio test unless otherwise instructed.

361. (A) $\sum x^n/n$.
   (B) $\sum x^n/n^2$.
   (C) $\sum x^n/n!$.
   (D) $\sum n!x^n$
   (E) $\sum x^n/2^n$.
   (F) $\sum x^n/(n \cdot 2^n)$.
   (G) $\sum nx^n$.

362. Find the radius of convergence of the power series $\displaystyle\sum_{n=1}^{\infty} \frac{(n!)^2}{(2n)!} x^n$.

363. Prove that, if a power series $\sum a_n x^n$ converges for $x = b$, then it converges absolutely for all x such that $|x| < |b|$.

364. If $\lim_{n \to +\infty} \sqrt[n]{|a_n|} = L > 0$, show that the radius of convergence of $\sum a_n x^n$ is $1/L$.

365. Find the radius of convergence of the binomial series
$$1 + \frac{m}{1}x + \frac{m(m-1)}{1 \cdot 2}x^2 + \frac{m(m-1)(m-2)}{1 \cdot 2 \cdot 3}x^3 + \cdots.$$

366. If $\sum a_n x^n$ has a radius of convergence r_1 and if $\sum b_n x^n$ has a radius of convergence $r_2 > r_1$, what is the radius of convergence of the sum $\sum (a_n + b_n)x^n$?

367. (A) Show that $\dfrac{1}{1+x} = 1 - x + x^2 - \cdots = \sum_{n=0}^{\infty} (-1)^n x^n$ for $|x| < 1$.

(B) Show that $\dfrac{1}{1+x^2} = 1 - x^2 + x^4 - \cdots = \sum_{n=0}^{\infty} (-1)^n x^{2n}$ for $|x| < 1$.

(C) Show that $\tan^{-1} x = x - \dfrac{x^3}{3} + \dfrac{x^5}{5} - \cdots = \sum_{n=0}^{\infty} \dfrac{(-1)^n x^{2n+1}}{2n+1}$ for $|x| < 1$.

(D) Find a power series representation for $\dfrac{1}{(1-x)^2}$.

(E) Find a power series representation for $\ln(1+x)$ for $|x| < 1$.

368. (A) Show that $e^x = \sum_{n=0}^{\infty} \dfrac{x^n}{n!}$ for all x.

(B) Find a power series representation for e^{-x}.

(C) Find a power series representation for $e^{-x^2/2}$.

369. Approximate $1/e$ correct to two decimal places.

370. (A) Find a power series representation for $\ln(1-x)$.

(B) Find a power series representation for $\ln\dfrac{1+x}{1-x}$.

(C) Use the power series for $\ln\dfrac{1+x}{1-x}$ to approximate $\ln 2$.

371. (A) Show directly that, if $y'' = -y$, and $y' = 1$, and $y = 0$ when $x = 0$, then $y = \sin x$.

(B) Show that $\sin x = \sum_{n=0}^{\infty} (-1)^n \dfrac{x^{2n+1}}{(2n+1)!}$.

(C) Show that $\cos x = \sum_{n=0}^{\infty} (-1)^n \dfrac{x^{2n}}{(2n)!}$.

372. (A) Show that $\ln 2 = 1 - \dfrac{1}{2} + \dfrac{1}{3} - \dfrac{1}{4} + \cdots = \sum_{n=1}^{\infty} \dfrac{(-1)^{n+1}}{n}$.

(B) Show that $\dfrac{\pi}{4} = 1 - \dfrac{1}{3} + \dfrac{1}{5} - \dfrac{1}{7} + \cdots = \sum_{n=0}^{\infty} \dfrac{(-1)^n}{2n+1}$.

373. Find a power series for $\sin^2 x$.

374. For what values of x can $\sin x$ be replaced by x if the allowable error is 0.0005?

375. Find the first five terms of the power series for $e^x \cos x$ by multiplication of power series.

376. Let $f(x) = \sum_{n=0}^{\infty} a_n x^n$. Show that $\dfrac{1}{1-x} f(x) = \sum_{n=0}^{\infty} (a_0 + a_1 + \cdots + a_n)x^n$.

377. Use the result of Question 376 to evaluate $\sum_{n=0}^{\infty} (n+1)x^n$.

378. Evaluate $x/2! + x^2/3! + x^3/4! + x^4/5! + \cdots$.

379. (A) For the binomial series (Question 365), $f(x) = 1 + mx + \dfrac{m(m-1)}{2!}x^2 + \cdots +$
$\dfrac{m(m-1)\cdots(m-n+1)}{n!} x^n + \cdots$, which is convergent for $|x| < 1$, show
that $(1+x) f'(x) = mf(x)$.

(B) Prove that the binomial series $f(x)$ of Question 379(A) is equal to $(1+x)^m$.

(C) Show that $\sqrt{1-x} = 1 - \dfrac{1}{2}x - \dfrac{1}{2\cdot4}x^2 - \dfrac{1\cdot3}{2\cdot4\cdot6}x^3$
$- \cdots - \dfrac{1\cdot3\cdots(2n-3)}{2^n \cdot n!}x^n - \cdots$.

(D) Derive the series $\dfrac{1}{\sqrt{1-x}} = 1 + \dfrac{1}{2}x + \dfrac{1\cdot3}{2.4}x^2 + \dfrac{1\cdot3\cdot5}{2\cdot4\cdot6}x^3 + \cdots$.

(E) Obtain the series $\sin^{-1} x = x + \dfrac{1}{2}\dfrac{x^3}{3} + \dfrac{1\cdot3}{2\cdot4}\dfrac{x^5}{5} + \dfrac{1\cdot3\cdot5}{2\cdot4\cdot6}\dfrac{x^7}{7} + \cdots$, $|x| < 1$.

(F) By means of the binomial series, approximate $\sqrt[5]{33}$ correct to three decimal places.

380. If infinitely many coefficients of a power series are nonzero integers, show that the radius of convergence $r \le 1$.

CHAPTER 39

Taylor and Maclaurin Series

381. (A) Find the Maclaurin series of e^x.

(B) Find the Maclaurin series for $\sin x$.

(C) Find the Maclaurin series for $\ln(1 - x)$.

(D) Compute the first three nonzero terms of the Maclaurin series for $e^{\cos x}$.

382. (A) Find the Taylor series for $\sin x$ about $\pi/4$.

(B) Calculate the Taylor series for $1/x$ about 1.

383. (A) If $f(x) = \sum_{n=0}^{\infty} a_n (x-a)^n$ for $|x - a| < r$, prove that $a_k = \dfrac{f^{(k)}(a)}{k!}$. In other words, if $f(x)$ has a power series expansion about a, that power series must be the Taylor series for $f(x)$ about a.

(B) Find the Maclaurin series for $\dfrac{1}{1+x}$.

(C) Obtain the Maclaurin series for $\cos^2 x$.

384. State Taylor's formula with Lagrange's form of the remainder and indicate how it is used to show that a function is represented by its Taylor series.

385. Show that $e = \sum_{n=0}^{\infty} \dfrac{1}{n!}$.

386. Estimate the error when $\sqrt{e} = e^{1/2}$ is approximated by the first four terms of the Maclaurin series for e^x.

387. Use the Maclaurin series to estimate e to within two-decimal-place accuracy.

388. If $f(x) = \sum\limits_{n=0}^{\infty} 2^n x^n$, find $f^{(33)}(0)$.

389. Approximate $\int_{0}^{1} e^{-x^2}\, dx$ to within two-decimal-place accuracy.

CHAPTER 40

Vectors in Space; Lines and Planes

390. (A) Find the equation of a sphere $\mathscr{S}$ of radius r and center (a, b, c).
(B) Describe the graph of the equation $x^2 + 4x + y^2 + z^2 - 8z = 5$.
(C) When does an equation $x^2 + y^2 + z^2 + Ax + By + Cz + D = 0$ represent a sphere?

391. Show that the three points $P(1, 2, 3)$, $Q(4, -5, 2)$, and $R(0, 0, 0)$ are the vertices of a right triangle.

392. Show that the points $P(2, -1, 5)$, $Q(6, 0, 6)$, and $R(14, 2, 8)$ are collinear.

393. Describe the intersection of the graphs of $x^2 + y^2 = 1$ and $z = 2$.

394. Find the direction cosines of $\mathbf{A} = 3\mathbf{i} + 12\mathbf{j} + 4\mathbf{k}$. (Recall that $\mathbf{i} = (1, 0, 0)$, $\mathbf{j} = (0, 1, 0)$, and $\mathbf{k} = (0, 0, 1)$.)

395. Find the angle θ between the vectors $\mathbf{A} = (1, 2, 3)$ and $\mathbf{B} = (2, -3, -1)$.

396. Find a value of c for which $\mathbf{A} = 3\mathbf{i} - 2\mathbf{j} + 5\mathbf{k}$ and $\mathbf{B} = 2\mathbf{i} + 4\mathbf{j} + c\mathbf{k}$ will be perpendicular.

397. Write the formula for the cross product $\mathbf{A} \times \mathbf{B}$, where $\mathbf{A} = (a_1, a_2, a_3)$ and $\mathbf{B} = (b_1, b_2, b_3)$.

398. Find a vector $\mathbf{N}$ that is perpendicular to the plane of the three points $P(1, -1, 4)$, $Q(2, 0, 1)$, and $R(0, 2, 3)$.

399. Find the volume of the parallelepiped formed by the vectors $\overline{PQ}$ and $\overline{PR}$ of Question 398 and the vector $\overline{PS}$ where $S = (3, 5, 7)$.

400. Establish the formula

$$\mathbf{A} \cdot (\mathbf{B} \times \mathbf{C}) = \begin{bmatrix} a_1 & a_2 & a_3 \\ b_1 & b_2 & b_3 \\ c_1 & c_2 & c_3 \end{bmatrix}$$

where $\mathbf{A} = (a_1, a_2, a_3)$, $\mathbf{B} = (b_1, b_2, b_3)$, $\mathbf{C} = (c_1, c_2, c_3)$.

401. Verify that $\mathbf{B} \times \mathbf{A} = -(\mathbf{A} \times \mathbf{B})$.

402. Show that the points $(0, 0, 0)$, (a_1, a_2, a_3), (b_1, b_2, b_3), and (c_1, c_2, c_3) are coplanar if and only if

$$\begin{vmatrix} a_1 & a_2 & a_3 \\ b_1 & b_2 & b_3 \\ c_1 & c_2 & c_3 \end{vmatrix} = 0.$$

403. (A) Find the vector representation, the parametric equations, and the rectangular equations for the line through the points $P(1, -2, 5)$ and $Q(3, 4, 6)$.
(B) Find the points at which the line of Problem 403(A) cuts the coordinate planes.

404. Write equations for the line through the point $(1, 2, -6)$ and parallel to the vector $(4, 1, 3)$.

405. By the methods of calculus, find the point $P_1(x, y, z)$ on the line $x = 3 + t$, $y = 2 + t$, and $z = 1 + t$ that is closest to the point $P_0(1, 2, 1)$, and verify that $\overrightarrow{P_0 P_1}$ is perpendicular to the line.

406. Find an equation of the plane containing the point $P_1(3, -2, 5)$ and perpendicular to the vector $\mathbf{N} = (4, 2, -7)$.

407. Find an equation for the plane through the points $P(1, 3, 5)$, $Q(-1, 2, 4)$, and $R(4, 4, 0)$.

408. Find the cosine of the angle θ between the planes $4x + 4y - 2z = 9$ and $2x + y + z = -3$.

409. Find an equation of the plane containing the point $P(1, 3, 1)$ and the line $\mathcal{L}: x = t, y = t, z = t + 2$.

410. (A) Show that the distance D from the point $P(x_1, y_1, z_1)$ to the plane $ax + by + cz + d = 0$ is given by $D = |ax_1 + by_1 + cz_1 + d|/ \sqrt{a^2 + b^2 + c^2}$.

   (B) Find the distance D from the point $(3, -5, 2)$ to the plane $8x - 2y + z = 5$.

411. Consider the sphere of radius 3 and center at the origin. Find the coordinates of the point P where the plane tangent to this sphere at $(1, 2, 2)$ cuts the x-axis.

412. Check that the planes $x - 2y + 2z = 1$ and $3x - y - z = 2$ intersect, and find their line of intersection.

413. Find an equation of a plane containing the intersection of the planes $3x - 2y + 4z = 5$ and $2x + 4y - z = 7$ and passing through the point $(2, 1, 2)$.

414. Find the coordinates of the point P at which the line $\dfrac{x+8}{9} = \dfrac{y-10}{-4} = \dfrac{z-9}{-2}$ cuts the plane $3x + 4y + 5z = 76$.

415. Find an equation of the line through $P(4, 2, -1)$ and perpendicular to the plane $6x - 3y + z = 5$.

CHAPTER 41

Functions of Several Variables

Multivariate Functions and Their Graphs

416. (A) Describe and sketch the graph of $\dfrac{x^2}{a^2}+\dfrac{y^2}{b^2}+\dfrac{z^2}{c^2}=1$ where $a, b, c > 0$.

(B) Describe and sketch the graph of $\dfrac{x^2}{a^2}+\dfrac{y^2}{b^2}-\dfrac{z^2}{c^2}=1$ where $a, b, c > 0$.

(C) Describe and sketch the graph of $\dfrac{z^2}{c^2}-\dfrac{x^2}{a^2}-\dfrac{y^2}{b^2}=1$ where $a, b, c > 0$.

(D) Describe and sketch the graph of $\dfrac{x^2}{a^2}+\dfrac{y^2}{b^2}=\dfrac{z^2}{c^2}$ where $a, b, c > 0$.

(E) Describe and sketch the graph of the function $f(x, y) = x^2 + y^2$.
(F) Describe and sketch the graph of the function $f(x, y) = 2x + 5y - 10$.
(G) Describe and sketch the graph of $z = y^2 - x^2$.

417. Find the volume of the ellipsoid $\dfrac{x^2}{a^2}+\dfrac{y^2}{b^2}+\dfrac{z^2}{c^2}=1$.

418. (A) Find $\displaystyle\lim_{(x,\,y)\to(0,\,0)} \dfrac{2xy^2}{x^2+y^2}$, if it exists.

(B) Find $\displaystyle\lim_{(x,\,y)\to(0,\,0)} \dfrac{2xy^2}{x^2+y^4}$, if it exists.

(C) Is it possible to define $f(x, y) = \dfrac{x^3+y^3}{x^2+y^2}$ at $(0, 0)$ so that $f(x, y)$ is continuous?

(D) Determine whether the function

$$f(x, y) = \begin{cases} \dfrac{xy}{x^2 + y^2} & \text{if } (x, y) \neq (0, 0) \\ 0 & \text{if } (x, y) = (0, 0) \end{cases}$$

is continuous at the origin.

Cylindrical and Spherical Coordinates

419. (A) Give the equations connecting rectangular and cylindrical coordinates of a point in space.

(B) Describe the surface with the cylindrical equation $r = k$.

(C) Describe the surface with the cylindrical equation $\theta = k$.

(D) Find cylindrical coordinates for the point with rectangular coordinates $(2, 2\sqrt{3}, 8)$.

(E) Find a rectangular equation for the surface with the cylindrical equation $\theta = \pi/3$.

(F) Find a rectangular equation for the surface with the cylindrical equation $r = 2 \sin \theta$.

420. (A) Write down the equations connecting spherical coordinates (ρ, ϕ, θ) with rectangular and cylindrical coordinates.

(B) Describe the surface with the equation $\rho = k$ in spherical coordinates.

(C) Describe the surface with the equation $\phi = k$ $(0 < k < \pi/2)$ in spherical coordinates.

(D) Find a set of spherical coordinates for the point whose rectangular coordinates are $(1, 1, \sqrt{6})$.

(E) Find the rectangular coordinates of the point with spherical coordinates $(4, 2\pi/3, \pi/3)$.

421. Find a spherical equation for the surface whose rectangular equation is $x^2 + y^2 + z^2 + 6z = 0$.

422. Describe the surface whose equation in spherical coordinates is $\rho \sin \phi = 3$.

CHAPTER 42

Partial Derivatives

423. If $f(x, y) = 4x^3 - 3x^2y^2 + 2x + 3y$, find the partial derivatives f_x and f_y.

424. Give an example of a function $f(x, y)$ such that $f_x(0, 0) = f_y(0, 0) = 0$, but f is not continuous at $(0, 0)$. Hence, the existence of the first partial derivatives does not ensure continuity.

425. (A) State a set of conditions under which the mixed partial derivatives $f_{xy}(x_0, y_0)$, and $f_{yx}(x_0, y_0)$ are equal.
(B) For $f(x, y) = 3x^2y - 2xy + 5y^2$, verify that $f_{xy} = f_{yx}$.

426. (A) For $f(x, y) = e^x \cos y$, verify that $f_{xy} = f_{yx}$.
(B) If $f(x, y) = 3x^2 - 2xy + 5y^3$, verify that $f_{xy} = f_{yx}$.
(C) If $f(x, y) = x^2 \cos y + y^2 \sin x$, verify that $f_{xy} = f_{yx}$.

427. (A) For $f(x, y) = 3x^4 - 2x^3y^2 + 7y$, find f_{xx}, f_{xy}, f_{yx}, and f_{yy}.
(B) If $f(x, y) = e^{xy}y^2 + \dfrac{x}{y}$, find f_{xx}, f_{xy}, f_{yx}, and f_{yy}.
(C) If $f(x, y, z) = x^2y + y^2z - 2xz$, find f_{xy}, f_{yx}, f_{xz}, f_{zx}, f_{yz}, and f_{zy}.

428. Give an example to show that the equation $f_{xy} = f_{yx}$ is not always valid.

429. If $z = e^{ax} \sin ay$, show that $\dfrac{\partial^2 z}{\partial x^2} + \dfrac{\partial^2 z}{\partial y^2} = 0$.

430. If $z = e^{-t}(\sin x + \cos y)$, show that $\dfrac{\partial^2 z}{\partial x^2} + \dfrac{\partial^2 z}{\partial y^2} = \dfrac{\partial z}{\partial t}$.

431. If $f(x, y) = g(x)h(y)$, show that $f_{xy} = f_{yx}$.

432. (A) Show that $f(x, t) = (x + at)^3$ satisfies the wave equation $a^2 f_{xx} = f_{tt}$.
  (B) Show that $f(x, t) = \sin(x + at)$ satisfies the wave equation $a^2 f_{xx} = f_{tt}$.
  (C) Show that $f(x, t) = e^{x - at}$ satisfies the wave equation $a^2 f_{xx} = f_{tt}$.

433. (A) If $u = f(x_1, \ldots, x_n)$ and $x_1 = h_1(t), \ldots, x_n = h_n(t)$, state the chain rule for du/dt.
  (B) If $u = x^2 - 2y^2 + z^3$ and $x = \sin t, y = e^t, z = 3t$, find du/dt.
  (C) If $w = \Phi(x, y, z)$ and $x = f(u, v), y = g(u, v), z = h(u, v)$, state the chain rule for $\partial w/\partial u$ and $\partial w/\partial v$.

434. How fast is the volume V of a rectangular box changing when its length l is 10 feet and increasing at the rate of 2 feet per second, its width w is 5 feet and decreasing at the rate of 1 feet per second, and its height h is 3 feet and increasing at the rate of 2 feet per second?

435. (A) Prove Euler's theorem: if $f(x, y)$ is homogeneous of degree n, then $xf_x + yf_y = nf$. (Recall that $f(x, y)$ is homogeneous of degree n if and only if $f(tx, ty) = t^n f(x, y)$ for all x, y and for all $t > 0$.)
  (B) Verify Euler's theorem (Question 435(A)) for the function $f(x, y) = xy^2 + x^2 y - y^3$.
  (C) Verify Euler's theorem (Question 435(A)) for the function $f(x, y) = \sqrt{x^2 + y^2}$.
  (D) Verify Euler's theorem (Question 435(A)) for the function $f(x, y, z) = 3xz^2 - 2xyz + y^2 z$.

436. If $z = 2x^2 - 3xy + 7y^2, x = \sin t, y = \cos t$, find dz/dt.

437. If $z = \ln(x^2 + y^2), x = e^{-t}, y = e^t$, find dz/dt.

438. If $z = f(x, y) = x^4 + 3xy - y^2$ and $y = \sin x$, find dz/dx.

439. If $z = f(x, y) = xy^2 + x^2 y$ and $y = \ln x$, find dz/dx and dz/dy.

440. If the radius r of a right circular cylinder is increasing at the rate of 3 inches per second and the altitude h is increasing at the rate of 2 inches per second, how fast is the surface area S changing when $r = 10$ inches and $h = 5$ inches?

441. If a point is moving on the curve of intersection of $x^2 + 3xy + 3y^2 = z^2$ and the plane $x - 2y + 4 = 0$, how fast is it moving when $x = 2$, if x is increasing at the rate of 3 units per second?

442. (A) Prove Leibniz's formula for differentiable functions $u(x)$ and $v(x)$,

(B) Verify Leibniz's formula (Question 442(A)) for $u = x$, $v = x^2$, and $f(x, y) = x^3 y^2 + x^2 y^3$.

443. (A) Show that the tangent plane to a surface $z = f(x, y)$ at a point (x_0, y_0, z_0) has a normal vector $(f_x(x_0, y_0), f_y(x_0, y_0), -1)$.

(B) If a surface has the equation $F(x, y, z) = 0$, show that a normal vector to the tangent plane at (x_0, y_0, z_0) is $(F_x(x_0, y_0, z_0), F_y(x_0, y_0, z_0), F_z(x_0, y_0, z_0))$.

444. Find an equation of the tangent plane to the sphere $x^2 + y^2 + z^2 = 1$ at the point $\left(\dfrac{1}{2}, \dfrac{1}{2}, 1/\sqrt{2} \right)$.

445. Find an equation of the tangent plane to $z^3 + xyz - 2 = 0$ at $(1, 1, 1)$.

446. Find an equation of the tangent plane to the ellipsoid $\dfrac{x^2}{a^2} + \dfrac{y^2}{b^2} + \dfrac{z^2}{c^2} = 1$ at a point (x_0, y_0, z_0).

CHAPTER 43

Directional Derivatives and the Gradient; Extreme Values

447. Given a function $f(x, y)$ and a unit vector **u**, define the *derivative of f in the direction* **u**, at a point (x_0, y_0), and state its connection with the gradient $\nabla f = (f_x, f_y)$.

448. Show that the direction of the gradient ∇f is the direction in which the derivative achieves its maximum, $|\nabla f|$, and the direction of $-\nabla f$ is the direction in which the derivative achieves its minimum, $-|\nabla f|$.

449. Find the derivative of $f(x, y) = 2x^2 - 3xy + 5y^2$ at the point $(1, 2)$ in the direction of the unit vector **u** making an angle of $45°$ with the positive x-axis.

450. Find the derivative of $z = x \ln y$ at the point $(1, 2)$ in the direction making an angle of $30°$ with the positive x-axis.

451. If the temperature is given by $f(x, y, z) = 3x^2 - 5y^2 + 2z^2$ and you are located $\left(\frac{1}{3}, \frac{1}{5}, \frac{1}{2}\right)$ and want to get cool as soon as possible, in which direction should you set out?

452. Prove that the gradient ∇F of a function $F(x, y, z)$ at a point $P(x_0, y_0, z_0)$ is perpendicular to the level surface of F going through P.

453. In what direction should one initially travel, starting at the origin, to obtain the most rapid rate of increase of the function $f(x, y, z) = (3 - x + y)^2 + (4x - y + z + 2)^3$?

454. If $z = f(x, y)$ has a relative maximum or minimum at a point (x_0, y_0), show that $\nabla z = \mathbf{0}$ at (x_0, y_0).

455. (A) Assume that $f(x, y)$ has continuous second partial derivatives in a disk containing the point (x_0, y_0) inside it. Assume also that (x_0, y_0) is a critical point of f— that is, $f_x = f_y = 0$ at (x_0, y_0). Let $\Delta \equiv f_{xx}f_{yy} - (f_{xy})^2$ (the Hessian determinant). State sufficient conditions for f to have a relative maximum or minimum at (x_0, y_0).

    (B) Using the assumptions and notation of Question 455(A), give examples to show that Case 3, where $\Delta - 0$, allows no conclusions to be drawn.

456. Find the relative maxima and minima of the function $f(x, y) = 2x + 4y - x^2 - y^2 - 3$.

457. Determine the values of p and q so that the sum S of the squares of the vertical distances of the points $(0, 2)$, $(1, 3)$, and $(2, 5)$ from the line $y = px + q$ shall be a minimum (method of least squares).

458. Find the absolute maximum and minimum of $f(x, y) = 4x^2 + 2xy - 3y^2$ on the unit square $0 \le x \le 1, 0 \le y \le 1$.

459. Find the absolute extrema of $f(x, y) = \sin x + \sin y + \sin (x + y)$.

460. Find the point(s) on the sphere $x^2 + y^2 + z^2 = 1$ farthest from the point $(2, 1, 2)$.

461. Find the point(s) on the cone $x^2 = y^2 + z^2$ nearest the point $(0, 1, 3)$.

CHAPTER 44

Multiple Integrals and Their Applications

462. (A) Evaluate the iterated integral $I = \int_0^{\pi/2} \int_0^{\cos\theta} \rho^2 \sin\theta \, d\rho \, d\theta$.

(B) Evaluate $I = \int_0^1 \int_y^1 e^{x^2} \, dx \, dy$.

463. Evaluate $I = \int_0^1 \int_{y^4}^{y^2} \sqrt{y/x} \, dx \, dy$.

464. (A) Evaluate $I = \iint_{\mathcal{R}} x \, dA$, where $\mathcal{R}$ is the region bounded by $y = x$ and $y = x^2$.

(B) Evaluate $I = \iint_{\mathcal{R}} y^2 \, dA$, where $\mathcal{R}$ is the region bounded by $y = 2x$, $y = 5x$, and $x = 2$.

465. Find the volume V under the plane $z = 3x + 4y$ and over the rectangle $\mathcal{R}$ $1 \le x \le 2$, $0 \le y \le 3$.

466. Find the volume V in the first octant bounded by $z = y^2$, $x = 2$, and $y = 4$.

467. Find $I = \iint_{\mathcal{R}} \sin\theta \, dA$, if $\mathcal{R}$ is the region outside the circle $r = 1$ and inside the cardioid $r = 1 + \cos\theta$ (see Figure A44.4 in the Answers section).

468. Use cylindrical coordinates to calculate the volume of a sphere of radius a.

469. Show that $\int_0^\infty e^{-x^2}\,dx = \dfrac{\sqrt{\pi}}{2}$.

470. Use spherical coordinates to find the volume of a sphere of radius a.

471. Find the mass of a circular plate $\mathcal{R}$ of radius a whose density is numerically equal to the distance from the center.

472. Find the center of mass of the first-quadrant part of the disk of radius a with center at the origin, if the density function is y.

473. Find the moments of inertia of the triangle bounded by $3x + 4y = 24$, $x = 0$, and $y = 0$, and having density 1.

474. Find the centroid $(\bar{x}, \bar{y})$ of the region in the first quadrant bounded by $y^2 = 6x$, $y = 0$, and $x = 6$ (Figure A44.5 in the Answers section).

CHAPTER 45

Vector Functions in Space; Divergence and Curl; Line Integrals

475. (A) For the space curve $\mathbf{R}(t) = (t, t^2, t^3)$, find a tangent vector and the tangent line at the point $(1, 1, 1)$.

(B) Find the speed of a particle tracing the curve of Question 475(A) at time $t = 1$. (The parameter t is usually, but not necessarily, interpreted as the time.)

476. Find a tangent vector, the tangent line, the speed, and the normal plane to the helical curve $\mathbf{R}(t) = (a \cos 2\pi t, a \sin 2\pi t, bt)$ at $t = 1$.

477. Prove that the angle θ between a tangent vector and the positive z-axis is the same for all points of the helix of Question 476.

478. If $\mathbf{F}(t) = (\sin t, \cos t, t)$ and $\mathbf{G}(t) = (t, 1, \ln t)$, find $\dfrac{d}{dt}[\mathbf{F}(t) \cdot \mathbf{G}(t)]$.

479. If $\mathbf{G}(3) = (1, 1, 2)$ and $\mathbf{G}'(3) = (3, -2, 5)$, find $\dfrac{d}{dt}[t^2\mathbf{G}(t)]$ at $t = 3$.

480. Let $\mathbf{F}(t) = \mathbf{G}(t) \times \mathbf{H}'(t)$. Prove $\mathbf{F}' = (\mathbf{G} \times \mathbf{H}') + (\mathbf{G}' \times \mathbf{H})$.

481. Prove that $\dfrac{d}{dt}[\mathbf{R}(t) \times \mathbf{R}'(t)] = \mathbf{R}(t) \times \mathbf{R}''(t)$.

482. If $\mathbf{G}'(t)$ is perpendicular to $\mathbf{G}(t)$ for all t, show that $|\mathbf{G}(t)|$ is constant—that is, the point $\mathbf{G}(t)$ lies on the surface of a sphere with center at the origin.

483. Derive the converse of Question 482: if $|\mathbf{G}(t)|$ is constant, then $\mathbf{G}(t) \cdot \mathbf{G}'(t) = 0$.

484. Find the principal unit normal vector $\mathbf{N}$ to the curve $\mathbf{R}(t) = (t, t^2, t^3)$ when $t = 1$.

485. Find a formula for the binormal vector $\mathbf{B} = \mathbf{T} \times \mathbf{N}$ in the case of the helix $\mathbf{R}(t) = (3 \cos 2t, 3 \sin 2t, 8t)$.

486. Find an equation of the *osculating plane* to the curve $\mathbf{R}(t) = (2t - t^2, t^2, 2t + t^2)$ at $t = 1$.

487. Show that a normal vector to the osculating plane of a curve $\mathbf{R}(t)$ is given by $\mathbf{R}' \times \mathbf{R}''$.

488. Find the curvature κ of the curve $\mathbf{R}(t) = \left(\sin t, \cos t, \dfrac{1}{2} t^2 \right)$ at $t = 0$.

489. Prove the following formula for the curvature: $\kappa = \dfrac{|\mathbf{R}' \times \mathbf{R}''|}{|\mathbf{R}'|^3}$.

490. Compute the divergence, div $\mathbf{F}$, for the vector field $\mathbf{F} = (xy, yz, xz)$.

491. For any vector field $\mathbf{F}(x, y, z) = (f(x, y, z), g(x, y, z), h(x, y, z))$, define curl $\mathbf{F}$.

492. Find curl $\mathbf{F}$ when $\mathbf{F} = (yz, xz, xy)$.

493. Show that, for any scalar function $f(x, y, z)$, div $\nabla f = f_{xx} + f_{yy} + f_{zz}$. (The latter sum, called the *Laplacian* of f, is often notated as $\nabla^2 f$.)

494. For any scalar function $f(x, y, z)$ with continuous mixed second partial derivatives, show that curl $\nabla f = 0$.

495. For a vector field $\mathbf{F}(x, y, z) = (f(x, y, z), g(x, y, z), h(x, y, z))$, where f, g, and h have continuous mixed second partial derivatives, show that div curl $\mathbf{F} = 0$.

496. For a scalar field f and a vector field $\mathbf{F}$, prove the product rule div $(f\mathbf{F}) = f$ div $\mathbf{F} + \nabla f \times \mathbf{F}$.

497. For a scalar field f and a vector field $\mathbf{F} = (\phi, \psi, \eta)$, prove the product rule curl $(f\mathbf{F}) = f\,\text{curl}\,\mathbf{F} + \nabla f \times \mathbf{F}$.

498. For vector fields $\mathbf{F} = (f, g, h)$ and $\mathbf{G} = (\phi, \psi, \eta)$, prove div $(\mathbf{F} \times \mathbf{G}) = \text{curl}\,\mathbf{F} \cdot \mathbf{G} - \mathbf{F} \cdot \text{curl}\,\mathbf{G}$.

499. Find the work W done by done by a force $\mathbf{F} = (xy, yz, xz)$ acting on an object moving along the curve $\mathbf{R}(t) = (t, t^2, t^3)$ for $0 \le t \le 1$.

500. Let $\mathscr{C}$ be any curve in the xy-plane. Show that $\int_{\mathscr{C}} y\,dx + x\,dy$ depends only on the endpoints of $\mathscr{C}$.

ANSWERS

Chapter 1: Inequalities

1. x may be positive or negative. **Case 1.** $x > 0$. $2/x < 3$. $2 < 3x$ [Multiply by x.], $\dfrac{2}{3} < x$

[Divide by 3.] **Case 2.** $x < 0$. $2/x < 3$. $2 > 3x$ [Multiply by x. Reverse the inequality.],

$\dfrac{2}{3} > x$ [Divide by 3.] Notice that this condition $\dfrac{2}{3} > x$ is satisfied whenever $x < 0$. Hence,

in the case where $x < 0$, the inequality is satisfied by all such x. Hence, $\dfrac{2}{3} < x$ or $x < 0$. As

shown in Figure A1.1, the solution is the union of the intervals $\left(\dfrac{2}{3}, \infty\right)$ and $(-\infty, 0)$.

$$0 \qquad\qquad \tfrac{2}{3}$$

Figure A1.1

2. We cannot simply multiply both sides by $x - 3$, because we do not know whether $x - 3$ is positive or negative. **Case 1.** $x - 3 > 0$ [This is equivalent to $x > 3$.] Multiplying the given inequality (1) by the positive quantity $x - 3$ preserves the inequality: $x + 4 < 2x - 6$, $4 < x - 6$ [Subtract x.], $10 < x$ [Add 6.] Thus, when $x > 3$, the given inequality holds when and only when $x > 10$. **Case 2.** $x - 3 < 0$ [This is equivalent to $x < 3$.] Multiplying the given inequality (1) by the negative quantity $x - 3$ reverses the inequality: $x + 4 > 2x - 6$, $4 > x - 6$ [Subtract x.], $10 > x$ [Add 6.] Thus, when $x < 3$, the inequality (1) holds when and only when $x < 10$. But $x < 3$ implies $x < 10$, and, therefore, the inequality (1) holds for all $x < 3$. Thus, $x > 10$ or $x < 3$. As shown in Figure A1.2, the solution is the union of the intervals $(10, \infty)$ and $(-\infty, 3)$.

$$0 \qquad 3 \qquad\qquad\qquad 10$$

Figure A1.2

3. Factor: $x^2 - 6x + 5 = (x - 1)(x - 5)$. Let $h(x) = (x - 1)(x - 5)$. To the left of $x = 1$, both $x - 1$ and $x - 5$ are negative and, therefore, $h(x)$ is positive. When we pass through $x = 1$, $x - 1$ changes sign and $h(x)$ becomes negative. When we move further to the right and pass through $x = 5$, $x - 5$ changes sign and $h(x)$ becomes positive again. Thus, $h(x)$ is positive for $x < 1$ and for $x > 5$. Hence $x > 5$ or $x < 1$. This is the union of the intervals $(5, \infty)$ and $(-\infty, 1)$.

4. $(x - 1)^2$ is always positive except when $x = 1$ (when it is 0). So, the only solutions occur when $x + 4 < 0$ and $x \neq 1$. $x < -4$ [In interval notation, $(-\infty, -4)$.]

5. See Figure A1.3. The key points for the function $K(x) = (2x + 1)(x - 3)(x + 7)$ are $x = -7$, $x = -\dfrac{1}{2}$, and $x = 3$. For x to the left of $x = -7$, all three factors are negative and, therefore, $K(x)$ is negative. When we pass from left to right through $x = -7$, $x + 7$ changes sign, and, therefore, $K(x)$ becomes positive. When we later pass through $x = -\dfrac{1}{2}$, $2x + 1$ changes sign, and, therefore, $K(x)$ becomes negative again. Finally, as we pass through $x = 3$, $x - 3$ changes sign, and $K(x)$ becomes and remains positive. Hence, $K(x)$ is negative when and only when $x < -7$ or $3 < x < 7$.

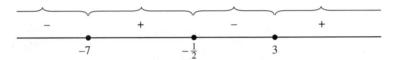

Figure A1.3

6. $x > x^2$ is equivalent to $x^2 - x < 0$, $x(x - 1) < 0$; hence one of x and $(x - 1)$ is positive and the other negative. Since $x > x - 1$, x must be positive and $x - 1$ must be negative (that is, $x - 1 < 0$, which implies $x < 1$). Thus, $0 < x < 1$.

7. $x^2 > x^3$ is equivalent to $x^3 - x^2 < 0$, $x^2(x - 1) < 0$, $x < 1$, and $x \neq 0$.

8. This is clearly true when x is negative and y positive, and false when x is positive and y negative. When x and y are both positive, or x and y are both negative, multiplication by the positive quantity xy yields the equivalent inequality $y < x$.

Chapter 2: Absolute Value

9. **(A)** $\dfrac{7}{3} > x > 1$ (Divide by -3 and reverse the inequalities.) In interval notation, the solution is the set $\left(1, \dfrac{7}{3}\right)$. $|5 - 3x| < 2$ if and only if $-2 < 5 - 3x < 2$, $-7 < -3x < -3$ [Subtract 5.]

   (B) Let us solve the negation of the given relation: $|3x - 2| < 1$. This is equivalent to $-1 < 3x - 2 < 1$, $1 < 3x < 3$ [Add 2.], $\dfrac{1}{3} < x < 1$ [Divide by 3].

The points not satisfying this condition correspond to x such that $x \leq \dfrac{1}{3}$ or $x \geq 1$.

(C) $|u| = -u$ when and only when $u \leq 0$. So, $|3 - x| = x - 3$ when and only when $3 - x \leq 0$; that is, $3 \leq x$.

(D) If $c > 0$, $|u| = c$ if and only if $u = \pm c$. So, $|2x + 3| = 4$ when and only when $2x + 3 = \pm 4$. There are two cases: **Case 1.** $2x + 3 = 4$. $2x = 1$, $x = \dfrac{1}{2}$. **Case 2.** $2x + 3 = -4$. $2x = -7$, $x = -\dfrac{7}{2}$.

So, either $x = \dfrac{1}{2}$ or $x = -\dfrac{7}{2}$.

10. (A) There are two cases: **Case 1.** $2x - 3 = x + 2$. $x - 3 = 2$, $x = 5$. **Case 2.** $2x - 3 = -(x + 2)$. $2x - 3 = -x - 2$, $3x - 3 = -2$, $3x = 1$, $x = \dfrac{1}{3}$.

So, either $x = 5$ or $x = \dfrac{1}{3}$.

(B) Since an absolute value is never negative, $2x - 1 \geq 0$. There are two cases: **Case 1.** $x + 7 \geq 0$. $2x - 1 = x + 7$, $x - 1 = 7$, $x = 8$. **Case 2.** $x + 7 < 0$. $2x - 1 = -(x + 7)$, $2x - 1 = -x - 7$, $3x - 1 = -7$, $3x = -6$, $x = -2$. But then, $2x - 1 = -5 < 0$.

So, the only solution is $x = 8$.

(C) This is equivalent to $-|x + 2| < 2x - 3 < |x + 2|$. There are two cases: **Case 1.** $x + 2 \geq 0$. $-(x + 2) < 2x - 3 < x + 2$, $-x - 2 < 2x - 3 < x + 2$, $1 < 3x$ and $x < 5$, $\dfrac{1}{3} < x < 5$. **Case 2:** $x + 2 < 0$. $-(x + 2) > 2x - 3 > x + 2$, $-x - 2 > 2x - 3 > x + 2$, $1 > 3x$ and $x > 5$, $\dfrac{1}{3} > x$ and $x > 5$ (Impossible). So, $\dfrac{1}{3} < x < 5$ is the solution.

(D) First solve $|3x + 1| < \dfrac{1}{3}$. This is equivalent to $-\dfrac{1}{3} < 3x + 1 < \dfrac{1}{3}$, $-\dfrac{4}{3} < 3x < -\dfrac{2}{3}$ (Subtract 1.), $-\dfrac{4}{9} < x < -\dfrac{2}{9}$ (Divide by 3.) The inequality $0 < |3x + 1|$ excludes the case where $0 = |3x + 1|$, that is, where $x = -\dfrac{1}{3}$.

All x for which $-\dfrac{4}{9} < x < -\dfrac{2}{9}$ except $x = -\dfrac{1}{3}$.

11. (A) The case $n = 2$ is the triangle inequality. Assume the result true for some n. By the triangle inequality and the inductive hypothesis,

$$|u_1 + u_2 + \cdots + u_n + u_{n+1}| \leq |u_1 + u_2 + \cdots + u_n| + |u_{n+1}| \leq (|u_1| + |u_2| + \cdots + |u_n|) + |u_{n+1}|$$

and, therefore, the result also holds for $n + 1$.

(B) $|u| = |v + (u - v)| \leq |v| + |u - v|$ (Triangle inequality.) Hence, $|u - v| \geq |u| - |v|$. Similarly, $|v - u| \geq |v| - |u|$. But, $|v - u| = |u - v|$. So, $|u - v| \geq$ (maximum of $|u| - |v|$ and $|v| - |u|$) $= ||u| - |v||$.

12. (A) This is equivalent to $\left|\dfrac{x^2 + 1}{x}\right| > 2$, $\dfrac{x^2 + 1}{|x|} > 2$ [Since $x^2 + 1 > 0$.], $x^2 + 1 > 2|x|$, $x^2 - 2|x| + 1 > 0$, $|x|^2 - 2|x| + 1 > 0$ [Since $x^2 = |x|^2$], $(|x| - 1)^2 > 0$, $|x| \neq 1$.

All x except $x = 1$ and $x = -1$.

(B) This is equivalent to $\left|\dfrac{x^2 + 1}{x}\right| < 4$, $x^2 + 1 < 4|x|$, $x^2 - 4|x| + 1 < 0$, $|x|^2 - 4|x| + 1 < 0$, $(|x| - 2)^2 < 3$ [completing the square], $||x| - 2| < \sqrt{3}$, $-\sqrt{3} < |x| - 2 < \sqrt{3}$, $2 - \sqrt{3} < |x| < 2 + \sqrt{3}$.

When $x > 0$, $2 - \sqrt{3} < x < 2 + \sqrt{3}$, and, when $x < 0$, $-2 - \sqrt{3} < x < -2 + \sqrt{3}$.

(C) When $x \geq 0$, this reduces to $x + 1 < x$, which is impossible. When $x < 0$, the inequality becomes $x + 1 < -x$, which is equivalent to $2x + 1 < 0$, or $2x < -1$, or $x < -\dfrac{1}{2}$.

13. From the definition of absolute value, $|a| = \pm a$ and $|b| = \pm b$. Hence, $|a| \cdot |b| = (\pm a) \cdot (\pm b) = \pm(ab)$. Since $|a| \cdot |b|$ is nonnegative, $|a| \cdot |b|$ must be $|ab|$.

14. (A) This is equivalent to $-|x - 1| \leq 3x - 2 \leq |x - 1|$. **Case 1.** $x - 1 \geq 0$. Then $-(x - 1) \leq 3x - 2 \leq x - 1$, $-x + 1 \leq 3x - 2 \leq x - 1$; the first inequality is equivalent to $\dfrac{3}{4} \leq x$ and the second to $x \leq \dfrac{1}{2}$. But this is impossible. **Case 2.** $x - 1 < 0$. $-x + 1 \geq 3x - 2 \geq x - 1$; the first inequality is equivalent to $x \leq \dfrac{3}{4}$ and the second to $x \geq \dfrac{1}{2}$. Hence, we have $\dfrac{1}{2} \leq x \leq \dfrac{3}{4}$.

(B) Case 1. $x \geq 5$. Then $x - 2 + x - 5 = 9$, $2x - 7 = 9$, $2x = 16$, $x = 8$. **Case 2.** $2 \leq x < 5$. Then $x - 2 + 5 - x = 9$, $3 = 9$, which is impossible. **Case 3.** $x < 2$. Then $2 - x + 5 - x = 9$, $7 - 2x = 9$, $2x = -2$, $x = -1$. So, the solutions are 8 and -1.

(C) Case 1. $5x + 1 \geq 0$, that is, $x \geq -\dfrac{1}{5}$. Then $4 - x \geq 5x + 1$, $3 \geq 6x$, $\dfrac{1}{2} \geq x$. Thus, we obtain the solutions $-\dfrac{1}{5} \leq x \leq \dfrac{1}{2}$. **Case 2.** $5x + 1 < 0$; that is, $x < -\dfrac{1}{5}$. Then $4 - x \geq -5x - 1$, $4x \geq -5$, $x \geq -\dfrac{5}{4}$. Thus, we obtain the solutions $-\dfrac{5}{4} \leq x < -\dfrac{1}{5}$. Hence, the set of solutions is $\left[-\dfrac{1}{5}, \dfrac{1}{2}\right] \cup \left[-\dfrac{5}{4}, -\dfrac{1}{5}\right] = \left[-\dfrac{5}{4}, \dfrac{1}{2}\right]$.

15. We argue geometrically from Figure A2.1. $|x - 1|$ is the distance of x from 1, and $|x - 3|$ is the distance of x from 3. The point $x = 2$ is equidistant from 1 and 3. Hence, the solutions consist of all $x \geq 2$.

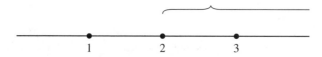

Figure A2.1

Chapter 3: Lines

16. **(A)** Remember that the slope m of the line through two points (x_1, y_1) and (x_2, y_2) is given by the equation $m = \dfrac{y_2 - y_1}{x_2 - x_1}$. Hence, the slope of the given line is $\dfrac{1 - 5}{7 - (-2)} = \dfrac{-4}{9} = -\dfrac{4}{9}$.

(B) The slope m of the given line is $(6 - 3)/(3 - 1) = \dfrac{3}{2}$. Recall that the point-slope equation of the line through point (x_1, y_1) and with slope m is $y - y_1 = m(x - x_1)$. Hence, one point-slope equation of the given line using the point $(1, 3)$ is $y - 3 = \dfrac{3}{2}(x - 1)$.

Another point-slope equation, using the point $(3, 6)$, is $y - 6 = \dfrac{3}{2}(x - 3)$.

(C) The line through $(1, 2)$ and $(1, 3)$ is vertical and, therefore, does not have a slope. Thus, there is no point-slope equation of the line.

(D) $y - 3 = 5(x - 1)$.

(E) Remember that the slope-intercept equation of a line is $y = mx + b$, where m is the slope and b is the y-intercept (that is, the y-coordinate of the point where the line cuts the y-axis). In this case, the slope $m = (8 - 4)/(4 - 2) = \dfrac{4}{2} = 2$.

Method 1. A point-slope equation of the line is $y - 8 = 2(x - 4)$. This is equivalent to $y - 8 = 2x - 8$, or, finally, to $y = 2x$.

Method 2. The slope-intercept equation has the form $y = 2x + b$. Since $(2, 4)$ lies on the line, we may substitute 2 for x and 4 for y. So, $4 = 2 \cdot 2 + b$, and, therefore, $b = 0$. Hence, the equation is $y = 2x$.

17. If a given line is vertical it has an equation $x = C$. In this case, we can let $A = 1$ and $B = 0$. If the given line is not vertical, it has a slope-intercept equation $y = mx + b$, or, equivalently, $-mx + y = b$. So, let $A = -m$, $B = 1$, and $C = b$. Conversely, assume that we are given an equation $Ax + By = C$, with A and B not both 0. If $B = 0$, the equation is equivalent to $x = C/A$, which is the equation of a vertical line. If $B \neq 0$, solve the equation for y: $y = -\dfrac{A}{B}x + \dfrac{C}{B}$. This is the slope-intercept equation of the line with slope $-\dfrac{A}{B}$ and y-intercept $\dfrac{C}{B}$.

10. Remember that two lines are parallel if and only if their slopes are equal. If we solve $3x + 4y = 2$ for y, namely, $y = -\dfrac{3}{4}x + \dfrac{1}{2}$, we obtain the slope-intercept equation for M. Hence, the slope of M is $-\dfrac{3}{4}$ and, therefore, the slope of the parallel line L also is $-\dfrac{3}{4}$. So, L has a slope-intercept equation of the form $y = -\dfrac{3}{4}x + b$. Since L goes through $(-1, 4)$, $4 = -\dfrac{3}{4} \cdot (-1) + b$, and, therefore, $b = 4 - \dfrac{3}{4} = \dfrac{13}{4}$. Thus, the equation of L is $y = -\dfrac{3}{4}x + \dfrac{13}{4}$.

19. If we solve $Ax + By = C$ for y, we obtain the slope-intercept equation $y = -\dfrac{A}{B}x + \dfrac{C}{B}$. So, the slope is $-A/B$. Given a parallel line, it must also have slope $-A/B$ and, therefore, has a slope-intercept equation $y = -\dfrac{A}{B}x + b$, which is equivalent to $\dfrac{A}{B}x + y = b$, and, thence to $Ax + By = bB$. Conversely, a line with equation $Ax + By = E$ must have slope $-A/B$ (obtained by putting the equation in slope-intercept form) and is, therefore, parallel to the line with equation $Ax + By = C$.

20. In Question 17, set $C/A = a$ and $C/B = b$. Notice that, when $y = 0$, the equation yields the value $x = a$, and, therefore, a is the x-intercept of the line, similarly for the y-intercept.

21. Solve $2x - 6y = 5$ for y, obtaining $y = \dfrac{1}{3}x - \dfrac{5}{6}$. So, the slope of L is $\dfrac{1}{3}$. Recall that two lines with slopes m_1 and m_2 are perpendicular if and only if $m_1 m_2 = -1$, or, equivalently, $m_1 = -1/m_2$. Hence, the slope of M is the negative reciprocal of $\dfrac{1}{3}$, that is, -3. The slope-intercept equation of M has the form $y = -3x + b$. Since $(1, 4)$ is on M, $4 = -3 \cdot 1 + b$. Hence, $b = 7$, and the required equation is $y = -3x + 7$.

22. Assume that $A_2 = rA_1$ and $B_2 = rB_1$, with $r \neq 0$. Then the equation of M is $rA_1x + rB_1y = C_2$, which is equivalent to $A_1x + B_1y = \dfrac{1}{r} \cdot C_2$. Then, by Question 19, M is parallel to L. Conversely, assume M is parallel to L. By solving the equations of L and M for y, we see that the slope of L is $-(A_1/B_1)$ and the slope of M is $-(A_2/B_2)$. Since M and L are parallel, their slopes are equal:

$$-\frac{A_1}{B_1} = -\frac{A_2}{B_2} \quad \text{or} \quad \frac{A_2}{A_1} = \frac{B_2}{B_1} = r$$

(In the special case where the lines are vertical, $B_1 = B_2 = 0$, and we can set $r = A_2/A_1$.)

23. (A) The slope m_1 of line $\overrightarrow{AB}$ is $(3-1)/(7-4) = \frac{2}{3}$. The slope m_2 of line $\overrightarrow{BC}$ is $(9-3)/(3-7) = -\frac{6}{4} = -\frac{3}{2}$.

Since m_2 is the negative reciprocal of m_1, the lines $\overrightarrow{AB}$ and $\overrightarrow{BC}$ are perpendicular. Hence, $\triangle ABC$ has a right angle at B.

(B) The slope of line $\overrightarrow{AB}$ is $(5-2)/[7-(-1)] = \frac{3}{8}$. The slope of line $\overrightarrow{BC}$ is $(2-0)/(-1-k) = -2/(1+k)$. The condition for $\triangle ABC$ to have a right angle at B is that lines $\overrightarrow{AB}$ and $\overrightarrow{BC}$ are perpendicular, which holds when and only when the product of their slopes is -1; that is, $\left(\frac{3}{8}\right)[-2/(1+k)] = -1$. This is equivalent to $6 - 8(1+k)$, or $8k = -2$, or $k = -\frac{1}{4}$.

24. (A) By the midpoint formula, the coordinates of the midpoint are the averages of the coordinates of the endpoints. In this case, the midpoint (x, y) is given by $([2+(-1)]/2, (5+3)/2) = \left(\frac{1}{2}, 4\right)$.

(B) The midpoint M of segment $\overline{BC}$ is $((8+2)/2, (1+3)/2) = (5, 2)$. So, $\overline{AM}$ is horizontal, with equation $y = 2$.

(C) The slope of $\overline{AC}$ is $(3-2)/(2-1) = 1$. Hence, the slope of the altitude is the negative reciprocal of 1, namely, -1. Thus, its slope-intercept equation has the form $y = -x + b$. Since $B(8, 1)$ is on the altitude, $1 = -8 + b$, and, so, $b = 9$. Hence, the equation is $y = -x + 9$.

25. Solving for y, we obtain the equation $y = -\frac{3}{2}x + 2$. For any fixed x, the vertical line with that x-coordinate cuts the line at the point Q where the y-coordinate is $-\frac{3}{2}x + 2$ (see Figure A3.1). The points along that vertical line and above Q have y-coordinates $y > -\frac{3}{2}x + 2$. This is equivalent to $2y > -3x + 4$, and thence to $3x + 2y > 4$.

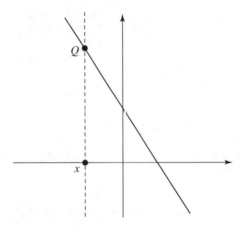

Figure A3.1

26. (A) The set of all nonvertical lines through $(0, 2)$.

(B) The family of mutually parallel lines of slope 3.

27. Given $\triangle ABC$, choose the coordinate system so that A and B lie on the x-axis and C lies on the y-axis (Figure A3.2). Let the coordinates of A, B, and C be $(u, 0)$, $(v, 0)$, and $(0, w)$. (***i***) The altitude from C to $\overrightarrow{AB}$ is the y-axis. (***ii***) The slope of $\overrightarrow{BC}$ is $-w/v$. So, the altitude from A to $\overrightarrow{BC}$ has slope v/w. Its slope-intercept equation has the form $y = (v/w)x + b$. Since $(u, 0)$ lies on the line, $0 = (v/w)(u) + b$; hence, its y-intercept $b = -vu/w$. Thus, this altitude intersects the altitude from C (the y-axis) at the point $(0, -vu/w)$. (***iii***) The slope of $\overrightarrow{AC}$ is $-w/u$. So, the altitude from B to $\overrightarrow{AC}$ has slope u/w, and its slope-intercept equation is $y = (u/w)x + b$. Since $(v, 0)$ lies on the altitude, $0 = (u/w)(v) + b$, and its y-intercept $b = -uv/w$. Thus, this altitude also goes through the point $(0, -vu/w)$.

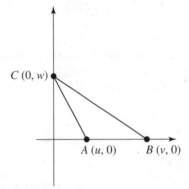

Figure A3.2

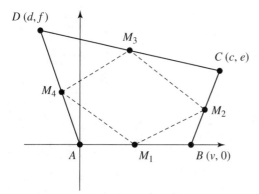

Figure A3.3

28. Refer to Figure A3.3. Let A be the origin and let B be on the x-axis, with coordinates $(v, 0)$. Let C be (c, e) and let D be (d, f). The midpoint M_1 of $\overline{AB}$ has coordinates $(v/2, 0)$, the midpoint M_2 of $\overline{BC}$ is $((c + v)/2, e/2)$, the midpoint M_3 of $\overline{CD}$ is $((c + d)/2, (e + f)/2)$, and the midpoint M_4 of $\overline{AD}$ is $(d/2, f/2)$.

$$\text{Slope of line } \overleftrightarrow{M_1M_2} = \frac{e/2 - 0}{(c+v)/2 - v/2} = \frac{e}{c} \quad \text{Slope of line } \overleftrightarrow{M_3M_4} = \frac{(e + f)/2 - f/2}{(c+d)/2 - d/2} = \frac{e}{c}$$

Thus, $\overleftrightarrow{M_1M_2}$ and $\overleftrightarrow{M_3M_4}$ are parallel. Similarly, the slopes of $\overleftrightarrow{M_2M_3}$ and $\overleftrightarrow{M_1M_4}$ both turn out to be $f/(d - v)$, and, therefore, $\overleftrightarrow{M_2M_3}$ and $\overleftrightarrow{M_1M_4}$ are parallel. Thus, $M_1M_2M_3M_4$ is a parallelogram. (Note two special cases. When $c = 0$, both $\overleftrightarrow{M_1M_2}$ and $\overleftrightarrow{M_3M_4}$ are vertical and, therefore, parallel. When $d = v$, both $\overleftrightarrow{M_1M_4}$ and $\overleftrightarrow{M_2M_3}$ are vertical and, therefore, parallel.)

29.

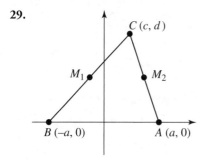

Figure A3.4

See Figure A3.4. Choose the x-axis so that it goes through A and B and let the origin be halfway between A and B. Let A be $(a, 0)$. Then B is $(-a, 0)$. Let C be (c, d). Then M_1 is $((c - a)/2, d/2)$, and M_2 is $((c + a)/2, d/2)$. By the distance formula,

$$\overline{AM}_1 = \sqrt{\left(a - \frac{c-a}{2}\right)^2 + \left(0 - \frac{d}{2}\right)^2} = \sqrt{\left(\frac{3a-c}{2}\right)^2 + \left(\frac{d}{2}\right)^2}$$

and
$$\overline{BM}_2 = \sqrt{\left[\frac{c+a}{2} - (-a)\right]^2 + \left(\frac{d}{2} - 0\right)^2} = \sqrt{\left(\frac{3a+c}{2}\right)^2 + \left(\frac{d}{2}\right)^2}$$

Setting $AM_1 = BM_2$ and squaring both sides, we obtain $[(3a - c)/2]^2 + (d/2)^2 = [(3a + c)/2]^2 + (d/2)^2$, and, simplifying, $(3a - c)^2 = (3a + c)^2$. So, $(3a + c)^2 - (3a - c)^2 = 0$, and, factoring the left-hand side, $[(3a + c) + (3a - c)] \cdot [(3a + c) - (3a - c)] = 0$; that is, $(6a) \cdot (2c) = 0$. Since $a \neq 0$, $c = 0$. Now the distance formula gives

$$\overline{CA} = \sqrt{(0-a)^2 + (d-0)^2} = \sqrt{[0-(-a)]^2 + (d-0)^2} = \overline{CB}$$

as required.

30. Remember that the distance from a point (x_1, y_1) to a line $Ax + By + C = 0$ is $|Ax_1 + By_1 + C|/\sqrt{A^2 + B^2}$. In our case, $A = 3$, $B = -4$, $C = 10$, and $\sqrt{A^2 + B^2} = \sqrt{25} = 5$. So the distance is $|3(1) - 4(2) - 10|/5 = \frac{15}{5} = 3$.

31. A point-slope equation of a line through $(4, -2)$ with slope m is $y + 2 = m(x - 4)$ or $mx - y - (4m + 2) = 0$. The distance of $(0, 0)$ from this line is $|4m + 2|/\sqrt{m^2 + 1}$. Hence, $|4m + 2|/\sqrt{m^2 + 1} = 2$. So $(4m + 2)^2 = 4(m^2 + 1)$, or $(2m + 1)^2 = m^2 + 1$. Simplifying, $m(3m + 4) = 0$, and, therefore, $m = 0$ or $m = -\frac{4}{3}$. The required equations are $y = -2$ and $4x + 3y - 10 = 0$.

32. Since the equation is linear, we can write it as $y = mx + b$. From the information about the freezing point of water, we see that $b = 32$. From the information about the boiling point, we have $212 = 100m + 32$, $180 = 100m$, $m = \frac{9}{5}$. So $y = \frac{9}{5}x + 32$.

Chapter 4: Circles

33. By the distance formula, a point (x, y) is on the circle if and only if $\sqrt{(x-a)^2 + (y-b)^2} = r$. Squaring both sides, we obtain the standard equation: $(x - a)^2 + (y - b)^2 = r^2$.

34. Complete the square in x and in y: $(x - 6)^2 + (y + 10)^2 + 15 = 36 + 100$. (Here the -6 in $(x - 6)$ is half of the coefficient, -12, of x in the original equation, and the $+10$ in $(y + 10)$ is half of the coefficient, 20, of y. The 36 and 100 on the right balance the squares of -6 and $+10$ that have in effect been added on the left.) Simplifying, we obtain $(x - 6)^2 + (y + 10)^2 = 121$, the standard equation of a circle with center at $(6, -10)$ and radius 11.

35. Let the center be $(-12, b)$. The distance formula yields $13 = \sqrt{(-12-0)^2 + (b-0)^2} = \sqrt{144 + b^2}$. So $144 + b^2 = 169$, $b^2 = 25$, and $b = \pm 5$. Hence, there are two circles, with equations $(x+12)^2 + (y-5)^2 = 169$ and $(x+12)^2 + (y+5)^2 = 169$.

36. The radius is the perpendicular distance from the center $(1, 3)$ to the line: $\dfrac{|5(1)-12(3)-8|}{13} = 3$. So the standard equation is $(x-1)^2 + (y-3)^2 = 9$.

37. Clearly, the indicated equation yields the equation of a circle that contains the intersection points. Conversely, given a circle $\mathscr{C} \neq \mathscr{C}_2$ that goes through those intersection points, take a point (x_0, y_0) of $\mathscr{C}$ that does not lie on $\mathscr{C}_2$ and substitute x_0 for x and y_0 for y in the indicated equation. By choice of (x_0, y_0) the coefficient of k is nonzero, so we can solve for k. If we then put this value of k in the indicated equation, we obtain an equation of a circle that is satisfied by (x_0, y_0) and by the intersection points of $\mathscr{C}_1$ and $\mathscr{C}_2$. Since three noncollinear points determine a circle, we have an equation for $\mathscr{C}$. [Again, it is the choice of (x_0, y_0) that makes the three points noncollinear, i.e., $k \neq -1$.]

38. Using Question 37, substitute $(3, 1)$ for (x, y) in the equation $(x^2 + y^2 - x - y - 2) + k(x^2 + y^2 + 4x - 4y - 8) = 0$. Then $4 + 10k = 0$, $k = -\dfrac{2}{5}$. So the desired equation can be written as

$$5(x^2 + y^2 - x - y - 2) - 2(x^2 + y^2 + 4x - 4y - 8) = 0 \text{ or } 3x^2 + 3y^2 - 13x + 3y + 6 = 0.$$

Chapter 5: Functions and Their Graphs

39. (A) The domain is the closed interval $[-2, 2]$, since $\sqrt{4-x^2}$ is defined when and only when $x^2 \leq 4$. The graph (Figure A5.1) is the upper half of the circle $x^2 + y^2 = 4$ with center at the origin and radius 2. The range is the closed interval $[0, 2]$.

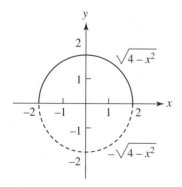

Figure A5.1

(B) The domain is the set of all real numbers. The range is the set of all nonnegative real numbers. The graph (Figure A5.2) is the graph of $y = |x|$ shifted one unit to the right.

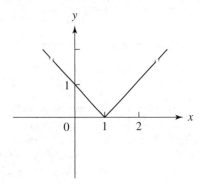

Figure A5.2

(C) The domain is the set of all nonzero real numbers, and the range is the same set. The graph (Figure A5.3) is the hyperbola $xy = 1$.

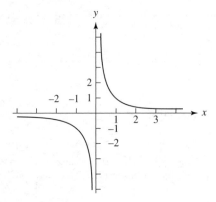

Figure A5.3

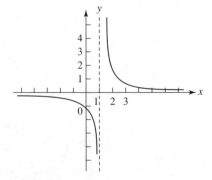

Figure A5.4

(D) The domain is the set of all real numbers $\neq 1$. The graph (Figure A5.4) is Figure A5.3 shifted one unit to the right. The range consists of all nonzero real numbers.

(E) The domain is the set of all real numbers, and the range is the same set. See Figure A5.5.

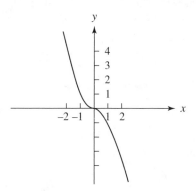

Figure A5.5

(F) The domain is the set of all real numbers except -2. Since $G(x) = \dfrac{(x+2)(x-2)}{x+2} = x - 2$ for $x \neq -2$, the graph (Figure A5.6) consists of all points on the line $y = x - 2$ except the point $(-2, -4)$. The range is the set of all real numbers except -4.

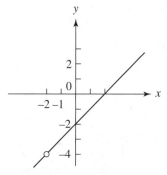

Figure A5.6

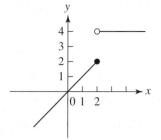

Figure A5.7

(G) The domain is the set of all real numbers. The graph (Figure A5.7) is made up of the left half of the line $y = x$ for $x \leq 2$ and the right half of the line $y = 4$ for $x > 2$. The range consists of all real numbers ≤ 2, plus the number 4.

(H) The domain is the set of all nonzero real numbers. The graph (Figure A5.8) is the right half of the line $y = 1$ for $x > 0$, plus the left half of the line $y = -1$ for $x < 0$. The range is $\{1, -1\}$.

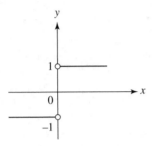

Figure A5.8

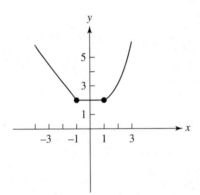

Figure A5.9

The domain is the set of all real numbers. The graph (Figure A5.9) is a continuous curve consisting of three pieces: the half of the line $y = 1 - x$ to the left of $x = -1$, the horizontal segment $y = 2$ between $x = -1$ and $x = 1$, and the part of the parabola $y = x^2 + 1$ to the right of $x = 1$. The range consists of all real numbers ≥ 2.

40. (A) Since some vertical lines cut the graph in more than one point, this cannot be the graph of a function.

(B) Since each vertical line cuts the graph in at most one point, this is the graph of a function.

41. (A) The domain consists of all real numbers except 2 and 3. To determine the range, set $y = \dfrac{1}{(x-2)(x-3)} = \dfrac{1}{x^2 - 5x + 6}$ and solve for x. $x^2 - 5x + \left(6 - \dfrac{1}{y}\right) = 0$. This has a solution when and only when $b^2 - 4ac = (-5)^2 - 4(1)\left(6 - \dfrac{1}{y}\right) = 25 - 24 + \dfrac{4}{y} = 1 + \dfrac{4}{y} \geq 0.$

This holds if and only if $4/y \geq -1$. This holds when $y > 0$, and, if $y < 0$, when $y \leq -4$. Hence the range is $(0, +\infty) \cup (-\infty, -4]$.

(B) x is in the domain if and only if $x^2 < 1$. Thus, the domain is $(-1, 1)$. To find the range, first note that $g(x) > 0$. Then set $y = 1/\sqrt{1-x^2}$ and solve for x. $y^2 = 1/(1-x^2)$, $x^2 = 1 - 1/y^2 \geq 0, 1 \geq 1/y^2$, $y^2 \geq 1$, $y \geq 1$. Thus, the range is $[1, +\infty)$.

(C) The domain is $(-1, +\infty)$. The graph consists of the open segment from $(-1, 0)$ to $(1, 2)$ plus the half-line of $y = 2$, with $x \geq 1$. Hence, the range is the half-open interval $(0, 2]$.

(D) The domain is $[0, 4)$. Inspection of the graph shows that the range is $[-1, 2]$.

(E) The domain is the set of all real numbers. To determine the range, note that $G(x) = 0$ if $x \geq 0$, and $G(x) = -2x$ if $x < 0$. Hence, the range consists of all nonnegative real numbers.

42. (A) Assume $f(u) = f(v)$. Then $\sqrt{u} = \sqrt{v}$. Square both sides; $u = v$. Thus, f is one-one.

(B) $f(-1) = 1 = f(1)$. Hence, f is not one-one.

(C) Assume $f(u) = f(v)$. Then $\dfrac{1}{u} = \dfrac{1}{v}$. Hence, $u = v$. Thus, f is one-one.

43. (A) $f(x+h) = (x+h)^2 - 2(x+h) = (x^2 + 2xh + h^2) - 2x - 2h$ So, $f(x+h) - f(x) = [(x^2 + 2xh + h^2) - 2x - 2h] - (x^2 - 2x) = 2xh + h^2 - 2h = h(2x + h - 2)$. Hence, $\dfrac{f(x+h) - f(x)}{h} = 2x + h - 2.$

(B) $f(x+h) = x + h + 4$. So, $f(x+h) - f(x) = (x+h+4) - (x+4) = h$. Hence, $\dfrac{f(x+h) - f(x)}{h} = 1.$

(C) $f(x+h) = (x+h)^3 + 1 = x^3 + 3x^2h + 3xh^2 + h^3 + 1$. So, $f(x+h) - f(x) = (x^3 + 3x^2h + 3xh^2 + h^3 + 1) - (x^3 + 1) = 3x^2h + 3xh^2 + h^3 = h(3x^2 + 3xh + h^2)$. Hence, $\dfrac{f(x+h) - f(x)}{h} = 3x^2 + 3xh + h^2.$

(D)
$$f(x+h) - f(x) = \sqrt{x+h} - \sqrt{x} = (\sqrt{x+h} - \sqrt{x})\frac{\sqrt{x+h} + \sqrt{x}}{\sqrt{x+h} + \sqrt{x}} = \frac{(x+h) - x}{\sqrt{x+h} + \sqrt{x}}$$
$$= \frac{h}{\sqrt{x+h} + \sqrt{x}}$$

So, $\dfrac{f(x+h)-f(x)}{h} = \dfrac{1}{\sqrt{x+h}+\sqrt{x}}$

(E) $f(x+h)-f(x) = \dfrac{1}{x+h} - \dfrac{1}{x} = \dfrac{x-(x+h)}{x(x+h)} = \dfrac{-h}{x(x+h)}$

Hence $\dfrac{f(x+h)-f(x)}{h} = -\dfrac{1}{x(x+h)}$

44. **(A)** Let $y = 2x+1$ and solve for x. $x = \dfrac{1}{2}(y-1)$. Thus, $f^{-1}(y) = \dfrac{1}{2}(y-1)$.

(B) Let $y = x^3$. Then $x = \sqrt[3]{y}$. So, $f^{-1}(y) = \sqrt[3]{y}$.

45. **(A)** $x^4 - 10x^2 + 9 = (x^2-9)(x^2-1) = (x-3)(x+3)(x-1)(x+1)$. Hence, the roots are $3, -3, 1, -1$.

(B) Inspection of the divisors of the constant term 32 reveals that -2 is a root. Division by $x+2$ yields the factorization

$$(x+2)(x^2-16) = (x+2)(x^2+4)(x^2-4) = (x+2)(x^2+4)(x-2)(x+2).$$

So, the roots are 2 and -2.

(C) Testing the divisors of 24 reveals the root -2. Dividing by $x+2$ yields the factorization $(x+2)(x^2+7x+12) = (x+2)(x+3)(x+4)$. Thus, the roots are $-2, -3$, and -4.

(D) -2 is a root. Dividing by $x+2$ yields the factorization $(x+2)(x^2-2x-1)$. The quadratic formula applied to x^2-2x-1 gives the additional roots $1 \pm \sqrt{2}$.

Chapter 6: Limits

46. Intuitively, this means that, as x gets closer and closer to a, $f(x)$ gets closer and closer to L. We can state this in more precise language as follows: For any $\varepsilon > 0$, there exists $\delta > 0$ such that, if $|x-a| < \delta$, then $|f(x)-L| < \varepsilon$. Here, we assume that, for any $\delta > 0$, there exists at least one x in the domain of $f(x)$ such that $|x-a| < \delta$.

47. **(A)** The numerator and denominator both approach 0. However, $u^2 - 25 = (u+5)$ $(u-5)$. Hence, $\dfrac{u^2-25}{u-5} = u+5$. Thus, $\lim\limits_{u \to 5} \dfrac{u^2-25}{u-5} = \lim\limits_{u \to 5}(u+5) = 10$.

(B) Both the numerator and denominator approach 0. However,

$x^3 - 1 = (x-1)(x^2+x+1)$. Hence, $\lim\limits_{x \to 1} \dfrac{x^3-1}{x-1} = \lim\limits_{x \to 1}(x^2+x+1) = 1+1+1 = 3$.

(C) $\lim\limits_{u\to0} 5u^2 - 4 = -4$ and $\lim\limits_{u\to0} (u+1) = 1$. Hence, by the quotient law for limits,

$$\lim_{u\to0} \frac{5u^2 - 4}{u+1} = \frac{-4}{1} = -4.$$

(D) Both the numerator and denominator approach 0. However, $x^2 - x - 12 = (x+3)(x-4)$. Hence, $\lim\limits_{x\to4} \dfrac{x^2 - x - 12}{x - 4} = \lim\limits_{x\to4} (x+3) = 7$.

(E) In this case, neither the numerator nor the denominator approaches 0. In fact, $\lim\limits_{x\to2} (x^3 - 5x^2 + 2x - 4) = -12$ and $\lim\limits_{x\to2} (x^2 - 3x + 3) = 1$. Hence, our limit is $\dfrac{-12}{1} = -12$.

(F) Both the numerator and denominator approach 0. "Rationalize" the numerator by multiplying both numerator and denominator by $\sqrt{x+3} + \sqrt{3}$:

$$\frac{\sqrt{x+3} - \sqrt{3}}{x} \cdot \frac{\sqrt{x+3} + \sqrt{3}}{\sqrt{x+3} + \sqrt{3}} = \frac{(x+3) - 3}{x(\sqrt{x+3} + \sqrt{3})} = \frac{1}{\sqrt{x+3} + \sqrt{3}}$$

So, we obtain $\lim\limits_{x\to0} \dfrac{1}{\sqrt{x+3} + \sqrt{3}} = \dfrac{1}{\sqrt{3} + \sqrt{3}} = \dfrac{1}{2\sqrt{3}}$.

(G) As $x \to 3$, from either the right or the left, $(x-3)^2$ remains positive and approaches 0. Hence, $1/(x-3)^2$, becomes larger and larger without bound and is positive. Hence, $\lim\limits_{x\to3} \dfrac{1}{(x-3)^2} = +\infty$, an improper limit.

(H) As $x \to 2$ from the right (that is, with $x > 2$), $x - 2$ approaches 0 and positive; therefore, $3/(x-2)$ approaches $+\infty$. However, as $x \to 2$ from the left (that is, with $x < 2$), $x - 2$ approaches 0 and is negative; therefore, $3/(x-2)$ approaches $-\infty$. Hence, nothing can be said about $\lim\limits_{x\to2} \dfrac{3}{x-2}$.

(Some people prefer to write $\lim\limits_{x\to2} \dfrac{3}{x-2} = \infty$ to indicate that the magnitude $\left|\dfrac{3}{x-2}\right|$ approaches $+\infty$.)

48. (A) $2x^{11} - 5x^6 + 3x^2 + 1 = x^{11}\left(2 - \dfrac{5}{x^5} + \dfrac{3}{x^9} + \dfrac{1}{x^{11}}\right)$. But $\dfrac{5}{x^5}$ and $\dfrac{3}{x^9}$ and $\dfrac{1}{x^{11}}$ all approach 0 as $x \to +\infty$. Thus, $2 - \dfrac{5}{x^5} + \dfrac{3}{x^9} + \dfrac{1}{x^{11}}$ approaches 2. At the same time x^{11} approaches $+\infty$. Hence, the limit is $+\infty$.

(B) $2x^3 - 12x^2 + x - 7 = x^3\left(2 - \dfrac{12}{x} + \dfrac{1}{x^2} - \dfrac{7}{x^3}\right)$. As $x \to -\infty$, $\dfrac{12}{x}$, $\dfrac{1}{x^2}$, and $\dfrac{7}{x^3}$ all

approach 0. Hence, $2 - \dfrac{12}{x} + \dfrac{1}{x^2} - \dfrac{7}{x^3}$ approaches 2. But x^3 approaches $-\infty$. Therefore,

the limit is $-\infty$. (Note that the limit will always be $-\infty$ when $x \to -\infty$ and the function is a polynomial of odd degree with a positive leading coefficient.)

(C) The numerator and denominator both approach ∞. Hence, we divide the numerator and denominator by x^2, the highest power of x in the denominator. We obtain

$$\lim_{x \to +\infty} \frac{2/x + 5/x^2}{1 - 7/x + 3/x^2} = \frac{\lim\limits_{x \to +\infty}(2/x) + \lim\limits_{x \to +\infty}(5/x^2)}{\lim\limits_{x \to +\infty} 1 - \lim\limits_{x \to +\infty}(7/x) + \lim\limits_{x \to +\infty}(3/x^2)} = \frac{0+0}{1-0+0} = \frac{0}{1} = 0$$

(D) Both the numerator and denominator approach 0. So we divide both of them by x^3, the highest power of x in the denominator.

$$\lim_{x \to +\infty} \frac{3 - 4/x^2 + 2/x^3}{7 + 5/x^3} = \frac{\lim\limits_{x \to \infty} 3 - \lim\limits_{x \to +\infty}(4/x^2) + \lim\limits_{x \to +\infty}(2/x^3)}{\lim\limits_{x \to +\infty} 7 + \lim\limits_{x \to +\infty}(5/x^3)} = \frac{3 - 0 + 0}{7 + 0} = \frac{3}{7}$$

(For a generalization, see Question 55(B).)

(E) Both the numerator and denominator approach ∞. So we divide both of them by x^3, the highest power of x in the denominator.

$$\lim_{x \to +\infty} \frac{4x^2 - 1/x^3}{3 + 7/x^3} = \frac{\lim\limits_{x \to +\infty} 4x^2 - \lim\limits_{x \to +\infty}(1/x^3)}{\lim\limits_{x \to +\infty} 3 + \lim\limits_{x \to +\infty}(7/x^3)} = \frac{\lim\limits_{x \to +\infty} 4x^2 - 0}{3 + 0} = \frac{\lim\limits_{x \to +\infty} 4x^2}{3} = +\infty$$

(For a generalization, see Question 55(C).)

(F) When $f(x)$ is a polynomial of degree n, it is useful to think of the degree of $\sqrt{f(x)}$ as being $n/2$. Thus, in this question, the denominator has a degree of 1, and, therefore, in line with the procedure that has worked before, we divide the numerator and denominator by x. Notice that, when $x > 0$, as it is when $x \to +\infty$, $x = \sqrt{x^2}$. So, we obtain

$$\lim_{x \to +\infty} \frac{4 - (1/x)}{\sqrt{(x^2 + 2)/x^2}} = \lim_{x \to +\infty} \frac{4 - (1/x)}{\sqrt{1 + (2/x^2)}} = \frac{\lim\limits_{x \to +\infty} 4 - \lim\limits_{x \to +\infty}(1/x)}{\sqrt{\lim\limits_{x \to +\infty} 1 + \lim\limits_{x \to +\infty}(2/x^2)}} = \frac{4 - 0}{\sqrt{1 + 0}} = 4$$

(G) We divide the numerator and denominator by $x^{3/2}$. Note that $x^{3/2} = \sqrt{x^3}$ when $x > 0$. So, we obtain

$$\lim_{x \to +\infty} \frac{7/\sqrt{x} - 4/x^{3/2}}{\sqrt{1 + 5/x^3}} = \frac{\displaystyle\lim_{x \to +\infty} (7/\sqrt{x}) - \lim_{x \to +\infty} (4/x^{3/2})}{\sqrt{1 + \displaystyle\lim_{x \to +\infty} (5/x^3)}} = \frac{0 - 0}{\sqrt{1 + 0}} = 0$$

(H) We divide the numerator and denominator by x^2. Note that $x^2 = \sqrt{x^4}$. We obtain

$$\lim_{x \to -\infty} \frac{3x + 2/x^2}{\sqrt{(x^4 - 2)/x^4}} = \lim_{x \to -\infty} \frac{3x + 2/x^2}{\sqrt{1 - 2/x^4}} = \frac{\displaystyle\lim_{x \to -\infty} 3x + \lim_{x \to -\infty} (2/x^2)}{\sqrt{1 - \displaystyle\lim_{x \to -\infty} (2/x^4)}} = \frac{\displaystyle\lim_{x \to -\infty} 3x + 0}{\sqrt{1 - 0}} = -\infty$$

49. (A) Remember that a vertical asymptote is a vertical line $x = c$ to which the graph gets closer and closer as x approaches c from the right or from the left. Hence, we obtain vertical asymptotes by setting the denominator $3x + 2 = 0$. Thus, the only vertical asymptote is the line $x = -\dfrac{2}{3}$. Recall that a horizontal asymptote is a line $y = d$ to which the graph gets closer and closer as $x \to +\infty$ or $x \to -\infty$. In this case, $\displaystyle\lim_{x \to \pm\infty} \frac{4x - 5}{3x + 2} = \lim_{x \to \pm\infty} \frac{4 - 5/x}{3 + 2/x} = \frac{4}{3}$. Thus, the line $y = \dfrac{4}{3}$ is a horizontal asymptote both on the right and the left.

(B) $x^2 - 2x - 3 = (x - 3)(x + 1)$. Hence, the denominator is 0 when $x = 3$ and when $x = -1$. So those lines are the vertical asymptotes. (Observe that the numerator is not 0 when $x = 3$ and when $x = -1$.) To obtain horizontal asymptotes, we compute $\displaystyle\lim_{x \to +\infty} \frac{2x + 3}{\sqrt{x^2 - 2x - 3}}$ and $\displaystyle\lim_{x \to -\infty} \frac{2x + 3}{\sqrt{x^2 - 2x - 3}}$. In both cases, we divide the numerator and denominator by x. The first limit becomes

$$\lim_{x \to +\infty} \frac{2 + 3/x}{\sqrt{(x^2 - 2x - 3)/x^2}} = \lim_{x \to +\infty} \frac{2 + 3/x}{\sqrt{1 - 2/x - 3/x^2}} = \frac{2 + 0}{\sqrt{1 - 0 - 0}} = 2$$

For the second limit, remember that $x = -\sqrt{x^2}$ when $x < 0$:

$$\lim_{x \to -\infty} \frac{2x + 3}{\sqrt{x^2 - 2x - 3}} = \lim_{x \to -\infty} \frac{2 + 3/x}{-\sqrt{(x^2 - 2x - 3)/x^2}} = \lim_{x \to -\infty} \frac{2 + 3/x}{-\sqrt{1 - 2/x - 3/x^2}} = \frac{2 + 0}{-\sqrt{1 - 0 - 0}} = -2$$

Hence, the horizontal asymptotes are $y = 2$ on the right and $y = -2$ on the left.

(C) The function is defined only for $x \geq 0$. There are no values $x = c$ such that $f(x)$ approaches ∞ as $x \to c$. So there are no vertical asymptotes. To find out whether there is a horizontal asymptote, we compute $\lim\limits_{x \to +\infty} \sqrt{x+1} - \sqrt{x}$:

$$\lim_{x \to +\infty} (\sqrt{x+1} - \sqrt{x}) \frac{\sqrt{x+1} + \sqrt{x}}{\sqrt{x+1} + \sqrt{x}} = \lim_{x \to +\infty} \frac{(x+1) - x}{\sqrt{x+1} + \sqrt{x}} = \lim_{x \to +\infty} \frac{1}{\sqrt{x+1} + \sqrt{x}} = 0$$

Thus, $y = 0$ is a horizontal asymptote on the right.

50. As x approaches 4 from the right, $x - 4 > 0$ and, therefore, $3/(x-4) > 0$; hence, since $3/(x-4)$ is getting larger and larger in magnitude, $\lim\limits_{x \to 4^+} [3/(x-4)] = +\infty$. As x approaches 4 from the left, $x - 4 < 0$, and, therefore, $3/(x-4) < 0$; hence, since $3/(x-4)$ is getting larger and larger in magnitude, $\lim\limits_{x \to 4^-} [3/(x-4)] = -\infty$.

51. $x^2 - 7x + 12 = (x-4)(x-3)$. As x approaches 3 from the right, $x - 3 > 0$, and, therefore, $1/(x-3) > 0$ and $1/(x-3)$ is approaching $+\infty$; at the same time, $1/(x-4)$ is approaching -1 and is negative. So, as x approaches 3 from the right, $1/(x^2 - 7x + 12)$ is approaching $-\infty$. Thus, $\lim\limits_{x \to 3^+} \dfrac{1}{x^2 - 7x + 12} = -\infty$. As x approaches 3 from the left, the only difference from the case just analyzed is that $x - 3 < 0$, and, therefore, $1/(x-3)$ approaches $-\infty$. Hence, $\lim\limits_{x \to 3^-} \dfrac{1}{x^2 - 7x + 12} = +\infty$.

52. $f(x+h) = 4(x+h)^2 - (x+h) = 4(x^2 + 2xh + h^2) - x - h = 4x^2 + 8xh + 4h^2 - x - h$. Hence, $f(x+h) - f(x) = (4x^2 + 8xh + 4h^2 - x - h) - (4x^2 - x) = 8xh + 4h^2 - h$. So, $\dfrac{f(x+h) - f(x)}{h} = \dfrac{8xh + 4h^2 - h}{h} = 8x + 4h - 1$.

Hence, $\lim\limits_{h \to 0} \dfrac{f(x+h) - f(x)}{h} = \lim\limits_{h \to 0} (8x + 4h - 1) = 8x - 1$.

53. $f(x+h) - f(x) = \sqrt{2(x+h)} - \sqrt{2x} = (\sqrt{2(x+h)} - \sqrt{2x}) \dfrac{\sqrt{2(x+h)} + \sqrt{2x}}{\sqrt{2(x+h)} + \sqrt{2x}}$

$$= \frac{2(x+h) - 2x}{\sqrt{2(x+h)} + \sqrt{2x}}$$

$$= \frac{2h}{\sqrt{2(x+h)} + \sqrt{2x}}$$

Hence $\qquad \lim\limits_{h \to 0} \dfrac{f(x+h) - f(x)}{h} = \lim\limits_{h \to 0} \dfrac{2}{\sqrt{2(x+h)} + \sqrt{2x}} = \dfrac{2}{2\sqrt{2x}} = \dfrac{1}{\sqrt{2x}}$

54. Rationalize the numerator:

$$\frac{\sqrt{x^2+5}-3}{x^2-2x}\cdot\frac{\sqrt{x^2+5}+3}{\sqrt{x^2+5}+3}=\frac{(x^2+5)-9}{x(x-2)[\sqrt{x^2+5}+3]}$$

$$=\frac{x^2-4}{x(x-2)(\sqrt{x^2+5}+3)}$$

$$=\frac{(x+2)(x-2)}{x(x-2)(\sqrt{x^2+5}+3)}$$

$$=\frac{x+2}{x(\sqrt{x^2+5}+3)}$$

We obtain $\lim\limits_{x\to2}\dfrac{x+2}{x(\sqrt{x^2+5}+3)}=\dfrac{4}{2(\sqrt{9}+3)}=\dfrac{1}{3}$.

55. (A) $f(x)=x^n\left(a_n+\dfrac{a_{n-1}}{x}+\cdots+\dfrac{a_1}{x^{n-1}}+\dfrac{a_0}{x^n}\right).$

Now, $\lim\limits_{x\to+\infty}\dfrac{a_n-1}{x}=\cdots=\lim\limits_{x\to+\infty}\dfrac{a_1}{x^{n-1}}=\lim\limits_{x\to+\infty}\dfrac{a_0}{x^n}=0$ So the sum inside the parentheses

approaches a_n. Since $\lim\limits_{x\to+\infty}x^n=+\infty$, $\lim\limits_{x\to+\infty}f(x)=+\infty$.

(B) Dividing the numerator and denominator by x^n,

$$f(x)=\frac{a_n+(a_{x-1}/x)+\cdots+(a_1/x^{n-1})+(a_0/x^n)}{b_n+(b_{n-1}/x)+\cdots+(b_1/x^{n-1})+(b_0/x^n)}$$

Since each a_{n-j}/x^j and b_{n-j}/x^j approaches 0, $\lim\limits_{x\to\pm\infty}f(x)=a_n/b_n$.

(C) Factoring out x^n from the numerator and then dividing the numerator and denominator by x^k, $f(x)$ becomes

$$x^{n-k}\left[\frac{a_n+(a_{n-1}/x)+\cdots+(a_1/x^{n-1})+(a_0/x^n)}{b_k+(b_{k-1}/x)+\cdots+(b_1/x^{k-1})+(b_0/x^k)}\right]$$

As $x\to+\infty$, all the quotients a_{n-j}/x^j and b_{k-j}/x^j approach 0, and, therefore, the quantity inside the parentheses approaches $a_n/b_k>0$. Since x^{n-k} approaches $+\infty$, $\lim\limits_{x\to+\infty}f(x)=+\infty$.

(D) Dividing the numerator and denominator by x^k,

$$f(x)=\frac{(a_n/x^{k-n})+(a_{n-1}/x^{k-n+1})+\cdots+(a_1/x^{k-1})+(a_0/x^k)}{b_k+(b_{k-1}/x)+\cdots+(b_1/x^{k-1})+(b_0/x^k)}.$$

Since each of the quotients a_{n-j}/x^{k-n+j} and b_{k-j}/x^j approaches 0, the denominator approaches $b_k > 0$, and the numerator approaches 0. Hence, $\lim\limits_{x \to \pm\infty} f(x) = 0$.

(E) By Question 55(B), the limit is $\dfrac{7}{4}$.

(F) By Question 55(C), the limit is $+\infty$.

(G) By Question 55(D), the limit is 0.

(H) Divide the numerator and denominator by $x^{2/3}$, which is essentially the "highest power of x" in the denominator (pay attention only to the term of highest order). We obtain $\dfrac{3x^{1/3} - 4/x^{2/3}}{\sqrt[3]{(x^2-1)/x^2}} = \dfrac{3x^{1/3} - 4/x^{2/3}}{\sqrt[3]{1-1/x^2}}$.

Since $1/x^2$ approaches 0, the denominator approaches 1. In the numerator, $4/x^{2/3}$ approaches 0. Since $x^{1/3}$ approaches $+\infty$, our limit is $+\infty$. (Note that the situation is essentially the same as in Question 55(C).)

(I) Divide the numerator and denominator by x, which is essentially the highest power in the denominator (forgetting about -2 in $x^3 - 2$). We obtain $\dfrac{2 + 1/x}{\sqrt[3]{(x^3 - 2)/x^3}} = \dfrac{2 + 1/x}{\sqrt[3]{1 - 2/x^3}}$.

Since $2/x^3$ and $1/x$ approach 0, our limit is 2. (This is essentially the same situation as in Question 55(B).)

Chapter 7: Continuity

56. $f(a)$ is defined, $\lim\limits_{x \to a} f(x)$ exists, and $\lim\limits_{x \to a} f(x) = f(a)$.

57. (A) $x = 0$ is a point of discontinuity because $\lim\limits_{x \to 0} f(x)$ does not exist. $x = 1$ is a point of discontinuity because $\lim\limits_{x \to 1} f(x) \neq f(1)$ (since $\lim\limits_{x \to 1} f(x) = 0$ and $f(1) = 2$).

(B) $f(x)$ is continuous everywhere. In particular, $f(x)$ is continuous at $x = 0$ because $f(0) = (0)^2 = 0$ and $\lim\limits_{x \to 0} f(x) = 0$.

(C) $f(x)$ is not continuous at $x = 0$ because $\lim\limits_{x \to 0} f(x)$ does not exist.

(D) Since $x^2 - 4 = (x-2)(x+2)$, $f(x) = x - 2$ if $x \neq -2$. So $f(x)$ is not continuous at $x = -2$ because $\lim\limits_{x \to -2} f(x) \neq f(-2)$ (since $f(-2) = 0$ but $\lim\limits_{x \to -2} f(x) = -4$ However, $x = -2$ is called a *removable discontinuity* because, if we redefine $f(x)$ at $x = -2$ by setting $f(-2) = -4$ then the new function is continuous at $x = -2$. (Compare Question 57(A).)

(E) Since $x^2 - 1 = (x-1)(x+1)$, $f(x) = x+1$ wherever it is defined. However, $f(x)$ is not defined when $x = 1$, since $(x^2 - 1)/(x-1)$ does not make sense when $x = 1$. Therefore, $f(x)$ is not continuous at $x = 1$.

(F) Since $x^2 - 9 = (x-3)(x+3)$, $f(x) = x+3$ for $x \neq 3$. However, $f(x) = x+3$ also when $x = 3$, since $f(3) = 6 = 3+3$. Thus, $f(x) = x+3$ for all x, and, therefore, $f(x)$ is continuous everywhere.

(G) $f(x)$ is discontinuous at $x = 1$ because $\lim_{x \to 1} f(x)$ does not exist. $f(x)$ is continuous at $x = 2$ because $f(2) = 2+1 = 3$ and $\lim_{x \to 2} f(x) = 3$. Obviously $f(x)$ is continuous for all other x.

(H) See Figure A7.1. $f(x) = \dfrac{3(x+1)}{(x+1)(x-4)} = \dfrac{3}{x-4}$. $f(x)$ is discontinuous at $x = 4$ and $x = -1$ because it is not defined at those points. (However, $x = -1$ is a removable discontinuity. If we let $f(-1) = -\dfrac{3}{5}$, the new function is continuous at $x = -1$.) The only vertical asymptote is $x = 4$. Since $\lim_{x \to \pm\infty} \dfrac{3x+3}{x^2 - 3x - 4} = 0$, the x-axis, $y = 0$, is a horizontal asymptote to the right and to the left.

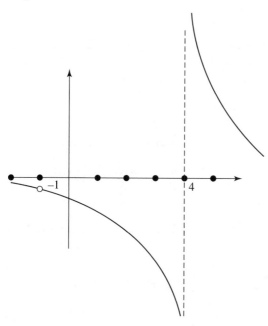

Figure A7.1

58. (A) $f(a)$ is defined, $\lim\limits_{x \to a^-} f(x)$ exists, and $\lim\limits_{x \to a^-} f(x) = f(a)$. **(B)** $f(a)$ is defined, $\lim\limits_{x \to a^+} f(x)$ exists, and $\lim\limits_{x \to a^+} f(x) = f(a)$.

59. At $x = 0$, $f(x)$ is not continuous on the left, since $\lim\limits_{x \to 0^-} f(x) = 3 \ne 1 = f(0)$. At $x = 0$, $f(x)$ is continuous on the right, since $\lim\limits_{x \to 0^+} f(x) = 1 = f(0)$. At $x = 2$, $f(x)$ is continuous neither on the left nor the right, since $\lim\limits_{x \to 2^-} f(x) = 2$, $\lim\limits_{x \to 2^+} f(x) = 0$, but $f(2) = 3$. At $x = 3$, $f(x)$ is continuous on the left, since $\lim\limits_{x \to 3^-} f(x) = 2 = f(3)$. At $x = 3$, $f(x)$ is not continuous on the right since $\lim\limits_{x \to 3^+} f(x) = 0 \ne f(3)$.

60. $f(x)$ is continuous, $f(1) = -1$, and $f(2) = 6$. Since $f(1) < 0 < f(2)$, the intermediate value theorem implies that there must be a number c in the interval $(1, 2)$ such that $f(c) = 0$.

61. $f(-4) = 0$, $f(0) = 4$, f is continuous on $[-4, 0]$, and $0 < \sqrt{7} < 4$. We must find a number c in $[-4, 0]$ such that $f(c) = \sqrt{7}$. So, $\sqrt{16 - c^2} = \sqrt{7}$, $16 - c^2 = 7$, $c^2 = 9$, $c = \pm 3$. Hence, the desired value of c is -3.

62. (A) No. $f(0) = 0$, but $\lim\limits_{x \to 0^+} f(x) = \lim\limits_{x \to 0^+} \dfrac{1}{x} = +\infty$.

(B) Yes. When continuity *over an interval* is considered, at the endpoints we are concerned with only the one-sided limit. So, although f is discontinuous at $x = 1$, the left-hand limit at 1 is 2 and $f(1) = 2$.

(C) No. The right-hand limit at $x = 1$ is $\lim\limits_{x \to 1^+} (x - 1) = 0$, whereas $f(1) = 2$.

63. Since $\lim\limits_{x \to 0^-} 3x^2 - 1 = -1$, the value of $cx + d$ at $x = 0$ must be -1; that is, $d = -1$. Since $\lim\limits_{x \to 1^+} \sqrt{x + 8} = 3$, the value of $cx + d$ at $x = 1$ must be 3; that is, $3 = c(1) - 1$, $c = 4$.

Chapter 8: The Derivative

64. (A) $f(x + \Delta x) = A(x + \Delta x) + B = Ax + A\,\Delta x + B$. Then $f(x + \Delta x) - f(x) = (Ax + A\,\Delta x + B) - (Ax + B) = A\,\Delta x$.

Hence, $\dfrac{f(x + \Delta x) - f(x)}{\Delta x} = A$. Thus, $f'(x) = \lim\limits_{\Delta x \to 0} \dfrac{f(x + \Delta x) - f(x)}{\Delta x} = \lim\limits_{\Delta x \to 0} A = A$.

(B) $f(x + \Delta x) = 2(x + \Delta x)^2 - 3(x + \Delta x) + 5 = 2[x^2 + 2x\,\Delta x + (\Delta x)^2] - 3x - 3\,\Delta x + 5 = 2x^2 + 4x\,\Delta x + 2(\Delta x)^2 - 3x - 3\,\Delta x + 5$. So, $f(x + \Delta x) - f(x) = [2x^2 + 4x\,\Delta x + 2(\Delta x)^2 - 3x - 3\,\Delta x + 5] - (2x^2 - 3x + 5) = 4x\,\Delta x + 2(\Delta x)^2 - 3\,\Delta x = (\Delta x)(4x + 2\,\Delta x - 3)$.

Thus, $\dfrac{f(x+\Delta x)-f(x)}{\Delta x} = 4x + 2\Delta x - 3$. Hence, $f'(x) = \lim\limits_{\Delta x \to 0} \dfrac{f(x+\Delta x)-f(x)}{\Delta x} =$

$\lim\limits_{\Delta x \to 0} (4x + 2\,\Delta x - 3) = 4x - 3$.

(C) $f(x+\Delta x) = (x+\Delta x)^3 = x^3 + 3x^2\,\Delta x + 3x(\Delta x)^2 + (\Delta x^3)$. So, $f(x+\Delta x) - f(x) =$ $[x^3 + 3x^2\,\Delta x + 3x(\Delta x)^2 + (\Delta x)^3] - x^3 = 3x^2\,\Delta x + 3x(\Delta x)^2 + (\Delta x)^3 = (\Delta x)(3x^2 + 3x\,\Delta x + (\Delta x)^2)$.

So $\dfrac{f(x+\Delta x)-f(x)}{\Delta x} = 3x^2 + 3x\,\Delta x + (\Delta x)^2$. Thus, $f'(x) = \lim\limits_{\Delta x \to 0} \dfrac{f(x+\Delta x)-f(x)}{\Delta x} =$

$\lim\limits_{\Delta x \to 0} [3x^2 + 3x\,\Delta x + (\Delta x)^2] = 3x^2$.

65. (A) $f'(x) = na_n x^{n-1} + (n-1)a_{n-1} x^{n-2} + \cdots + 2a_2 x + a_1$.

   (B) $f'(x) = 35x^4 - 12x^3 + 12x + 3$.

66. (A) $D_x[f(x) + g(x)] = D_x f(x) + D_x g(x)$

   $D_x[f(x) \cdot g(x)] = f(x) \cdot D_x g(x) + g(x) \cdot D_x f(x)$

   $D_x\left[\dfrac{f(x)}{g(x)}\right] = \dfrac{g(x) \cdot D_x f(x) - f(x) \cdot D_x g(x)}{[g(x)]^2}$

   (Note the various ways of denoting a derivative: $f'(x), D_x f(x), \dfrac{dy}{dx}, y'$.)

   (B) $F'(x) = (5x^3 - 20x + 13)(24x^5 + 10x^4 - 14x + 2) + (4x^6 + 2x^5 - 7x^2 + 2x)(15x^2 - 20)$. (In such cases, do not bother to carry out the tedious multiplications unless a particular question requires it.)

   (C) $G'(x) = \dfrac{(x^2 + 7)(3) - (3x - 2)(2x)}{(x^2 + 7)^2} = \dfrac{3x^2 + 21 - 6x^2 + 4x}{(x^2 + 7)^2} = \dfrac{-3x^2 + 4x + 21}{(x^2 + 7)^2}$.

   (D) (i) $-40x^4 + 3\sqrt{3}x^2 + 4\pi x$.

   (ii) $102x^{50} + 36x^{11} - 28 + \sqrt[3]{7}$.

67. (A) When $x = 3$, $f(x) = 45$. So the point is $(3, 45)$. Recall that the slope of the tangent line is the derivative $f'(x)$, evaluated for the given value of x. But $f'(x) = 12x^2 - 14x$. Hence, $f'(3) = 12(9) - 14(3) = 66$. Thus, the slope-intercept equation of the tangent line has the form $y = 66x + b$. Since the point $(3, 45)$ is on the tangent line, $45 = 66(3) + b$, and, therefore, $b = -153$. Thus, the equation is $y = 66x - 153$.

   (B) The derivative is $y' = 5x^4 + 4$. Hence, the slope of the tangent line at a point $A(x_0, y_0)$ of the graph is $5x_0^4 + 4$. The line $\overline{AB}$ has slope $\dfrac{(x_0^5 + 4x_0 - 3) - 1}{x_0 - 0} = \dfrac{x_0^5 + 4x_0 - 4}{x_0}$.

So the line $\overline{AB}$ is the tangent line if and only if $(x_0^5 + 4x_0 - 4)/x_0 = 5x_0^4 + 4$. Solving, $x_0 = -1$. So there is only one point $(-1, -8)$.

68. The normal line is the line perpendicular to the tangent line. Since $y' = 3x^2 - 2x$, the slope of the tangent line at $x = 1$ is $3(1)^2 - 2(1) = 1$. Hence, the slope of the normal line is the negative reciprocal of 1, namely -1. Thus, the required slope-intercept equation has the form $y = -x + b$. On the curve, when $x = 1$, $y = (1)^3 - (1)^2 = 0$. So the point $(1, 0)$ is on the normal line, and, therefore, $0 = -1 + b$. Thus, $b = 1$, and the required equation is $y = -x + 1$.

69. Recall the definition of the derivative: When $f(x) = 5x^4$, $f'(x) = \lim\limits_{\Delta x \to 0} \dfrac{5(x + \Delta x)^4 - 5x^4}{\Delta x}$.

In particular, for $x = \dfrac{1}{3}$, $f'\left(\dfrac{1}{3}\right) = \lim\limits_{\Delta x \to 0} \dfrac{5(\frac{1}{3} + \Delta x)^4 - 5(\frac{1}{3})^4}{\Delta x}$. If we replace Δx by h in this limit, we obtain the limit to be evaluated, which is therefore equal to $f'\left(\dfrac{1}{3}\right)$. But $f'(x) = 20x^3$. So the value of the limit is $20\left(\dfrac{1}{3}\right)^3 = \dfrac{20}{27}$.

70. $y' = x^2 - 1$ is the slope of the tangent line. To be parallel to the line $y = 3x$ having slope 3, it also must have slope 3. Hence, $x^2 - 1 = 3$, $x^2 = 4$, $x = \pm 2$. Thus, the points are $\left(2, \dfrac{2}{3}\right)$ and $\left(-2, -\dfrac{2}{3}\right)$.

71. (A) $f(x + \Delta x) - f(x) = \{[f(x + \Delta x) - f(x)]/\Delta x\}\,\Delta x$. Thus,

$$\lim_{\Delta x \to 0}[f(x + \Delta x) - f(x)] = \lim_{\Delta x \to 0} \frac{f(x + \Delta x) - f(x)}{\Delta x} \cdot \lim_{\Delta x \to 0} \Delta x = f'(x) \cdot 0 = 0.$$

Hence, $0 = \lim\limits_{\Delta x \to 0}[f(x + \Delta x) - f(x)] = \lim\limits_{\Delta x \to 0} f(x + \Delta x) - \lim\limits_{\Delta x \to 0} f(x) = \lim\limits_{\Delta x \to 0} f(x + \Delta x) - f(x).$

So $\lim\limits_{\Delta x \to 0} f(x + \Delta x) = f(x)$, and f is continuous at x.

(B) Consider the function $f(x) = |x|$ at $x = 0$. Clearly, f is continuous everywhere.

However, $\dfrac{f(0 + \Delta x) - f(0)}{\Delta x} = \dfrac{|\Delta x| - 0}{\Delta x} = \dfrac{|\Delta x|}{\Delta x}$. When $\Delta x > 0$, $|\Delta x|/\Delta x = 1$, and, when $\Delta x < 0$, $|\Delta x|/\Delta x = -1$.

Therefore, $\lim\limits_{\Delta x \to 0} \dfrac{|\Delta x|}{\Delta x} = f'(0)$ does not exist.

72. The slope of the tangent line is the derivative $f'(x) = 9x^2 - 22x - 15$. The tangent line is horizontal when and only when its slope is 0. Hence, we set $9x^2 - 22x - 15 = 0$, $(9x + 5)(x - 3) = 0$; $x = 3$ or $x = -\dfrac{5}{9}$. Thus, the desired points are $(3, 0)$ and $\left(-\dfrac{5}{9}, \dfrac{16384}{243}\right)$.

73. The graph (Figure A8.1), reveals a sharp point at $x = 3$, $y = 0$, where there is no unique tangent line. Thus the function is not differentiable at $x = 3$. (This can be verified in a more rigorous way by considering the Δ-definition.)

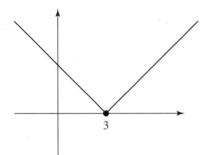

Figure A8.1

Chapter 9: The Chain Rule

74. $(f \circ g)(x) = f(g(x)) = f(x^3) = (x^3)^2 + 2(x^3) - 5 = x^6 + 2x^3 - 5$

$(g \circ f)(x) = g(f(x)) = g(x^2 + 2x - 5) = (x^2 + 2x - 5)^3$

75. Let $g(x) = 3x - 5$ and let $f(x) = \sqrt{x}$. Then $(f \circ g)(x) = f(g(x)) = f(3x - 5) = \sqrt{3x - 5}$.

76.

$(f \circ g)(x) = f(g(x)) = f\left(\dfrac{1}{x-1}\right) = \left(\dfrac{2}{x-1}\right)$ and $(g \circ f)(x) = g(f(x)) = g(2x) = \dfrac{1}{2x-1}$.

So we must solve $\dfrac{2}{x-1} = \dfrac{1}{2x-1}$, $4x - 2 = x - 1$, $3x = 1$, $x = \dfrac{1}{3}$.

77. (A) $(f \circ g)'(x) = f'(g(x)) \cdot g'(x)$.

(B) $\dfrac{dy}{dx} = \dfrac{dy}{du} \cdot \dfrac{du}{dx}$. Here the first occurrence of y refers to y as a function of x, while the second occurrence of y (on the right side) refers to y as a function of u.

(C) Use the chain rule. Think of the function as a composition $(f \circ g)(x)$ where $f(x) = x^4$ and $g(x) = x^3 - 2x^2 + 7x - 3$. Then $f'(x) = 4x^3$ and $g'(x) = 3x^2 - 4x + 7$. Hence, $\dfrac{d}{dx}(x^3 - 2x^2 + 7x - 3)^4 = 4(x^3 - 2x^2 + 7x - 3)^3 \cdot (3x^2 - 4x + 7)$.

(D) We can write $\dfrac{1}{(3x^2 + 5)^4} = (3x^2 + 5)^{-4}$. Now we can use the chain rule. Remember that $\dfrac{d}{dx} x^r = rx^{r-1}$ for any real number r. In particular, $\dfrac{d}{dx} x^{-4} = -4x^{-5}$. By the chain rule, $\dfrac{d}{dx}(3x^2 + 5)^{-4} = -4(3x^2 + 5)^{-5} \cdot (6x) = -\dfrac{24x}{(3x^2 + 5)^5}$.

(E) We can write $\sqrt{2x+7} = (2x+7)^{1/2}$. By the chain rule,

$$\frac{d}{dx}(2x+7)^{1/2} = \frac{1}{2}(2x+7)^{-1/2}\cdot(2) = (2x+7)^{-1/2} = \frac{1}{(2x+7)^{1/2}} = \frac{1}{\sqrt{2x+7}}.$$

$$\left(\text{Here, we have used }\frac{d}{dv}v^{1/2} = \frac{1}{2}v^{-1/2} \text{ and } \frac{d}{dx}(2x+7) - 2.\right)$$

(F) Use the chain rule. $\dfrac{d}{dx}\left(\dfrac{x+2}{x-3}\right)^3 = 3\left(\dfrac{x+2}{x-3}\right)^2\cdot\dfrac{d}{dx}\left(\dfrac{x+2}{x-3}\right)$. Here we must

calculate $\dfrac{d}{dx}\left(\dfrac{x+2}{x-3}\right)$ by the quotient rule: $\dfrac{d}{dx}\left(\dfrac{x+2}{x-3}\right) = \dfrac{(x-3)\cdot 1 - (x+2)\cdot 1}{(x-3)^2} = -\dfrac{5}{(x-3)^2}$.

Hence, $\dfrac{d}{dx}\left(\dfrac{x+2}{x-3}\right)^3 = 3\left(\dfrac{x+2}{x-3}\right)^2\cdot\left[-\dfrac{5}{(x-3)^2}\right] = -15\dfrac{(x+2)^2}{(x-3)^3}$.

78. Think of this function as a product of $(4x^2-3)^2$ and $(x+5)^3$, and first apply the product rule: $\dfrac{d}{dx}[(4x^2-3)^2(x+5)^3] = (4x^2-3)^2\cdot\dfrac{d}{dx}(x+5)^3 + (x+5)^3\cdot\dfrac{d}{dx}(4x^2-3)^2$. By the chain rule, $\dfrac{d}{dx}(x+5)^3 = 3(x+5)^2\cdot 1 = 3(x+5)^2$, and $\dfrac{d}{dx}(4x^2-3)^2 = 2(4x^2-3)\cdot(8x) = 16x(4x^2-3)$. Thus, $\dfrac{d}{dx}[(4x^2-3)^2(x+5)^3] = (4x^2-3)^2\cdot 3(x+5)^2 + (x+5)^3\cdot 16x(4x^2-3)$.

We can factor out $(4x^2-3)$ and $(x+5)^2$ to obtain $(4x^2-3)(x+5)^2[3(4x^2-3) + 16x(4x+5)] = (4x^2-3)(x+5)^2(12x^2-9+16x^2+80x) = (4x^2-3)(x+5)^2(28x^2+80x-9)$.

79. By the quotient rule, $y' = \dfrac{(x^2+1)\dfrac{d}{dx}\sqrt{x-1} - \sqrt{x-1}(2x)}{(x^2+1)^2}$.

By the chain rule, $\dfrac{d}{dx}\sqrt{x-1} = \dfrac{d}{dx}(x-1)^{1/2} = \dfrac{1}{2}(x-1)^{-1/2} = \dfrac{1}{2\sqrt{x-1}}$.

Thus, $y' = \dfrac{(x^2+1)\dfrac{1}{2\sqrt{x-1}} - 2x\sqrt{x-1}}{(x^2+1)^2}$.

When $x = 2$, $\sqrt{x-1} = 1$, and therefore, at the point $\left(2, \dfrac{1}{5}\right)$, $y' = -\dfrac{3}{50}$. Hence, a

point-slope equation of the tangent line is $y - \dfrac{1}{5} = -\dfrac{3}{50}x - 2)$. Solving for y, we obtain

the slope-intercept equation $y = -\dfrac{3}{50}x + \dfrac{8}{25}$.

80. $y = (x^2 + 16)^{1/2}$. Hence, by the chain rule,

$$y' = \frac{1}{2}(x^2 + 16)^{-1/2} \cdot \frac{d}{dx}(x^2 + 16) = \frac{1}{2}(x^2 + 16)^{-1/2} \cdot (2x) = x(x^2 + 16)^{-1/2} = \frac{x}{\sqrt{x^2 + 16}}.$$

At the point $(3, 5)$, $\sqrt{x^2 + 16} = 5$, and, therefore, $y' = \dfrac{3}{5}$. This is the slope tangent
line. Hence, the slope of the normal line is $-\dfrac{5}{3}$, and a point-slope equation for it is
$y - 5 = -\dfrac{5}{3}(x - 3)$. Solving for y, we obtain the slope-intercept equation $y = -\dfrac{5}{3}x + 10$.

81. $\dfrac{dy}{dz} = \dfrac{dy}{dx} \cdot \dfrac{dx}{dz} = 3x^2 \cdot (6z) = 18zx^2 = 18z(3z^2 + 5)^2$.

82. By the chain rule, $H'(x) = F'(G(x)) \cdot G'(x)$. Hence, $H'(3) = F'(G(3)) \cdot G'(3) = F'(7) \cdot 6 = 2 \cdot 6 = 12$.

83. $F(x) = (1 + x^2)^{4/3}$. By the chain rule,

$$F'(x) = \frac{4}{3}\left(1 + x^2\right)^{1/3} \cdot \frac{d}{dx}(1 + x^2) = \frac{4}{3}(1 + x^2)^{1/3} \cdot (2x) = \frac{8}{3}x\sqrt[3]{1 + x^2}.$$

84. We are asked to find the value of dy/dt when $t = 4$. $dy/dx = 3x^2 - 3 = 3(x^2 - 1)$, and $dx/dt = 1/(4\sqrt{t})$.

Hence, $\dfrac{dy}{dt} = \dfrac{dy}{dx} \cdot \dfrac{dx}{dt} = \dfrac{3(x^2 - 1)}{4\sqrt{t}}$ when $t = 4$, $x = 4$, and $\dfrac{dy}{dt} = 3(16 - 1)/(4 \cdot 2) = \dfrac{45}{8}$
per unit of time.

Chapter 10: Trigonometric Functions and Their Derivatives

85. Consider a circle with a radius of one unit (Figure A10.1). Let the center be C, and let CA and CB be two radii for which the intercepted arc $\overarc{AB}$ of the circle has length 1. Then the central angle $\angle ABC$ has a measure of one radian.

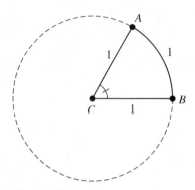

Figure A10.1

86. 2π radians is the same as 360 degrees. Hence, 1 radian = $180/\pi$ degrees, and 1 degree = $\pi/180$ radians. So if an angle has a measure of D degrees and R radians, then D = $(180/\pi)$ R and $R = (\pi/180)D$.

87. We use the formula $R = (\pi/180)D$. Hence 30° = $\pi/6$ radians, 45° = $\pi/4$ radians, 60° = $\pi/3$ radians, 90° = $\pi/2$ radians, 120° = $2\pi/3$ radians, 135° = $3\pi/4$ radians, 180° = π radians, 270° = $3\pi/2$ radians, 360° – 2π radians.

88. We use the formula $D = (180/\pi)$ R. Thus, $3\pi/5$ radians = 108° and $5\pi/6$ radians = 150°.

89. The arc length s, the radius r, and the central angle θ (measured in radians) are related by the equation $s = r\theta$. In this case, $r = 10$ inches and $\theta = \pi/5$. Hence, $s = 2\pi$ inches.

90. See Figure A10.2. $\pi/3$ radians = 60°, and the minus sign indicates that a 60° rotation is to be taken in the clockwise direction. (Positive angles correspond to counter-clockwise rotations.)

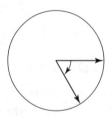

Figure A10.2

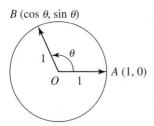

$B (\cos\theta, \sin\theta)$

θ

1

O 1

$A (1, 0)$

Figure A10.3

91. Refer to Figure A10.3. Place an arrow $\overrightarrow{OA}$ of unit length so that its initial point O is the origin of a coordinate system and its endpoint A is $(1, 0)$. Rotate $\overrightarrow{OA}$ about the point O through an angle with radian measure θ. Let $\overrightarrow{OB}$ be the final position of the arrow after the rotation. Then $\cos\theta$ is defined to be the x-coordinate of B, and $\sin\theta$ is defined to be the y-coordinate of B.

92.

θ	$\sin\theta$	$\cos\theta$
0	0	1
$\pi/6$	$1/2$	$\sqrt{3}/2$
$\pi/4$	$\sqrt{2}/2$	$\sqrt{2}/2$
$\pi/3$	$\sqrt{3}/2$	$1/2$
$\pi/2$	1	0
π	0	-1
$3\pi/2$	-1	0
2π	0	1

Notice that $9\pi/4 = 2\pi + \pi/4$, and the sine and cosine functions have a period of 2π; that is, $\sin(\theta + 2\pi) = \sin\theta$ and $\cos(\theta + 2\pi) = \cos\theta$. Hence, $\sin(9\pi/4) = \sin(\pi/4) = \sqrt{2}/2$ and $\cos(9\pi/4) = \cos(\pi/4) = \sqrt{2}/2$.

93. (A) In general, $\cos(-\theta) = \cos\theta$. Hence, $\cos(-\pi/6) = \cos(\pi/6) = \sqrt{3}/2$. **(B)** In general, $\sin(-\theta) = -\sin\theta$. Hence, $\sin(-\pi/6) = -\sin(\pi/6) = -\dfrac{1}{2}$. **(C)** $2\pi/3 = \pi/2 + \pi/6$. We use the identity $\cos(\theta + \pi/2) = -\sin\theta$. Thus, $\cos(2\pi/3) = -\sin(\pi/6) = -\dfrac{1}{2}$. **(D)** We use the identity $\sin(\theta + \pi/2) = \cos\theta$. Thus, $\sin(2\pi/3) = \cos(\pi/6) = \sqrt{3}/2$.

94. We use the values calculated in Question 92 to draw Figure A10.4.

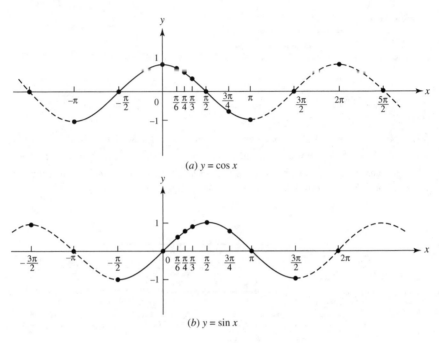

(a) $y = \cos x$

(b) $y = \sin x$

Figure A10.4

95. Because $\cos 3(x + 2\pi/3) = \cos (3x + 2\pi) = \cos 3x$, the function is of period $p = 2\pi/3$. Hence, the length of each wave is $2\pi/3$. The number f of waves over an interval of length 2π is 3. (In general, this number f, called the *frequency* of the function, is given by the equation $f = 2\pi/p$.) The graph is indicated in Figure A10.5.

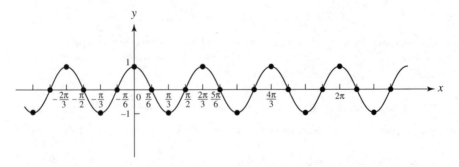

Figure A10.5

96. The period $p = \pi/2$. (In general, $p = 2\pi/b$, where b is the coefficient of x.) The coefficient 1.5 is the *amplitude*, the greatest height above the x-axis reached by points of the graph. The graph looks like Figure A10.6.

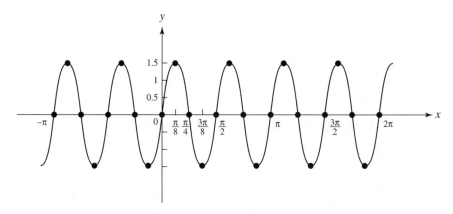

Figure A10.6

97. (A) $\displaystyle\lim_{x \to 0} \frac{\sin 3x}{x} = \lim_{x \to 0} 3 \frac{\sin 3x}{3x} = 3 \cdot \lim_{x \to 0} \frac{\sin 3x}{3x} = 3 \cdot \lim_{\theta \to 0} \frac{\sin \theta}{\theta} = 3 \cdot 1 = 3.$

(B) $\displaystyle\lim_{x \to 0} \frac{\sin 2x}{\sin 3x} = \lim_{x \to 0} \left(\frac{\sin 2x}{2x} \cdot \frac{3x}{\sin 3x} \cdot \frac{2}{3} \right)$

$\displaystyle = \lim_{x \to 0} \frac{\sin 2x}{2x} \cdot \lim_{x \to 0} \frac{3x}{\sin 3x} \cdot \frac{2}{3}$

$\displaystyle = \lim_{\theta \to 0} \frac{\sin \theta}{\theta} \cdot \lim_{\theta \to 0} \frac{\theta}{\sin \theta} \cdot \frac{2}{3} = 1 \cdot 1 \cdot \frac{2}{3} = \frac{2}{3}.$

(C) $\displaystyle\lim_{x \to 0} \frac{1 - \cos x}{x} = \lim_{x \to 0} \frac{1 - \cos x}{x} \cdot \frac{1 + \cos x}{1 + \cos x}$

$\displaystyle = \lim_{x \to 0} \frac{1 - \cos^2 x}{x(1 + \cos x)}$

$\displaystyle = \lim_{x \to 0} \frac{\sin^2 x}{x(1 + \cos x)} = \lim_{x \to 0} \frac{\sin x}{x} \cdot \lim_{x \to 0} \frac{\sin x}{1 + \cos x} = 1 \cdot \frac{0}{2} = 0.$

98. (A) By the identity $\sin (u + v) = \sin u \cos v + \cos u \sin v$, $\sin(x + \Delta x) = \sin x \cos(\Delta x) + \cos x \sin(\Delta x)$. Hence, $\sin (x + \Delta x) - \sin x = \sin x[\cos(\Delta x) - 1] + \cos x \sin(\Delta x)$, and

$$\frac{\sin(x + \Delta x) - \sin x}{\Delta x} = \sin x \cdot \frac{\cos(\Delta x) - 1}{\Delta x} + \cos x \cdot \frac{\sin(\Delta x)}{\Delta x}.$$

Thus, $\dfrac{d}{dx}(\sin x) = \lim\limits_{\Delta x \to 0} \dfrac{\sin(x + \Delta x) - \sin x}{\Delta x}$

$$= \sin x \cdot \lim\limits_{\Delta x \to 0} \dfrac{\cos(\Delta x) - 1}{\Delta x} + \cos x \cdot \lim\limits_{\Delta x \to 0} \dfrac{\sin(\Delta x)}{\Delta x}$$

$$= (\sin x)(0) + (\cos x)(1) = \cos x.$$

Here, we have used $\lim\limits_{\theta \to 0} \dfrac{\sin \theta}{\theta} = 1$ and $\lim\limits_{\theta \to 0} \dfrac{\cos \theta - 1}{\theta} = 0$ (Question 97(C).)

(B) By the identity $\cos x = \sin\left(\dfrac{\pi}{2} - x\right)$, $\dfrac{d}{dx}(\cos x) = \dfrac{d}{dx}\left[\sin\left(\dfrac{\pi}{2} - x\right)\right] =$

$\cos\left(\dfrac{\pi}{2} - x\right) \cdot \dfrac{d}{dx}\left(\dfrac{\pi}{2} - x\right)$ [chain rule] $= \sin x \cdot (-1)\left[\sin x = \cos\left(\dfrac{\pi}{2} - x\right)\right] = -\sin x.$

(C) $\sin 3x$ is a composite function of $3x$ and the sine function. By the chain rule and the fact that $\dfrac{d}{dx}(\sin x) = \cos x$, $\dfrac{d}{dx}(\sin 3x) = \cos 3x \cdot \dfrac{d}{dx}(3x) = \cos 3x \cdot 3 = 3\cos 3x.$

(D) $\cos^2 x = (\cos x)^2$. Hence, by the chain rule, $\dfrac{d}{dx}(\cos^2 x) = 2(\cos x) \cdot \dfrac{d}{dx}\cos x =$ $2\cos x \cdot (-\sin x) = -2\sin x \cos x = -\sin 2x.$

(E) $\sqrt{\sin x} = (\sin x)^{1/2}$. By the chain rule, $\dfrac{d}{dx}(\sqrt{\sin x}) = \dfrac{1}{2}(\sin x)^{-1/2} \cdot \dfrac{d}{dx}(\sin x) =$ $\dfrac{1}{2\sqrt{\sin x}} \cdot \cos x = \dfrac{\cos x}{2\sqrt{\sin x}}.$

99. The slope of the tangent line is the derivative y'. By the chain rule, since $\sin^2 x = (\sin x)^2$, $y' = 2(\sin x) \cdot \dfrac{d}{dx}(\sin x) = 2\sin x \cos x$. When $x = \pi/3$, $\sin x = \sqrt{3}/2$ and $\cos x = \dfrac{1}{2}$. So $y' = 2 \cdot \sqrt{3}/2 \cdot \dfrac{1}{2} = \sqrt{3}/2$. At the point where $x = \pi/3$, $y = (\sqrt{3}/2)^2 = \dfrac{3}{4}$. So a point-slope equation of the tangent line is $y - \dfrac{3}{4} = (\sqrt{3}/2)(x - \pi/3)$.

100. (A) Remember that $\tan x = \sin x / \cos x$ and $\sec x = 1/\cos x$. By the quotient rule,

$$\dfrac{d}{dx}(\tan x) = \dfrac{d}{dx}\left(\dfrac{\sin x}{\cos x}\right) = \dfrac{(\cos x)\dfrac{d}{dx}(\sin x) - (\sin x)\dfrac{d}{dx}(\cos x)}{(\cos x)^2}$$

$$= \dfrac{(\cos x)(\cos x) - (\sin x)(-\sin x)}{(\cos x)^2} = \dfrac{\cos^2 x + \sin^2 x}{(\cos x)^2}$$

$$= \dfrac{1}{(\cos x)^2} = \sec^2 x.$$

(B) Note that $\tan(\pi/3) = \sin(\pi/3)/\cos(\pi/3) = (\sqrt{3}/2)/\frac{1}{2} = \sqrt{3}$, and $\sec(\pi/3) =$
$1/\cos(\pi/3) = 1/\frac{1}{2} = 2$. By the chain rule, $y = 2(\tan x) \cdot \frac{d}{dx}(\tan x) = 2(\tan x)(\sec^2 x)$. Thus,
when $x = \pi/3$, $y' = 2\sqrt{3} \cdot 4 = 8\sqrt{3}$, so the slope of the tangent line is $8\sqrt{3}$. Hence, a
point-slope equation of the tangent line is $y - 3 = 8\sqrt{3}(x - \pi/3)$.

(C) By the chain rule,

$$\frac{d}{dx}(\sec x) = \frac{d}{dx}(\cos x)^{-1} = -(\cos x)^{-2} \cdot \frac{d}{dx}(\cos x) = -\frac{1}{\cos^2 x} \cdot (-\sin x)$$

$$= \frac{\sin x}{\cos^2 x} = \frac{1}{\cos x} \cdot \frac{\sin x}{\cos x} = \sec x \tan x.$$

101. By the chain rule, $y' = 3\left[2\sec x \cdot \frac{d}{dx}(\sec x)\right] = 3(2\sec x \cdot \sec x \cdot \tan x) = 6\sec^2 x \tan x$.
So the slope of the tangent line is $y' = 6\left(\frac{4}{3}\right)(\sqrt{3}/3) = 8\sqrt{3}/3$. Hence, the slope of the normal line is the negative reciprocal $-\sqrt{3}/8$. Thus, a point-slope equation of the normal line
is $y - 4 = -(\sqrt{3}/8)(x - \pi/6)$.

102. $\frac{\tan x}{x} = \frac{\sin x}{\cos x}\cdot\frac{1}{x} = \frac{\sin x}{x}\cdot\frac{1}{\cos x}$. Hence, $\lim_{x\to 0}\frac{\tan x}{x} = \lim_{x\to 0}\frac{\sin x}{x}\cdot\lim_{x\to 0}\frac{1}{\cos x} = 1\cdot\frac{1}{1} = 1$.

103. A line is horizontal when and only when its slope is 0. The slope of the tangent line
is $y' = D_x(\sec x) = \sec x \tan x$. Hence, we must solve $\sec x \tan x = 0$. Since $\sec x = 1/\cos x$,
$\sec x$ is never 0. Hence, $\tan x = 0$. But, since $\tan x = \sin x/\cos x$, $\tan x = 0$ is equivalent to
$\sin x = 0$. The latter occurs when and only when $x = n\pi$ for some integer n.

Chapter 11: Rolle's Theorem, the Mean Value Theorem, and the Sign of the Derivative

104. If f is continuous over a closed interval $[a, b]$ and differentiable on the open interval
(a, b), and if $f(a) = f(b) = 0$, then there is at least one number c in (a, b) such that $f'(c) = 0$.

105. $f(x)$ is clearly differentiable everywhere, and $f(-1) = f(3) = 0$. Hence, Rolle's
theorem applies. $f'(x) = 2x - 2$. Setting $f'(x) = 0$, we obtain $x = 1$. Thus, $f'(1) = 0$ and
$-1 < 1 < 3$.

106. There is a discontinuity at $x = 1$, since $\lim_{x\to 1} f(x)$ does not exist. Hence, Rolle's
theorem does not apply.

107. $f(x)$ is differentiable within $(0, 8)$ but not at 0. However, it is continuous at $x = 0$ and, therefore, throughout $[0, 8]$. Also, $f(0) = f(8) = 0$. Hence, Rolle's theorem applies. $f'(x) = 2/3\sqrt[3]{x} - 2/3(\sqrt[3]{x})^2$. Setting $f'(x) = 0$, we obtain $x = 1$, which is between 0 and 8.

108. (A) If $f(x)$ is continuous on the closed interval $[a, b]$ and differentiable on the open interval (a, b), then there is a number c in (a, b) such that $f'(c) = \dfrac{f(b) - f(a)}{b - a}$.

(B) $f'(x) = 2$. Hence, the mean value theorem applies. Note that $\dfrac{f(4) - f(1)}{4 - 1} = \dfrac{11 - 5}{4 - 1} = 2$. Thus, we can take c to be any point in $(1, 4)$.

(C) $f'(x) = 6x - 5$, and the mean value theorem applies. Setting $6c - 5 = \dfrac{f(5) - f(2)}{5 - 2} = \dfrac{51 - 3}{3} = 16$, we find $c = \dfrac{21}{6} = \dfrac{7}{2}$, which lies between 2 and 5.

(D) $f(x)$ is continuous for $x \geq 0$ and differentiable for $x > 0$. Thus, the mean value theorem is applicable.

$f'(x) = \dfrac{3}{4\sqrt[4]{x}}$. Setting $\dfrac{3}{4\sqrt[4]{c}} = \dfrac{f(16) - f(0)}{16 - 0} = \dfrac{8 - 0}{16} = \dfrac{1}{2}$, we find $c = \dfrac{81}{16}$, which lies between 0 and 16.

109. Assume $a < u < v < b$. Then the mean value theorem applies to $f(x)$ on the closed interval (u, v). So for some c between u and v, $f'(c) = [f(v) - f(u)]/(v - u.)$ Hence, $f(v) - f(u) = f'(c)(v - u)$. Since $u < v$, $v - u > 0$. By hypothesis, $f'(c) > 0$. Hence, $f(v) - f(u) > 0$, and $f(v) > f(u)$. Thus, $f(x)$ is increasing in (a, b).

110. (A) $f'(x) = 3$. Hence, $f(x)$ is increasing everywhere.

(B) $f'(x) = 2x - 4$. Since $2x - 4 > 0 \leftrightarrow x > 2$, $f(x)$ is increasing when $x > 2$. Similarly, since $2x - 4 < 0 \leftrightarrow x < 2$, $f(x)$ is decreasing when $x < 2$.

(C) $f'(x) = 3x^2 - 18x + 15 = 3(x - 5)(x - 1)$. The key points are $x = 1$ and $x = 5$. $f'(x) > 0$ when $x > 5$, $f'(x) < 0$ for $1 < x < 5$, and $f'(x) > 0$ when $x < 1$. Thus, $f(x)$ is increasing when $x < 1$ or $x > 5$, and it is decreasing when $1 < x < 5$.

(D) $f(x)$ is defined for $x \neq 0$. $f'(x) = 1 - (1/x^2)$. Hence, $f'(x) < 0 \leftrightarrow 1 < 1/x^2$, which is equivalent to $x^2 < 1$. Hence, $f(x)$ is decreasing when $-1 < x < 0$ or $0 < x < 1$, and it is increasing when $x > 1$ or $x < -1$.

111. $f(0) = -4 < 0$, and $f(1) = 2 > 0$. Hence, by the intermediate value theorem, $f(x) = 0$ for some x between 0 and 1. $f'(x) = 15x^2 - 4x + 3$. By the quadratic formula, we see that $f'(x)$ has no real roots and is, therefore, always positive. Hence, $f(x)$ is an increasing function and, thus, can take on the value 0 at most once.

112. Let $f(x) = x^3 + 2x - 5$. Since $f(0) = -5 < 0$ and $f(2) = 7 > 0$, the intermediate value theorem tells us that there is a root of $f(x) = 0$ between 0 and 2. Since $f'(x) = 3x^2 + 2 > 0$ for all x, $f(x)$ is an increasing function and, therefore, can assume the value 0 at most once. Hence, $f(x)$ assumes the value 0 exactly once.

113. **(A)** Let $a < x \le b$. The mean value theorem applies to $f(x)$ on the interval $[a, x]$. Hence, there exists a c between a and x such that $f'(c) = \dfrac{f(x) - f(a)}{x - a}$. Since $f'(c) = 0$, $f(x) = f(a)$. Hence, $f(x)$ has the value $f(a)$ throughout the interval.

　(B) Let $h(x) = f(x) - g(x)$. Then $h'(x) = 0$ for all x in $[a, b]$. By Question 113(A), there is a constant K such that $h(x) = K$ for all x in $[a, b]$. Hence, $f(x) = g(x) + K$ for all x in $[a, b]$.

Chapter 12: Higher-Order Derivatives and Implicit Differentiation

114. $y' = 3\pi x^2 - 7$, $y'' = 6\pi x$, $y''' = 6\pi$, and $y^{(n)} = 0$ for $n \ge 4$.

115. 　$y = (3 + x)^{-1}$.

$$y' = -(3 + x)^{-2} = -\frac{1}{(3 + x)^2}.$$

$$y'' = 2(3 + x)^{-3} = \frac{2}{(3 + x)^3}.$$

$$y''' = -6(3 + x)^{-4} = -\frac{6}{(3 + x)^4}.$$

The general pattern is $y^{(n)} = (-1)^n (n!)(3 + x)^{-(n+1)} = (-1)^n (n!)\dfrac{1}{(3 + x)^{n+1}}$.

116. $y' = \cos x$, $y'' = -\sin x$, $y''' = -\cos x$, $y^{(4)} = \sin x$, and then the pattern of these four functions keeps on repeating.

117. By implicit differentiation, $2x + 2yy' = 0$, $y' = -x/y$. By the quotient rule,

$$y'' = -\frac{y \cdot 1 - x \cdot y'}{y^2} = -\frac{y - x(-x/y)}{y^2} = -\frac{y^2 + x^2}{y^3} = -\frac{a^2}{y^3}.$$

118. Use implicit differentiation. (∗) $2x + 2(xy' + y) + 6yy' = 0$. When $y = 1$, the original equation yields $x^2 + 2x + 3 = 2$, $x^2 + 2x + 1 = 0$, $(x + 1)^2 = 0$, $x + 1 = 0$, $x = -1$. Substitute -1 for x and 1 for y in (∗), which results in $-2 + 2(-y' + 1) + 6y' = 0$; so, $y' = 0$ when $y = 1$. To find y'', first simplify (∗) to $x + xy' + y + 3yy' = 0$, and then differentiate implicitly to get $1 + (xy'' + y') + y' + 3(yy'' + y'y') = 0$. In this equation, substitute -1 for x, 1 for y, and 0 for y', which results in $1 - y'' + 3y'' = 0$, $y'' = -\dfrac{1}{2}$.

119. Use implicit differentiation to get $2b^2x + 2a^2yy' = 0$, $y' = -(b^2/a^2)(x/y)$. Now differentiate by the quotient rule.

$$y'' = -\frac{b^2}{a^2}\left(\frac{y - xy'}{y^2}\right) = -\frac{b^2}{a^2}\frac{y - x[(-b^2/a^2)(x/y)]}{y^2}$$

$$= -\frac{b^2}{a^2}\frac{a^2y^2 + b^2x^2}{a^2y^3} = -\frac{b^2}{a^2}\frac{a^2b^2}{a^2y^3} = -\frac{b^4}{a^2y^3}.$$

Chapter 13: Maxima and Minima

120. If $f'(c) = 0$ and $f''(c) < 0$, then $f(x)$ has a relative maximum at c. (See Figure A13.1(a).) If $f'(c) = 0$ and $f''(c) > 0$, then $f(x)$ has a relative minimum at c. (See Figure A13.1(b).) If $f'(c) = 0$ and $f''(c) = 0$, we cannot draw any conclusions at all.

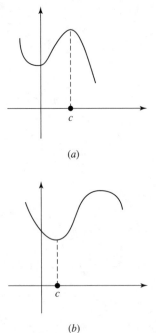

(a)

(b)

Figure A13.1

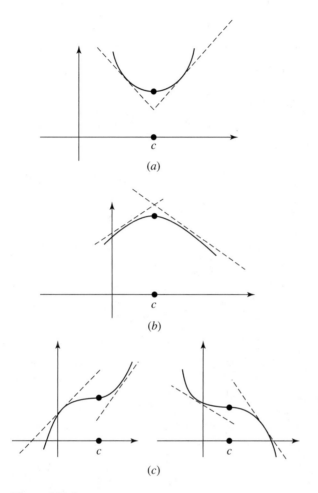

Figure A13.2

121. Assume $f'(c) = 0$. If f' is negative to the left of c and positive to the right of c—the case $\{-, +\}$—then f has a relative minimum at c. (See Figure A13.2(a).) If f' is positive to the left of c and negative to the right of c—the case $\{+, -\}$—then f has a relative maximum at c. (See Figure A13.2(b).) If f' has the same sign to the left and to the right of c—$\{+, +\}$ or $\{-, -\}$—then f has an inflection point at c. (See Figure A13.2(c).)

122. (A) Recall that a critical number is a number c such that $f(c)$ is defined and either $f'(c) = 0$ or $f'(c)$ does not exist. Now $f'(x) = -2 + 2x$. So we set $-2 + 2x = 0$. Hence, the only critical number is $x = 1$. But $f''(x) = 2$. In particular, $f''(1) = 2 > 0$. Hence, by the second-derivative test, $f(x)$ has a relative minimum at $x = 1$.

(B) $f'(x) = 3x^2 - 10x - 8 = (3x + 2)(x - 4)$. Hence, the critical numbers are $x = 4$ and $x = -\dfrac{2}{3}$. Now $f''(x) = 6x - 10$. So $f''(4) = 14 > 0$, and, by the second-derivative test, there is a relative minimum at $x = 4$. Similarly, $f''\left(-\dfrac{2}{3}\right) = -14$; therefore, there is a relative maximum at $x = -\dfrac{2}{3}$.

(C) $f'(x) = x \cdot 3(x - 1)^2 + (x - 1)^3 = (x - 1)^2(3x + x - 1) = (x - 1)^2(4x - 1)$. So the critical numbers are $x = 1$ and $x = \dfrac{1}{4}$. Now $f''(x) = (x - 1)^2 \cdot 4 + 2(x - 1)$

$(4x - 1) = 2(x - 1)[2(x - 1) + 4x - 1] = 2(x - 1)(6x - 3) = 6(x - 1)(2x - 1)$. Thus,

$f''\left(\dfrac{1}{4}\right) = 6\left(-\dfrac{3}{4}\right)\left(-\dfrac{1}{2}\right) = \dfrac{9}{4} > 0$, and, therefore, by the second-derivative test, there is a

relative minimum when $x = \dfrac{1}{4}$. On the other hand, $f''(1) = 6 \cdot 0 \cdot 1 = 0$, and, therefore, the second-derivative test, is inapplicable. Let us use the first-derivative test, $f'(x) = (x - 1)^2(4x - 1)$. For $x \neq 1$, $(x - 1)^2$ is positive. Since $4x - 1$ has the value 3 when $x = 1$, $4x - 1 > 0$ just to the left and to the right of 1. Hence, $f'(x)$ is positive both on the left and on the right of $x = 1$, and this means that we have the case $\{+, +\}$. By the first-derivative test, there is an inflection point at $x = 1$.

(D) $f'(x) = \cos x - 1$. The critical numbers are the solutions of $\cos x = 1$, and these are the numbers $x = 2\pi n$ for any integer n. Now $f''(x) = -\sin x$. So $f''(2\pi n) = -\sin(2\pi n) = -0 = 0$, and, therefore, the second-derivative test is inapplicable. Let us use the first-derivative test. Immediately to the left and right of $x = 2\pi n$, $\cos x < 1$, and, therefore, $f'(x) = \cos x - 1 < 0$. Hence, the case $\{-, -\}$ holds, and there is an inflection point at $x = 2\pi n$.

123. $f'(x) = \dfrac{2}{3}(x - 1)^{-1/3} = \dfrac{2}{3}[1 / (x - 1)^{1/3}]$. There are no values of x for which $f'(x) = 0$, but $x = 1$ is a critical number, since $f'(1)$ is not defined. Try the first-derivative test (which is also applicable when $f'(c)$ is not defined). To the left of $x = 1$, $(x - 1)$ is negative, and, therefore, $f'(x)$ is negative. To the right of $x = 1$, $(x - 1)$ is positive, and, therefore, $f(x)$ is positive. Thus, the case $\{-, +\}$ holds, and there is a relative minimum at $x = 1$.

124. (A) Find all the critical numbers of $f(x)$ in $[a, b]$. List all these critical numbers, c_1, $c_2, \ldots$, and add the endpoints a and b to the list. Calculate $f(x)$ for each x in the list. The largest value thus obtained is the maximum value of $f(x)$ on $[a, b]$, and the minimal value thus obtained is the minimal value of $f(x)$ on $[a, b]$.

x	a	b	c_1	c_2	$\cdots$	c_n
$f(x)$	$f(a)$	$f(b)$	$f(c_1)$	$f(c_2)$	$\cdots$	$f(c_n)$

(B) $f'(x) = 8x - 7$. Solving $8x - 7 = 0$, we find the critical $x = \dfrac{7}{8}$, which lies in the interval. So we list $\dfrac{7}{8}$ and the endpoints -2 and 3 in a table and calculate the corresponding values $f(x)$. The absolute maximum 33 is assumed at $x = -2$. The absolute minimum $-\dfrac{1}{16}$ is assumed at $x = \dfrac{7}{8}$.

x	-2	3	$\frac{7}{8}$
$f(x)$	33	18	$-\frac{1}{16}$

(C) $f'(x) = 12x^2 - 16x = 4x(3x - 4)$. So the critical numbers are $x = 0$ and $x = \dfrac{4}{3}$. But $x = \dfrac{4}{3}$ does not lie in the interval. Hence, we list only 0 and the endpoints -1 and 1 and calculate the corresponding values of $f(x)$. So the absolute maximum 1 is achieved at $x = 0$, and the absolute minimum -11 is achieved at $x = -1$.

x	-1	1	0
$f(x)$	-11	-3	1

(D) $f'(x) = 4x^3 - 6x^2 - 2x - 4 = 2(2x^3 - 3x^2 - x - 2)$. We first search for roots of $2x^3 - 3x^2 - x - 2$ by trying integral factors of the constant term 2. It turns out that $x = 2$ is a root. Dividing $2x^3 - 3x^2 - x - 2$ by $x - 2$, we obtain the quotient $2x^2 + x + 1$. By the quadratic formula, the roots of the latter are $x = (-1 \pm \sqrt{-7})/4$, which are not real. Thus, the only critical number is $x = 2$. So, listing 2 and the endpoints 0 and 4, we calculate the corresponding values of $f(x)$. Thus, the absolute maximum 99 is attained at $x = 4$, and the absolute minimum -9 at $x = 2$.

x	0	4	2
$f(x)$	3	99	-9

(E) $f'(x) = \dfrac{(x+2)(3x^2) - x^3}{(x+2)^2} = \dfrac{3x^3 + 6x^2 - x^3}{(x+2)^2} = \dfrac{2x^3 + 6x^2}{(x+2)^2} = \dfrac{2x^2(x+3)}{(x+2)^2}$.

Thus, the critical numbers are $x = 0$ and $x = -3$. However, $x = -3$ is not in the given interval. So we list 0 and the endpoints -1 and 1. The absolute maximum $\dfrac{1}{3}$ is assumed at $x = 1$, and the absolute minimum -1 is assumed at $x = -1$.

x	0	-1	1
$f(x)$	0	-1	$\frac{1}{3}$

(F) $f'(x) = \cos x + 1$. For a critical number, $\cos x + 1 = 0$, or $\cos x = -1$. The only solution of this equation in $[0, 2\pi]$ is $x = \pi$. We list π and the two endpoints 0 and 2π and compute the values of $f(x)$. Hence, the absolute maximum 2π is achieved at $x = 2\pi$, and the absolute minimum 0 at $x = 0$.

x	π	0	2π
$f(x)$	π	0	2π

125. $f'(x) = 2(x - a_1) + 2(x - a_2) + \cdots + 2(x - a_n)$. Setting this equal to 0 and solving for x, $x = (a_1 + a_2 + \cdots + a_n)/n$. Now $f''(x) = 2n > 0$. So, by the second-derivative test, there is a relative minimum at $x = (a_1 + a_2 + \cdots + a_n)/n$. However, since this is the *only* relative extremum, the graph of the continuous function $f(x)$ must go up on both sides of $(a_1 + a_2 + \cdots + a_n)/n$ and must keep on going up (since, if it ever turned around and started going down, there would have to be another relative extremum).

126. (A) Note that $f(0) = 0$ and $f(x)$ is positive for $x > 0$. Hence, 0 is the absolute minimum.

$$f'(x) = \frac{(x^2+1)^{3/2} - x(\frac{3}{2})(x^2+1)^{1/2} \cdot (2x)}{(x^2+1)^3} = \frac{(x^2+1)^{1/2}[(x^2+1) - 3x^2]}{(x^2+1)^3} = \frac{1 - 2x^2}{(x^2+1)^{5/2}}.$$

Setting $f'(x) = 0$, we have $2x^2 = 1$, $x^2 = \dfrac{1}{2}$, $x = \pm\sqrt{2}/2$. So the only critical number in $[0, +\infty)$ is $x = \sqrt{2}/2$. At that point, the first derivative test involves the case $\{+, -\}$, and, therefore, there is a relative maximum at $x = \sqrt{2}/2$, where $y = 2\sqrt{3}/9$. Since this is the only critical number in the given interval, the relative maximum is actually an absolute maximum.

(B) $f'(x) = 2 \cos x + 2 \cos 2x$. Setting $f'(x) = 0$, we obtain $\cos x + \cos 2x = 0$. Since $\cos 2x = 2 \cos^2 x - 1$, we have $2 \cos^2 x + \cos x - 1 = 0$, $(2 \cos x - 1)(\cos x + 1) = 0$, $\cos x = -1$ or $\cos x = \dfrac{1}{2}$. In the given interval, the solution of $\cos x = -1$ is $x = \pi$, and the solutions of $\cos x = \dfrac{1}{2}$ are $x = \pi/3$ and $x = 5\pi/3$. We tabulate the values of $f(x)$ for these critical numbers and the endpoints. So the absolute maximum is $3\sqrt{3}/2$, attained at $x = \pi/3$, and the absolute minimum is $-3\sqrt{3}/2$, attained at $x = 5\pi/3$.

x	0	$\pi/3$	π	$5\pi/3$	2π
$f(x)$	0	$3\sqrt{3}/2$	0	$-3\sqrt{3}/2$	0

(C) Since $\lim\limits_{x \to 1^+} f(x) = +\infty$ and $\lim\limits_{x \to 1^-} f(x) = -\infty$ no absolute maximum or minimum exists.

Chapter 14: Related Rates

127.

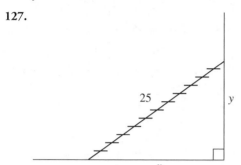

Figure A14.1

Let y be the distance of the top of the ladder from the ground, and let x be the distance of the bottom of the ladder from the base of the wall (Figure A14.1). By the Pythagorean theorem, $x^2 + y^2 = (25)^2$. Differentiating with respect to time t, $2x \cdot D_t < x + 2y \cdot D_t$ $y = 0$; so, $x \cdot D_t x + y \cdot D_t y = 0$. The given information tells us that $D_t y = -1$ foot per second. (Since the ladder is sliding down the wall, y is decreasing, and, therefore, its derivative is negative.) When $x = 7$, substitution in $x^2 + y^2 = (25)^2$ yields $y^2 = 576$, $y = 24$. Substitution in $\cdot D_t x + y \cdot D_t y = 0$ yields $7 \cdot D_t x + 24 \cdot (-1) = 0$, $D_t x = \dfrac{24}{7}$ per second.

128. Let V be the volume of wheat at time t, and let h be the depth of the wheat in the tank. Then $V = \pi(10)^2 h$. So, $D_t V = 100\pi \cdot D_t h$. But we are given that $D_t V = 314$ cubic feet per minute. Hence, $314 = 100\pi \cdot D_t h$, $D_t h = 314/(100\pi)$. If we approximate π by 3.14, then $D_t h = 1$. Thus, the depth of the wheat is increasing at the rate of 1 cubic foot per minute.

129.

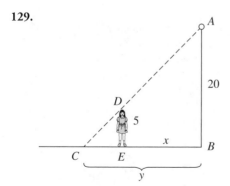

Figure A14.2

Let x be the distance of the girl from the base of the post, and let y be the distance of the tip of her shadow from the base of the post (Figure A14.2). $\triangle ABC$ is similar to $\triangle DEC$.

Hence, $AB/DE = y/(y - x)$, $\dfrac{20}{5} = y/(y - x)$, $4 = y/(y - x)$, $4y - 4x = y$, $3y = 4x$. Hence, $3 \cdot$
$D_t y = 4 \cdot D_t x$. But we are told that $D_t x = -6$ feet per second. (Since she is walking toward

the base, x is decreasing, and $D_t x$ is negative.) So $3 \cdot D_t y = 4 \cdot (-6)$, $D_t y = -8$. Thus, the
tip of the shadow is moving at the rate of 8 feet per second toward the base of the post.

130.

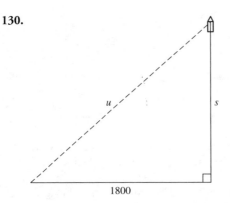

Figure A14.3

Let u be the distance from the rocket to the observer, as shown in Figure A14.3. By the
Pythagorean theorem, $u^2 = s^2 + (1800)^2$. Hence, $2u \cdot D_t u = 2s \cdot D_t s$, $u \cdot D_t u = s \cdot D_t s$. When
$s = 2400$, $u^2 = (100)^2 \cdot (900)$, $u = 100 \cdot 30 = 3000$. Since $s = 400t - 16t^2$, when $s = 2400$,
$2400 = 400t - 16t^2$, $t^2 - 25t + 150 = 0$, $(t - 10)(t - 15) = 0$. So, on the way up, the rocket
is at 2,400 feet when $t = 10$. But $D_t s = 400 - 32t$. So, when $t = 10$, $D_t s = 400 - 32 \cdot 10 =$
80. Substituting in $u \cdot D_t u = s \cdot D_t s$, we obtain $3000 \cdot D_t u = 2400 \cdot 80$, $D_t u = 64$. So the
distance from the rocket to the observer is increasing at the rate of 64 feet per second when
$t = 10$.

131. At time t, let x be the horizontal distance of the plane from the point directly over
R, and let u be the distance between the plane and the station. Then $u^2 = x^2 + (4)^2$. So $2u \cdot$
$D_t u = 2x \cdot D_t x$, $u \cdot D_t u = x \cdot D_t x$. When $u = 5$, $(5)^2 = x^2 + (4)^2$, $x = 3$, and we are also told
that $D_t u$ is 300. Substituting in $u \cdot D_t u = x \cdot D_t x$, $5 \cdot 300 = 3 \cdot D_t x$, $D_t x = 500$ kilometers
per hour.

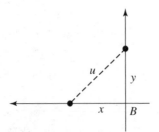

Figure A14.4

132. Refer to Figure A14.4. Let the time t be measured in hours after 9 A.M. Let x be the number of miles that the first boat is west of the buoy at time t, and let y be the number of miles that the second boat is north of the buoy at time t. Let u be the distance between the boats at time t. For any time $t \geq 1$, $u^2 = x^2 + y^2$. Then $2u \cdot D_t u = 2x \cdot D_t x + 2y \cdot D_t y$, $u \cdot D_t u = x \cdot D_t x + y \cdot D_t y$. We are given that $D_t x = 3$ and $D_t y = 5$. So $u \cdot D_t u = 3x + 5y$.

At 11:30 A.M. the first boat has traveled $2\frac{1}{2}$ hours at 3 miles per hour; so $x = \frac{15}{2}$. Similarly, the second boat has traveled at 5 miles per hour for $1\frac{1}{2}$ hours since passing the buoy;

so $y = \frac{15}{2}$. Also, $u^2 = \left(\frac{15}{2}\right)^2 + \left(\frac{15}{2}\right)^2 = \frac{225}{2}$, $u = 15/\sqrt{2}$. Substituting in $u \cdot D_t u = 3x + 5y$,

$(15/\sqrt{2}) \cdot D_t u = 3 \cdot \frac{15}{2} + 5 \cdot \frac{15}{2} = 60$, $D_t u = 4\sqrt{2} \approx 5.64$ miles per hour.

133.

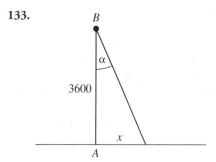

Figure A14.5

Let x be the distance from A to the point on the shore hit by the beacon, and let α be the angle between the line from the lighthouse B to A and the beacon (Figure A14.5). Then $\tan \alpha = x/3600$, so $\sec^2 \alpha \cdot D_t \alpha = \frac{1}{3600} \cdot D_t x$. We are told that $D_t \alpha = 4\pi$. When the beacon hits point A, $\alpha = 0$, $\sec \alpha = 1$, so $4\pi = \frac{1}{3600} D_t x$, $D_t x = 14{,}400\pi$ feet per minute $= 240\pi$ feet per second.

Chapter 15: Curve Sketching (Graphs)

134. $f'(x) = 3x^2 + 30x + 6$, $f''(x) = 6x + 30 = 6(x + 5)$. Thus, $f''(x) > 0$ when $x > -5$; hence, the graph is concave upward for $x > -5$. Since $f''(x) < 0$ for $x < -5$, the graph is concave downward for $x < -5$. Hence, there is an inflection point where the concavity changes at $(5, 531)$.

135. $f'(x) = 4x^3 + 54x^2 + 240x + 1$, $f''(x) = 12x^2 + 108x + 240 = 12(x^2 + 9x + 20) = 12(x + 4)(x + 5)$. Thus, the important points are $x = -4$ and $x = -5$. For $x > -4$, $x + 4$ and $x + 5$ are positive, and therefore, so is $f''(x)$. For $-5 < x < -4$, $x + 4$ is negative and $x + 5$ is positive; hence, $f''(x)$ is negative. For $x < -5$, both $x + 4$ and $x + 5$ are negative, and, therefore, $f''(x)$ is positive. Therefore, the graph is concave upward for $x > -4$ and for $x < -5$. The graph is concave downward for $-5 < x < -4$. Thus, the inflection points are $(-4, 1021)$ and $(-5, 1371)$.

136. $f'(x) = 3x^2 - 10x - 8 = (3x + 2)(x - 4)$. $f''(x) = 6x - 10$. The critical numbers are $x = -\dfrac{2}{3}$ and $x = 4$. $f''\left(-\dfrac{2}{3}\right) = -14 < 0$, hence, $x = -\dfrac{2}{3}$ yields a relative maximum. $f''(4) - 14 > 0$; hence, $x = 4$ yields a relative minimum. There is an inflection point at $x = \dfrac{5}{3}$.

137. $f(x) = 1 - 1/(x^2 + 1)$. So $f'(x) = 2x/(x^2 + 1)^2$. The only critical number is $x = 0$. Use the first-derivative test. To the right of 0, $f'(x) > 0$, and to the left of 0, $f'(x) < 0$. Thus, we have the case $\{-, +\}$, and, therefore, $x = 0$ yields a relative minimum. Using the quotient rule, $f''(x) = 2(1 - 3x^2)/(x^2 + 1)^3$. So there are inflection points at $x = \pm\ 1/\sqrt{3}$, $y = \dfrac{1}{4}$.

138. $f'(x) = 4x^3 + 12x^2 = 4x^2(x + 3)$ and $f''(x) = 12x^2 + 24x = 12x(x + 2)$. The critical numbers are $x = 0$ and $x = -3$. $f''(0) = 0$, so we have to use the first-derivative test: $f'(x)$ is positive to the right and left of 0; hence, there is an inflection point at $x = 0$, $y = 0$. $f''(-3) - 36 > 0$; hence, there is a relative minimum at $x = -3$, $y = -27$. Solving $f''(x) = 0$, we see that there is another inflection point at $x = -2$, $y = -16$. Since $f(x) = x^3(x + 4)$, the graph intersects the x-axis only at $x = 0$ and $x = -4$. As $x \to \pm\infty$, $f(x) \to +\infty$. The graph is shown in Figure A15.1.

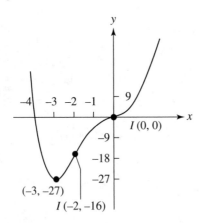

Figure A15.1

139. $f'(x) = 15x^4 - 60x^2 = 15x^2(x^2 - 4) = 15x^2(x - 2)(x + 2)$, and $f''(x) = 60x^3 - 120x = 60x(x^2 - 2) = 60x(x - \sqrt{2})(x + \sqrt{2})$. The critical numbers are 0, 2, −2. $f''(0) = 0$. So we must use the first-derivative test for $x = 0$. $f'(x)$ is negative to the right and left of $x = 0$; hence, we have the $\{-, -\}$ case and there is an inflection point at $x = 0$, $y = 0$. For $x = 2$, $f''(2) = 240 > 0$; thus, there is a relative minimum at $x = 2$, $y = -64$. Similarly, $f''(-2) = -240 < 0$, so there is a relative maximum at $x = -2$, $y = 64$. There are also inflection points at $x = \sqrt{2}$, $y = -28\sqrt{2} \approx -39.2$, and at $x = -\sqrt{2}$, $y = 28\sqrt{2} \approx 39.2$. As $x \to +\infty$, $f(x) \to +\infty$. As $x \to -\infty$, $f(x) \to -\infty$. See Figure A15.2.

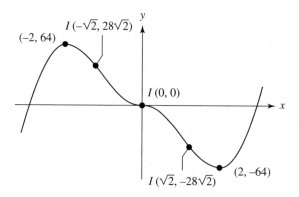

Figure A15.2

140. $f'(x) = 2x - 2/x^2 = 2(x^3 - 1)/x^2 = 2(x - 1)(x^2 + x + 1)/x^2$, and $f''(x) = 2 + 4/x^3$. By the quadratic formula, $x^2 + x + 1$ has no real roots. Hence, the only critical number is $x = 1$. Since $f''(1) = 6 > 0$, there is a relative minimum at $x = 1$, $y = 3$. There is a vertical asymptote at $x = 0$. As $x \to 0^+$, $f(x) \to +\infty$. As $x \to 0^-$, $f(x) \to -\infty$. There is an inflection point where $2 + 4/x^3 = 0$—namely, at $x = -\sqrt[3]{2}$; the graph is concave downward for $-\sqrt[3]{2} < x < 0$ and concave upward for $x < -\sqrt[3]{2}$. As $x \to +\infty$, $f(x) \to -\infty$. As $x \to -\infty$, $f(x) \to +\infty$. See Figure A15.3.

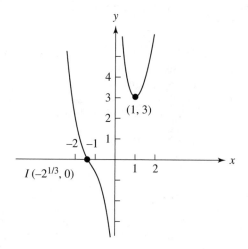

Figure A15.3

141. Writing $f(x) = x^{-1} - 3x^{-3}$, we obtain $f'(x) = -1/x^2 + 9/x^4 = -(x - 3)(x + 3)/x^4$. Similarly, $f''(x) = -2(18 - x^2)/x^5$. So the critical numbers are 3, -3. $f''(3) = -\dfrac{2}{27} < 0$. Thus, there is a relative maximum at $x = 3$, $y = \dfrac{2}{9}$. $f''(-3) = \dfrac{2}{27} > 0$. Thus, there is a

relative minimum at $x = -3$, $y = -\dfrac{2}{9}$. There is a vertical asymptote at $x = 0$. As $x \to 0^+$,
$f(x) \to -\infty$. As $x \to 0^-$, $f(x) \to +\infty$. As $x \to +\infty$, $f(x) \to 0$. As $x \to -\infty$, $f(x) \to 0$. Thus,
the x-axis is a horizontal asymptote on the right and on the left. There are inflection
points where $x^2 = 18$—that is, at $x = \pm 3\sqrt{2} \approx \pm 4.2$, $y = \pm \dfrac{5}{36}\sqrt{2} \approx \pm 0.2$. See Figure A15.4.

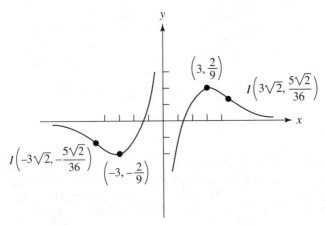

Figure A15.4

142. Since $f''(x) < 0$, the graph must be concave downward. This eliminates (*a*), (*c*), and
(*e*). Since $f'(x) > 0$, the slope of the tangent line must be positive. This eliminates (*b*). The
only possibility is (*d*).

143. Since $\sin(x + \pi) = -\sin x$, $f(x)$ has a period of π. So we need only show the graph
for $-\pi/2 \le x \le \pi/2$. Now $f'(x) = 2 \sin x \cdot \cos x = \sin 2x$. $f''(x) = 2 \cos 2x$. Within $[-\pi/2,$
$\pi/2]$, we only have the critical numbers 0, $-\pi/2$, $\pi/2$. $f''(0) = 2 > 0$; hence, there is a
relative minimum at $x = 0$, $y = 0$. $f''(\pi/2) = -2 < 0$; hence, there is a relative maximum at
$x = \pi/2$, $y = 1$ and, similarly, at $x = -\pi/2$, $y = 1$. Inflection points occur where $f''(x) = 2$
$\cos 2x = 0$, $2x = \pm \pi/2$, $x = \pm \pi/4$, $y = \dfrac{1}{2}$. The graph is shown in Figure A15.5.

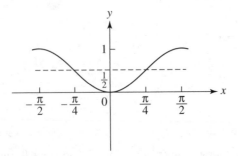

Figure A15.5

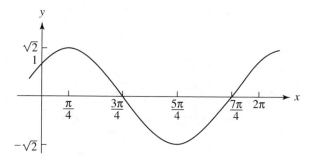

Figure A15.6

144. $f(x)$ has a period of 2π. Hence, we need only consider the interval $[0, 2\pi]$. $f'(x) = \cos x - \sin x$, and $f''(x) = -(\sin x + \cos x)$. The critical numbers occur where $\cos x = \sin x$ or $\tan x = 1$, $x = \pi/4$ or $x = 5\pi/4$. $f''(\pi/4) = -(\sqrt{2}/2 + \sqrt{2}/2) = -\sqrt{2} < 0$. So there is a relative maximum at $x = \pi/4$, $y = \sqrt{2}$. $f''(5\pi/4) = -(-\sqrt{2}/2 - \sqrt{2}/2) = \sqrt{2} > 0$. Thus, there is a relative maximum at $x = 5\pi/4$, $y = -\sqrt{2}$. The inflection points occur where $f''(x) = -(\sin x + \cos x) = 0$, $\sin x = -\cos x$, $\tan x = -1$, $x = 3\pi/4$ or $x = 7\pi/4$, $y = 0$. See Figure A15.6.

145. $f(x) = \dfrac{x}{(x-1)(x+1)}$.

$$f'(x) = \frac{(x^2 - 1) - x(2x)}{(x^2 - 1)^2} = -\frac{1 + x^2}{(x^2 - 1)^2}.$$

$$f''(x) = -\frac{(x^2 - 1)^2(2x) - (1 + x^2)[2(x^2 - 1) \cdot 2x]}{(x^2 - 1)^4}$$

$$= -\frac{2x[(x^2 - 1) - (1 + x^2) \cdot 2]}{(x^2 - 1)^3} = \frac{2x(3 + x^2)}{(x^2 - 1)^3}.$$

There are no critical numbers. There are vertical asymptotes at $x = 1$ and $x = -1$. As $x \to 1^+$, $f(x) \to +\infty$. As $x \to 1^-$, $f(x) \to -\infty$. As $x \to -1^+$, $f(x) \to +\infty$. As $x \to -1^-$, $f(x) \to -\infty$. As $x \to \pm\infty$, $f(x) = (1/x)/(1 - 1/x^2) \to 0$. Hence, the x-axis is a horizontal asymptote to the right and left. There is an inflection point at $x = 0$, $y = 0$. The concavity is upward for $x > 1$ and for $-1 < x < 0$, where $f''(x) > 0$; elsewhere, the concavity is downward. See Figure A15.7.

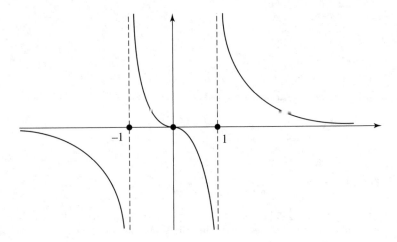

Figure A15.7

146. $f(x) = 3x^{2/3}\left(\dfrac{1}{5}x - 1\right)$. $f'(x) = x^{2/3} - 2x^{-1/3} = x^{-1/3}(x-2) = (x-2)/\sqrt[3]{x}$.
$f''(x) = \dfrac{2}{3}x^{-1/3} + \dfrac{2}{3}x^{-4/3} = \dfrac{2}{3}x^{-4/3}(x+1) = \dfrac{2}{3}(x+1)/\sqrt[3]{x^4}$. There are critical numbers at 2
and 0. $f''(2) > 0$; hence, there is a relative minimum at $x = 2$, $y = 3\sqrt[3]{4}\left(-\dfrac{3}{5}\right) \approx -3.2$.

Near $x = 0$, $f'(x)$ is positive to the left and negative to the right, so we have the case $\{+, -\}$

of the first-derivative test and there is a relative maximum at $x = 0$, $y = 0$. As $x \to +\infty$,
$f(x) \to +\infty$. As $x \to -\infty$, $f(x) \to -\infty$. Note that the graph cuts the x-axis at the solution

$x = 5$ of $\dfrac{1}{5}x - 1 = 0$. There is an inflection point at $x = -1$, $y = -3.6$. The graph is concave

downward for $x < -1$ and concave upward elsewhere. Observe that there is a cusp at the
origin. See Figure A15.8.

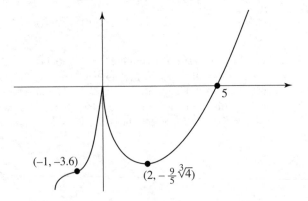

$(-1, -3.6)$

$\left(2, -\dfrac{9}{5}\sqrt[3]{4}\right)$

Figure A15.8

147. $f'(x) = 15x^4 - 15x^2 = 15x^2(x^2 - 1) = 15x^2(x-1)(x+1)$, and $f''(x) = 15(4x^3 - 2x)$ $= 30x(2x^2 - 1)$. The critical numbers are $0, \pm 1$. $f''(1) = 30 > 0$, so there is a relative minimum at $x = 1, y = -1$. $f''(-1) = -30 < 0$, so there is a relative maximum at $x = -1, y = 3$. Near $x = 0, f'(x)$ is negative to the right and left of $x = 0$ (since $x^2 > 0$ and $x^2 - 1 < 0$). Thus, we have the case $\{-, -\}$ of the first-derivative test, and therefore, there is an inflection point at $x = 0, y = 1$. As $x \to +\infty, f(x) \to +\infty$. As $x \to -\infty, f(x) \to -\infty$. There are also inflection points at the solutions of $2x^2 - 1 = 0, x = \pm\sqrt{2}/2 \approx \pm 0.7$. See Figure A15.9.

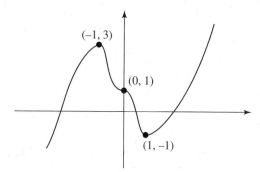

$(-1, 3)$

$(0, 1)$

$(1, -1)$

Figure A15.9

Chapter 16: Applied Maximum and Minimum Problems

148. Refer to Figure 16.1. Let u be the distance between $(0, 1)$ and a point (x, y) on the hyperbola. Then $u = \sqrt{x^2 + (y-1)^2}$. To minimize u, it suffices to minimize $u^2 = x^2 + (y-1)^2 = 2 + y^2 + (y-1)^2$. Since $x^2 = y^2 + 2$, y can be any real number. $D_y(u^2) = 2y + 2(y-1) = 4y - 2$. Also, $D_y^2(u^2) = 4$. The only critical number is $\dfrac{1}{2}$, and, since the second derivative is positive, there is a relative minimum at $y = \dfrac{1}{2}, x = \pm\dfrac{3}{2}$. Since there is only one critical number, this point yields the absolute minimum.

149. The volume $k = \pi r^2 h$. The amount of material $M = 2\pi r^2 + 2\pi rh$. (This is the area of the top and bottom, plus the lateral area.) So $M = 2\pi r^2 + 2\pi r(k/\pi r^2) = 2\pi r^2 + 2k/r$. Then $D_r M = 4\pi r - 2k/r^2$, $D_r^2 M = 4\pi + 4k/r^3$. Solving $4\pi r - 2k/r^2 = 0$, we find that the only critical number is $r = \sqrt[3]{k/2\pi}$. Since the second derivative is positive, this yields a relative minimum that, by the uniqueness of the critical number, is an absolute minimum. Note that $k = \pi r^2 h = \pi r^3(h/r) = \pi(k/2\pi)(h/r)$. Hence, $h/r = 2$.

150. Let R be the point where the boat lands, and let O be the center of the circle. Since $\triangle OPR$ is isosceles, $PR = 2\cos\theta$. The arc length $\overset{\frown}{RQ} = 2\theta$. Hence, the time $T = PR/1.5 + \overset{\frown}{RQ}/3 = \dfrac{4}{3}\cos\theta + \dfrac{2}{3}\theta$. So $D_\theta T = -\dfrac{4}{3}\sin\theta + \dfrac{2}{3}$. Setting $D_\theta T = 0$, we find

$\sin\theta = \dfrac{1}{2}, \theta = \pi/6$. Since T is a continuous function on the closed interval $[0, \pi/2]$, we can use the tabular method. List the critical number $\pi/6$ and the endpoints 0 and $\pi/2$, and compute the corresponding values of T. The smallest of these values is the absolute minimum. Clearly, $\pi/3 < \dfrac{4}{3}$, so it is easy to check that $\pi/3 < (6\sqrt{3}+\pi)/9$. (Assume the contrary and obtain the false consequence that $\pi > 3\sqrt{3}$). Thus, the absolute minimum is attained when $\theta = \pi/2$. That means that the man walks all the way.

θ	$\pi/6$	0	$\pi/2$
T	$(6\sqrt{3}+\pi)/9$	$\frac{4}{3}$	$\pi/3$

151. Let x and y be the dimensions. Then $16 = 2x + 2y$, $8 = x + y$. Thus, $0 \le x \le 8$. The area $A = xy = x(8-x) = 8x - x^2$, so $D_x A = 8 - 2x$, $D_x^2 A = -2$. Hence, the only critical number is $x = 4$. We can use the tabular method. Then the maximum value 16 is attained when $x = 4$. When $x = 4$, $y = 4$. Thus, the rectangle is a square.

x	4	0	8
A	16	0	0

152. Let x be the side of the square that is cut out. The length will be $8 - 2x$, the width $3 - 2x$, and the height x. Hence, the volume $V = x(3 - 2x)(8 - 2x)$; so $D_x V = (1)(3 - 2x)$ $(8 - 2x) + x(-2)(8 - 2x) + x(3 - 2x)(-2) = 4(3x - 2)(x - 3)$, and $D_x^2 V = 24x - 44$. Setting $D_x V = 0$, we find $x = \dfrac{2}{3}$ or $x = 3$. Since the width 3 of the cardboard is greater than $2x$, we must have $x < \dfrac{3}{2}$. Hence, the value $x = 3$ is impossible. Thus, we have a unique critical number $x = \dfrac{2}{3}$, and, for that value, the second derivative turns out to be negative. Hence, that critical number determines an absolute maximum for the volume.

153. Let x be the distance from A to C. Then the cost of running the line is
$$f(x) = 1000x + 2000\sqrt{144 + (5-x)^2}. \quad f'(x) = 1000 - \frac{2000(5-x)}{\sqrt{144+(5-x)^2}}, \text{ and } f''(x) =$$
$$2000\frac{144 + 2(5-x)^2}{[144+(5-x)^2]^{3/2}} > 0. \text{ Setting } f'(x) = 0 \text{ and solving for } x, 48 = (x-5)^2, x = 5 \pm 4\sqrt{3}.$$
Since x cannot be negative or greater than 5, neither critical number is feasible. So the minimum occurs at an endpoint. Since $f(0) = 26{,}000$ and $f(5) = 29{,}000$, the minimum occurs at $x = 0$.

Chapter 17: Rectilinear Motion

154. (A) To say that the object is released from rest means that the initial velocity is $v_0 = 0$, so its position after t seconds is $s_0 - 16t^2$. The difference between that position and its initial position s_0 is $16t^2$.

(B) By Part (A), $64 = 16t^2$. Hence, $t^2 = 4$, and, since t is positive, $t = 2$.

(C) If t is the time until it hits the bottom, $256 = 16t^2$, so $t^2 = 16$, $t = 4$.

(D) Let t be the time until the object hits the ground. Since the building is 400 feet tall, $400 = 16t^2$, $t^2 = 25$, $t = 5$. The velocity $v = D_t s$. Since $s = s_0 - 16t^2$, $v = -32t$. When $t = 5$, $v = -160$. Thus, the speed $|v|$ is 160 feet per second. To change to mi/h, we calculate as follows:

$$x \text{ feet per second} = 60x \text{ feet per minute} = 3600x \text{ feet per hour} = \frac{3600x}{5280} \text{ miles per hour}$$

$$= \frac{15x}{22} \text{ miles per hour} \approx 0.68x \text{ miles per hour}$$

In particular, when $x = 160$ feet per second, the speed is about 108.8 miles per hour.

155. Since s increases as we move right, the car moves right when $v = D_t s > 0$ and moves left when $v = D_t s < 0$. $v = 36t^2 - 36t + 9 = 9(4t^2 - 4t + 1) = 9(2t - 1)^2$. Since $v > 0$ (except at $t = 0.5$, where $v = 0$), the car always moves to the right and never changes direction. (It slows down to an instantaneous velocity of 0 at $t = 0.5$ seconds but then immediately speeds up again.)

156. The velocity $v = D_t x = 10 - 4t$. Thus, $v > 0$ when $t < 2.5$, and $v < 0$ when $t > 2.5$. Hence, the particle is moving right for $t < 2.5$ and it is moving left for $t > 2.5$. The distance d_r that it covers while it is moving right from $t = 0$ to $t = 2.5$ is $x(2.5) - x(0) = 12.5 - 0 = 12.5$. The distance d_ℓ that it covers while it is moving left from $t = 2.5$ to $t = 3$ is $x(2.5) - x(3) = 12.5 - 12 = 0.5$. Hence, the total distance is $d_r + d_\ell = 12.5 + 0.5 = 13$.

157. Its height $s = s_0 + v_0 t - 16t^2$. In this case, $s_0 = 0$ and v_0 is unknown, so $s = v_0 t - 16t^2$. We are told that $s = 0$ when $t = 20$. Hence, $0 = v_0(20) - 16(20)^2$, $v_0 = 320$ feet per second.

158. (A) Set $6t - t^2 = t^2 - 4t$. Then $t^2 - 5t = 0$, $t(t - 5) = 0$, $t = 0$ or $t = 5$. **(B)** The velocities are $f'(t) = 6 - 2t$ and $g'(t) = 2t - 4$. Setting $6 - 2t = 2t - 4$, we have $t = 2.5$. **(C)** When they meet at $t = 0$, $f'(t) = f'(0) = 6$, and $g'(t) = g'(0) = -4$. Since $f'(0)$ and $g'(0)$ have opposite signs, they are moving in opposite directions when $t = 0$. When they meet at $t = 5$, $f'(t) = f'(5) = -4$ and $g'(t) = g'(5) = 6$. Hence, when $t = 5$, they are moving in opposite directions.

159. $v = D_t s = 3t^2 - 12t + 9 = 3(t^2 - 4t + 3) = 3(t-1)(t-3)$. Since the velocity changes sign at $t = 1$ and $t = 3$, the particle changes direction at those times.

160. $v = D_t s = 40 - 32t$, $D_t^2 s = -32$. **(A)** To find out when the ball hits the ground, we set $s = 40t - 16t^2 = 0$. Then $t = 0$ or $t = 2.5$. So the ball hits the ground after 2.5 seconds. **(B)** When $t = 1$, $v = 8$ feet per second. **(C)** Set $v = 40 - 32t = 0$. Then $t = 1.25$. Since the second derivative is negative, this unique critical number yields an absolute maximum. When $t = 1.25$, $s = 25$ feet.

(B) $s = s_0 + v_0 t - 16t^2$. In this case, $s_0 = 0$. So $s = v_0 t - 16t^2$, $v = D_t s = v_0 - 32t$, $a = D_t v = D_t^2 s = -32$. So the unique critical number is $t = v_0/32$, and, since the second derivative is negative, this yields the maximum height. Thus, the time of the upward flight is $v_0/32$. The object hits the ground again when $s = v_0 t - 16t^2 = 0$, $v_0 = 16t$, $t = v_0/16$. Hence, the total time of the flight was $v_0/16$, and half of that time, $v_0/32$, was used up in the upward flight. Hence, the time taken on the way down was also $v_0/32$.

(C) By Question 160, the object hits the ground after $v_0/16$ seconds. At that time, $v = v_0 - 32t = v_0 - 32(v_0/16) = -v_0$. Thus, the velocity when it hits the ground is the negative of the initial velocity, and, therefore, the speeds are the same.

161. For the first stone, $s = 256 - 16t^2$. It hits the ground when $0 = s = 256 - 16t^2$, $t^2 = 16$, $t = 4$ seconds. Since the second stone was thrown 2 seconds later than the first and hit the ground at the same time as the first, the second stone's flight took 2 seconds. So, for the second stone, $0 = 256 + v_0(2) - 16(2)^2$, $v_0 = -192$ feet per second.

Chapter 18: Approximation by Differentials

162. (A) Let x be a number in the domain of f, let Δx be a small change in the value of x, and let $\Delta y = f(x + \Delta x) - f(x)$ be the corresponding change in the value of the function. Then the approximation principle asserts that $\Delta y \approx f'(x) \cdot \Delta x$; that is, Δy is very close to $f'(x) \cdot \Delta x$ for small values of Δx.

(B) Let $f(x) = \sqrt{x}$, let $x = 49$, and let $\Delta x = 2$. Then $x + \Delta x = 51$, $\Delta y = f(x + \Delta x) - f(x) = \sqrt{51} - \sqrt{49} = \sqrt{51} - 7$. Note that $f'(x) = \dfrac{1}{2\sqrt{x}} = \dfrac{1}{2 \cdot 7} = \dfrac{1}{14}$. The approximation principle tells us that $\Delta y \approx f'(x) \cdot \Delta x$, $\sqrt{51} - 7 \approx \dfrac{1}{14} \cdot 2$, $\sqrt{51} \approx 7 + \dfrac{1}{7} \approx 7.14$. (Checking a table of square roots shows that this is actually correct to two decimal places.)

(C) Let $f(x) = \sqrt[3]{x}$, $x = 125$, $\Delta x = -2$. Then $x + \Delta x = 123$, $\Delta y = \sqrt[3]{123} - \sqrt[3]{125} = \sqrt[3]{123} - 5$. $f'(x) = \dfrac{1}{3(\sqrt[3]{x})^2} = \dfrac{1}{3 \cdot (5)^2} = \dfrac{1}{75}$. So by the approximation principle, $\sqrt[3]{123} - 5 \approx \dfrac{1}{75} \cdot (-2) = -\dfrac{2}{75}$. $\sqrt[3]{123} \approx 5 - \dfrac{2}{75} \approx 5 - 0.03 = 4.97$. (This is actually correct to two decimal places.)

163. $V = s^3$. By the approximation principle, $|\Delta V| \approx 3s^2 \cdot |\Delta s|$. So $\dfrac{|\Delta V|}{V} \approx \dfrac{3s^2 |\Delta s|}{s^3} = \dfrac{3|\Delta s|}{s} \le 3(0.03) = 0.09$. So 9 percent is an approximate bound on the percentage error in the volume.

164. $V = \dfrac{4}{3}\pi r^3$, $D_r V = 4\pi r^2$. By the approximation rule, $\Delta V \approx 4\pi r^2 \cdot \Delta r$. Since $\Delta V = 8,000,000$ and $r = 4000$, we have $8,000,000 \approx 4\pi(4000)^2 \cdot \Delta r$, $\Delta r \approx 1/8(8\pi) \approx 0.0398$ mile ≈ 210 feet.

165. $dy = D_x y \cdot dx = \left(\dfrac{3}{2}x^{1/2}\right)(2) = \left(\dfrac{3}{2}\sqrt{4}\right)(2) = 6$. (Here we appeal to the definition of dy; there is no approximation involved.)

166. $V = s^3$. Let $s = 5$. $D_s V = 3s^2 = 75$. By the approximation principle, $\Delta V \approx 75 \cdot \Delta s$. We desire $|\Delta V| \le 3$—that is, $75 \cdot |\Delta s| \le 3$, $|\Delta s| \le \dfrac{1}{25} = 0.04$.

167. Let $f(x) = x^n$. Then $f'(x) = nx^{n-1}$ By the approximation principle, $\Delta y \approx nx^{n-1}\Delta x$. Hence, $\left|\dfrac{\Delta y}{y}\right| \approx \left|\dfrac{nx^{n-1}\Delta x}{x^n}\right| = n\left|\dfrac{\Delta x}{x}\right|$.

Chapter 19: Antiderivatives (Indefinite Integrals)

168. (A) By the chain rule, $D_x((g(x))^{r+1}) = (r+1)(g(x))^r \cdot g'(x)$. Hence, $\int (g(x))^r g'(x)\, dx = \dfrac{1}{r+1}(g(x))^{r+1} + C$, where C is an arbitrary constant.

(B) $\int x^r\, dx = \dfrac{1}{r+1} x^{r+1} + C$, since $D_x(x^{r+1}) = (r+1)x^r$.

(C) $\int (3\sin x + 5\cos x)\, dx = 3(-\cos x) + 5\sin x + C = -3\cos x + 5\sin x + C$.

(D) $\int (7\sec^2 x - \sec x \tan x)\, dx = 7\tan x - \sec x + C$.

(E) $\int (\csc^2 x + 3x^2)\, dx = -\cot x + x^3 + C$.

169. (A) Use substitution. Let $u = 7x + 4$. Then $du = 7\, dx$, and $\int \sqrt{7x+4}\, dx = \int \sqrt{u}\,\dfrac{1}{7}\, du = \dfrac{1}{7}\int u^{1/2}\, du = \dfrac{1}{7}\left(\dfrac{2}{3}\right)u^{3/2} + C = \dfrac{2}{21}(7x+4)^{3/2} + C = \dfrac{2}{21}(\sqrt{7x+4})^3 + C$.

(B) Let $u = \sin 3x$. By the chain rule, $du = 3 \cos 3x\, dx$. So

$$\int \frac{\cos 3x}{\sin^2 3x}\, dx = \int \frac{1}{u^2} \cdot \frac{1}{3}\, du = \frac{1}{3} \int u^{-2}\, du = \frac{1}{3}(-u^{-1}) + C = -\frac{1}{3u} + C = -\frac{1}{3 \sin 3x} + C$$

$$= -\frac{1}{3} \csc 3x + C.$$

170. $D_t v = a = 2t - 3$. So, $v = \int (2t - 3)\, dt = t^2 - 3t + C$. Since $v = 4$ when $t = 0$, $C = 4$.

Thus, $v = t^2 - 3t + 4$. Since $v = D_t s$, $s = \int (t^2 - 3t + 4)\, dt = \frac{1}{3}t^3 - \frac{3}{2}t^2 + 4t + C_1$. Since

$s = 0$ when $t = 0$, $C_1 = 0$. Thus, $s = \frac{1}{3}t^3 - \frac{3}{2}t^2 + 4t$. Changes of direction occur where

s reaches a relative maximum or minimum. To look for critical numbers for s, we set $v = 0$. The quadratic formula shows that $v = 0$ has no real roots. (Alternatively, note that

$t^2 - 3t + 4 = \left(t - \frac{3}{2}\right)^2 + \frac{7}{4} > 0$.) Hence, the particle never changes direction. Since it is

moving to the right at $t = 0$, it always moves to the right.

171. Let $t = 0$ be the time the brakes were applied, let the positive s direction be the direction that the car was traveling, and let the origin $s = 0$ be the point at which the brakes were applied. Then the acceleration $a = -22$. So, $v = \int a\, dt = -22t + C$. The velocity

at $t = 0$ was 45 miles per hour, which is the same as $\frac{45 \cdot 5280}{3600} = 66$ feet per second.

Hence, $C = 66$. Thus, $v = -22t + 66$. Then $s = \int v\, dt = -11t^2 + 66t + C_1$. Since $s = 0$ when $t = 0$, $C_1 = 0$ and $s = -11t^2 + 66t$. The car stops when $v = 0$—that is, when $t = 3$. At $t = 3$, $s = 99$. So the car stops in 3 seconds and travels 99 feet during that time.

172. $v = (t - 2)(t + 1)$. Hence, $v = 0$ when $t = 2$ or $t = -1$. Since $a = D_t v = 2t - 1$ is equal to 3 when $t = 2$, the position s of the particle is a relative minimum when $t = 2$. So the particle moves to the left from $t = 1$ to $t = 2$, and to the right from $t = 2$ to $t = 4$. Now

$s = \int v\, dt = \frac{1}{3}t^3 - \frac{1}{2}t^2 - 2t + C$. By direct computation, $s(1) = -\frac{13}{6} + C$, $s(2) = -\frac{10}{3} + C$,

and $s(4) = \frac{16}{3} + C$. Hence, the distance traveled from $t = 1$ to $t = 2$ is $|s(1) - s(2)| = \frac{7}{6}$,

and the distance traveled from $t = 2$ to $t = 4$ is $|s(2) - s(4)| = \frac{26}{3}$. Thus, the total distance

traveled is $\frac{59}{6}$.

173. Let $u = \sec x$, $du = \sec x \tan x\, dx$. Then $\int \sec^5 x \tan x\, dx = \int u^4\, du = \frac{1}{5}u^5 + C = \frac{1}{5}\sec^5 x + C.$

174. Remember the trigonometric identity $\cos^2 x = (1 + \cos 2x)/2$. Hence,

$$\int \cos^2 x \, dx = \frac{1}{2}\int (1 + \cos 2x)\, dx = \frac{1}{2}\left(x + \frac{1}{2}\sin 2x\right) + C = \frac{1}{2}(x + \sin x \cdot \cos x) + C.$$ For the

last equation, we used the trigonometric identity $\sin 2x = 2 \sin x \cos x$.

Chapter 20: The Definite Integral and the Fundamental Theorem of Calculus

175. Divide the interval $[0, b]$ into n equal subintervals of length b/n by the points $0 = x_0 < b/n < 2b/n < \cdots < nb/n = x_n = b$. In the ith subinterval choose x_i^* to be the right-hand

endpoint ib/n. Then an approximating sum is $\displaystyle\sum_{i=1}^{n} \frac{ib}{n}\cdot\frac{b}{n} = \frac{b^2}{n^2}\sum_{i=1}^{n} i = \frac{b^2}{n^2}\frac{n(n+1)}{2} = \frac{b^2}{2}\left(1 + \frac{1}{n}\right).$

As $n \to +\infty$, the approximating sum approaches $b^2/2$, which is, therefore, the value of the integral.

176. The integral is equal to the sum of the areas above the x-axis and under the graph, minus the sum of the areas under the x-axis and above the graph. Hence, $\displaystyle\int_0^5 f(x)\, dx = A_2 - A_1 - A_3.$

177. (A) $\displaystyle\int (3x^2 - 2x + 1)\, dx = x^3 - x^2 + x.$ (We omit the arbitrary constant in all such

cases.) So $\displaystyle\int_{-1}^{3} (3x^2 - 2x + 1)\, dx = (x^3 - x^2 + x)]_{-1}^{3} = (3^3 - 3^2 + 3) - [(-1)^3 - (-1)^2 + (-1)] = 21 - (-3) = 24.$

(B) $\displaystyle\int \cos x \, dx = \sin x.$ Hence, $\displaystyle\int_0^{\pi/4} \cos x \, dx = \sin x]_0^{\pi/4} = \sin\frac{\pi}{4} - \sin 0 = \frac{\sqrt{2}}{2} - 0 = \frac{\sqrt{2}}{2}.$

178. (A)

$$A = \int_{\pi/6}^{\pi/3} \sin x \, dx = (-\cos x)]_{\pi/6}^{\pi/3} = \left(-\cos\frac{\pi}{3}\right) - \left(-\cos\frac{\pi}{6}\right) = \left(-\frac{1}{2}\right) - \left(-\frac{\sqrt{3}}{2}\right) = \frac{\sqrt{3}-1}{2}.$$

(B) $\displaystyle A = \int_0^3 (x^2 + 4x)\, dx = \left(\frac{1}{3}x^3 + 2x^2\right)\Big]_0^3 = \left[\frac{1}{3}(3)^3 + 2(3)^2\right] = 9 + 18 = 27.$

(C) $\displaystyle A = \int_0^{\pi/2} \sin^2 x \cos x \, dx = \frac{1}{3}\sin^3 x \Big]_0^{\pi/2} = \frac{1}{3}[\sin^3(\pi/2) - \sin^3 0] = \frac{1}{3}.$

179. (A) $\displaystyle\int_0^{\pi/2} \cos x \sin x \, dx = \frac{1}{2}\sin^2 x \Big]_0^{\pi/2} = \frac{1}{2}[\sin^2(\pi/2) - \sin^2 0] = \frac{1}{2}$ (using Question

168(A) to find the antiderivative).

(B) $\displaystyle\int_0^{\pi/4} \tan x \sec^2 x \, dx = \frac{1}{2}\tan^2 x \Big]_0^{\pi/4} = \frac{1}{2}[\tan^2(\pi/4) - \tan^2 0] = \frac{1}{2}(1 - 0) = \frac{1}{2}.$

(C) Let $u = x + 2$, $x = u - 2$, $du = dx$. When $x = -1$, $u = 1$, and when $x = 2$, $u = 4$.
Then, by change of variables, $\int_{-1}^{2} \sqrt{x+2}\, x^2\, dx = \int_{1}^{4} \sqrt{u}(u-2)^2\, du = \int_{1}^{4} \sqrt{u}(u^2 - 4u + 4)\, du =$

$\int_{1}^{4} (u^{5/2} - 4u^{3/2} + 4u^{1/2})\, du = \left[\frac{2}{7} u^{7/2} - 4\left(\frac{2}{5}\right) u^{5/2} + 4\left(\frac{2}{3}\right) u^{3/2} \right]_{1}^{4} = 2u^{3/2} \left(\frac{1}{7} u^2 - \frac{4}{5} u + \frac{4}{3} \right) \Big]_{1}^{4}$

$-2 \left[8 \left(\frac{16}{7} - \frac{16}{5} + \frac{4}{3} \right) \left(\frac{1}{7} - \frac{4}{5} + \frac{4}{3} \right) \right] - 2 \left(\frac{127}{7} - \frac{124}{5} + \frac{28}{3} \right) - \frac{562}{105}$

180. By definition, the average value of a function $f(x)$ on an interval $[a, b]$ is
$\frac{1}{b-a} \int_{a}^{b} f(x)\, dx$. Hence, we must compute $\int_{0}^{1} \sqrt[3]{x}\, dx = \int_{0}^{1} x^{1/3}\, dx = \frac{3}{4} x^{4/3} \big]_{0}^{1} = \frac{3}{4}(1-0) = \frac{3}{4}$.

181. (A) If a function f is continuous on $[a, b]$, it assumes its average value in $[a, b]$—
that is, $\frac{1}{b-a} \int_{a}^{b} f(x)\, dx = f(c)$ for some c in $[a, b]$.

(B) $\frac{1}{b-a} \int_{a}^{b} f(x)\, dx = \int_{1}^{2} (x+2)\, dx = \left(\frac{1}{2} x^2 + 2x \right) \Big]_{1}^{2} = (2+4) - \left(\frac{1}{2} + 2 \right) = \frac{7}{2}$. But
$\frac{7}{2} = x + 2$ when $x = \frac{3}{2}$, and $1 < \frac{3}{2} < 2$.

182. Let the initial and final times be t_1 and t_2, with $T = t_2 - t_1$. The average velocity is

$$\frac{1}{t_2 - t_1} \int_{t_1}^{t_2} v\, dt = \frac{1}{T} x \Big]_{t_1}^{t_2} = \frac{1}{T}[x(t_2) - x(t_1)] = \frac{1}{T}(x_2 - x_1).$$

Thus, as usual, the average velocity is the distance (more precisely, the displacement) divided by the time.

183. (A) Let $g(x) = \int_{a}^{x} f(t)\, dt$. Then $g(x + \Delta x) - g(x) = \int_{a}^{x+\Delta x} f(t)\, dt - \int_{a}^{x} f(t)\, dt =$
$\int_{x}^{x+\Delta x} f(t)\, dt$. By the mean-value theorem for integrals, the last integral is $\Delta x \cdot f(x^*)$ for
some x^* between x and $x + \Delta x$. Hence,

$\frac{g(x + \Delta x) - g(x)}{\Delta x} = f(x^*)$ and $D_x \left[\int_{a}^{x} f(t)\, dt \right] = \lim_{\Delta x \to 0} \frac{g(x + \Delta x) - g(x)}{\Delta x} = \lim_{\Delta x \to 0} f(x^*)$.

But as $\Delta x \to 0$, $x^* \to x$, and, by the continuity of f, $\lim_{\Delta x \to 0} f(x^*) = f(x)$.

(B) $D_x \left[\int_{x}^{b} f(t)\, dt \right] = D_x \left[-\int_{b}^{x} f(t)\, dt \right] = -D_x \left[\int_{b}^{x} f(t)\, dt \right] = -f(x)$ (by Question
183(A)).

184. See Figure A20.1. $\int_0^c \sin x\, dx = \dfrac{1}{3} \int_c^\pi \sin x\, dx$, $-\cos x]_0^c = \dfrac{1}{3}(-\cos x)]_c^\pi$, $-(\cos c - \cos 0)$

$$= -\dfrac{1}{3}(\cos \pi - \cos c),\ \cos c - 1 = \dfrac{1}{3}(-1 - \cos c),\ 3\cos c - 3$$

$$= -1 - \cos c,\ 4\cos c = 2,\ \cos c = \dfrac{1}{2},\ c = \pi/3.$$

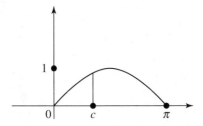

Figure A20.1

185. $x = \int v\, dt = \int \cos 3t\, dt = \dfrac{1}{3}\sin 3t + C$. But $x = 0$ when $t = 0$. Hence, $C = 0$ and

$x = \dfrac{1}{3}\sin 3t$. The average value of x on $[0, \pi/3]$ is

$$\dfrac{1}{\pi/3}\int_0^{\pi/3} \dfrac{1}{3}\sin 3t\, dt = \dfrac{1}{\pi}\left(-\dfrac{1}{3}\cos 3t\right)\Bigg]_0^{\pi/3} = -\dfrac{1}{3\pi}(\cos \pi - \cos 0) = -\dfrac{1}{3\pi}(-1 - 1) = \dfrac{2}{3\pi}.$$

186. (A) Let $f(x) \geq 0$ be integrable on $[a, b]$. Divide $[a, b]$ into n equal parts of length $\Delta x = (b - a)/n$, by means of points $x_1, x_2, \ldots, x_{n-1}$. Then

$$\int_a^b f(x)\, dx \approx \dfrac{\Delta x}{2}\left[f(a) + f(b) + 2\sum_{i=1}^{n-1} f(x_i)\right].$$

(B) Let $f(x)$ be integrable and nonnegative on $[a, b]$. Divide $[a, b]$ into $n = 2k$ equal subintervals of length $\Delta x = (b - a)/n$. Then

$$\int_a^b f(x)\, dx \approx \dfrac{\Delta x}{2}\,[f(a) + 4f(a + \Delta x) + 2f(a + 2\Delta x) + 4f(a + 3\Delta x) + 2f(a + 4\Delta x) + \cdots +$$
$$2f(a + (2k - 2)\Delta x) + 4f(a + (2k - 1)\Delta x) + f(b)].$$

(C) We obtain, with $\Delta x = \dfrac{1}{4}$, $\dfrac{1}{12}\left[0^4 + 4\left(\dfrac{1}{4}\right)^4 + 2\left(\dfrac{1}{2}\right)^4 + 4\left(\dfrac{3}{4}\right)^4 + 1^4\right] = \dfrac{1}{12}$

$\left(\dfrac{1}{64} + \dfrac{1}{8} + \dfrac{81}{64} + 1\right) = \dfrac{154}{768} \approx 0.2005$, which is close to the exact value $\displaystyle\int_0^1 x^4\,dx = \dfrac{1}{5}x^5\Big]_0^1 =$

$\dfrac{1}{5} - 0.2$

(D) $\displaystyle\int_0^1 x^2\,dx \approx \dfrac{1}{20}\left(0^2 + 1^2 + 2\sum_{i=1}^{9}\dfrac{i^2}{100}\right) = \dfrac{1}{20}\left(1 + \dfrac{1}{50}\sum_{i=1}^{9}i^2\right)$

$= \dfrac{1}{20}\left(1 + \dfrac{1}{50}\cdot\dfrac{9\cdot 10\cdot 19}{6}\right)$ (by Question 186(A))

$= \dfrac{1}{20}\left(\dfrac{201}{30}\right) = 0.335$

which is close to the exact value $\dfrac{1}{3}$.

187. The graph of $y = \sqrt{a^2 - x^2}$ this upper half of the circle $x^2 + y^2 = a^2$ with center at the origin and radius a. $\displaystyle\int_{-a}^{a}\sqrt{a^2 - x^2}$ is, therefore, the area of the semicircle—that is, $\pi a^2/2$.

188. The area is twice the area above the x-axis and under the ellipse, which is given by

$\displaystyle\int_{-a}^{a} y\,dx = \int_{-a}^{a}\dfrac{b}{a}\sqrt{a^2 - x^2}\,dx = \dfrac{b}{a}\int_{-a}^{a}\sqrt{a^2 - x^2}\,dx = \dfrac{b}{a}\dfrac{\pi a^2}{2}$ (by Question 187).

$= \dfrac{\pi ab}{2}$

Hence, the total area inside the ellipse is πab.

189. By the disk formula,

$V = \pi\displaystyle\int_{-1}^{1}[1^2 - (1 - \sqrt{1 - x^2})^2]\,dx = \pi\int_{-1}^{1}[1 - (1 - 2\sqrt{1 - x^2} + 1 - x^2)]\,dx$

$= \pi\displaystyle\int_{-1}^{1}(2\sqrt{1 - x^2} + x^2 - 1)\,dx = 2\pi\int_{-1}^{1}\sqrt{1 - x^2}\,dx + \pi\left(\dfrac{1}{3}x^3 - x\right)\Big]_{-1}^{1}$

$= 2\pi\left(\dfrac{1}{2}\pi\right) + \pi\left[\left(\dfrac{1}{3} - 1\right) - \left(-\dfrac{1}{3} + 1\right)\right] = \pi^2 - \dfrac{4}{3}\pi.$

(The integral $\displaystyle\int_{-1}^{1}\sqrt{1 - x^2}\,dx = \dfrac{1}{2}\pi$ by Question 187.)

Chapter 21: Area and Arc Length

190. See Figure A21.1. The base of the region is the y-axis. The area is given by the integral

$$\int_1^3 2y^2 \, dy = \frac{2}{3} y^3 \bigg]_1^3 = \frac{2}{3}(27-1) = \frac{52}{3}.$$

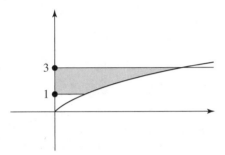

Figure A21.1

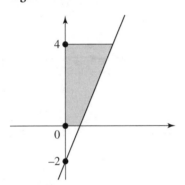

Figure A21.2

191. See Figure A21.2. The region has a base on the y-axis. We must solve $y = 3x - 2$ for x:
$x = \frac{1}{3}(y+2)$. Then the area is $\int_0^4 \frac{1}{3}(y+2) \, dy = \frac{1}{3}\left(\frac{1}{2}y^2 + 2y\right)\bigg]_0^4 = \frac{1}{3}(8+8) = \frac{16}{3}.$

192. (A) See Figure A21.3. First we find the points of intersection: $y = -y^2 + 6$, $y^2 + y - 6 = 0$,
$(y-2)(y+3) = 0$, $y = 2$ or $y = -3$. Thus, the points of intersection are $(-4, 2)$ and $(-9, -3)$.
It is more convenient to integrate with respect to y, with the parabola as the upper boundary
and the line as the lower boundary. The area is given by the integral $\int_{-3}^{2} [-y^2 - (y-6)] \, dy =$

$$\left(-\frac{1}{3}y^3 - \frac{1}{2}y^2 + 6y\right)\bigg]_{-3}^{2} = \left(-\frac{8}{3} - 2 + 12\right) - \left(9 - \frac{9}{2} - 18\right) = 19 + \frac{11}{6} = \frac{125}{6}.$$

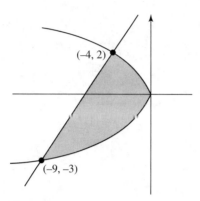

Figure A21.3

(B) See Figure A21.4. First we find the points of intersection: $-4 = x^2 - x - 6$, $x^2 - x - 2 = 0$, $(x - 2)(x + 1) = 0$, $x = 2$ or $x = -1$. Thus, the intersection points are $(2, -4)$ and $(-1, -4)$. The upper boundary of the region is $y = -4$, and the lower boundary is the parabola. The area is given by $\int_{-1}^{2} [-4 - (x^2 - x - 6)]\, dx = \int_{-1}^{2} (2 - x^2 + x)\, dx =$

$$\left(2x - \frac{1}{3}x^3 + \frac{1}{2}x^2 \right)\Bigg]_{-1}^{2} = \left(4 - \frac{8}{3} + 2 \right) - \left(-2 + \frac{1}{3} + \frac{1}{2} \right) = \frac{9}{2}.$$

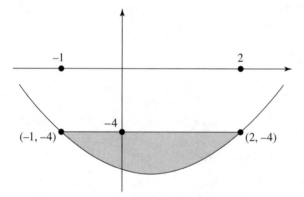

Figure A21.4

193. Recall that the arc length formula is $L = \int_{a}^{b} \sqrt{1 + (y')^2}\, dx$. In this case,

$$y' = \frac{1}{2}x^3 - \frac{1}{2}\frac{1}{x^3} = \frac{1}{2}\left(\frac{x^6 - 1}{x^3} \right) \quad (y')^2 = \frac{(x^6 - 1)^2}{4x^6} = \frac{x^{12} - 2x^6 + 1}{4x^6}.$$

Hence, $1 + (y')^2 = \dfrac{4x^6 + x^{12} - 2x^6 + 1}{4x^6} = \dfrac{x^{12} + 2x^6 + 1}{4x^6} = \left(\dfrac{x^6 + 1}{2x^3} \right)^2.$

Thus,

$$L = \int_1^2 \frac{x^6 + 1}{2x^3}\, dx = \frac{1}{2}\int_1^2 (x^3 + x^{-3})\, dx = \frac{1}{2}\left(\frac{x^4}{4} - \frac{1}{2}x^{-2}\right)\Bigg]_1^2 = \frac{1}{2}\left[\left(4 - \frac{1}{8}\right) - \left(\frac{1}{4} - \frac{1}{2}\right)\right] = \frac{33}{16}.$$

194. By implicit differentiation, $\frac{2}{3}x^{-1/3} + \frac{2}{3}y^{-1/3}y' = 0$, $y' = -(x^{-1/3}/y^{-1/3}) = -(y^{1/3}/x^{1/3})$.

So, $(y')^2 = y^{2/3}/x^{2/3}$. Hence, $1 + (y')^2 = 1 + y^{2/3}/x^{2/3} = (x^{2/3} + y^{2/3})/x^{2/3} = 4/x^{2/3}$. Therefore,

$$L = \int_1^8 \frac{2}{x^{1/3}}\, dx = 2\int_1^8 x^{-1/3}\, dx = 2 \cdot \frac{3}{2}x^{2/3}\Bigg]_1^8 = 3(4-1) = 9.$$

195. The area is $\int_0^\pi \sin x\, dx = -\cos x\,]_0^\pi = -(-1-1) = 2.$

Chapter 22: Volume

196. Consider the upper semicircle $y = \sqrt{r^2 - x^2}$ (Figure A22.1). If we rotate it about the x-axis, the sphere of radius r results. By the disk formula, $V = \pi \int_{-r}^r y^2\, dx = \pi \int_{-r}^r (r^2 - x^2)\, dx =$

$$\pi\left(r^2 x - \frac{1}{3}x^3\right)\Bigg]_{-r}^r = \pi\left[\left(r^3 - \frac{1}{3}r^3\right) - \left(-r^3 + \frac{1}{3}r^3\right)\right] = \frac{4}{3}\pi r^3$$

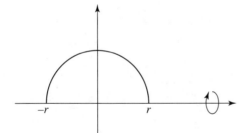

Figure A22.1

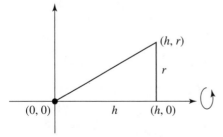

Figure A22.2

197. Refer to Figure A22.2. Consider the right triangle with vertices $(0, 0)$, $(h, 0)$, and (h, r). If this is rotated about the x-axis, a right circular cone of height h and radius of base r results. Note that the hypotenuse of the triangle lies on the line $y = (r/h)x$. Then, by the disk formula,

$$V = \pi \int_0^h y^2 \, dx = \pi \int_0^h \frac{r^2}{h^2} x^2 \, dx = \frac{\pi r^2}{h^2} \cdot \frac{1}{3} x^3 \bigg]_0^h = \frac{\pi r^2}{h^2} \cdot \frac{1}{3} h^3 = \frac{1}{3} \pi r^2 h.$$

198. (A) See Figure A22.3. The upper curve is $y = 1$, and the lower curve is $y = x^3$. We use the circular ring formula: $V = \pi \int_0^1 [1^2 - (x^3)^2] \, dx = \pi \left(x - \frac{1}{7} x^7 \right) \bigg]_0^1 = \pi \left(1 - \frac{1}{7} \right) = \frac{6}{7} \pi.$

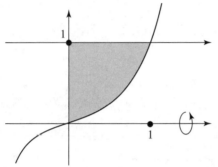

Figure A22.3

(B) We integrate along the y-axis from 0 to 1. The upper curve is $x = y^{1/3}$, the lower curve is the y-axis, and we use the disk formula: $V = \pi \int_0^1 x^2 \, dy = \pi \int_0^1 y^{2/3} \, dy = \pi \cdot \frac{3}{5} y^{5/3} \bigg]_0^1 = \frac{3}{5} \pi.$

(C) We shall consider only the region above the x-axis (Figure A22.4) and then, by symmetry, double the result. We use the cylindrical shell formula: $V = 2\pi \int_0^a xy \, dx = 2\pi \int_0^a x\sqrt{r^2 - x^2}$
$dx = 2\pi \cdot \left(-\frac{1}{2} \right) \int_0^a (r^2 - x^2)^{1/2} (-2x) dx = -\pi \cdot \frac{2}{3} (r^2 - x^2)^{3/2} \big]_0^a = -\frac{2\pi}{3} [(r^2 - a^2)^{3/2} - (r^2)^{3/2}] =$
$\frac{2\pi}{3} [r^3 - (r^2 - a^2)^{3/2}]$. We multiply by 2 to obtain the answer $\frac{4\pi}{3} [r^3 - (r^2 - a^2)^{3/2}]$.

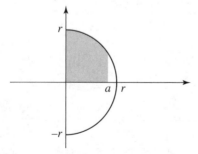

Figure A22.4

(D) See Figure A22.5. We use the disk formula along the y-axis: $V = \pi \int_a^r x^2 \, dy = \pi \int_a^r (r^2 -$

$y^2) dy = \pi \left(r^2 y - \frac{1}{3} y^3 \right) \Big]_a^r = \pi \left[\left(r^3 - \frac{1}{3} r^3 \right) - \left(r^2 a - \frac{1}{3} a^3 \right) \right] = \pi \left(\frac{2}{3} r^3 - ar^2 + \frac{1}{3} a^3 \right).$

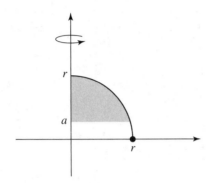

Figure A22.5

(E) Refer to Figure A22.6. We deal with the region in the first quadrant and then double it.
Use the cylindrical shell formula: $V = 2\pi \int_{b-a}^{b+a} xy \, dy = 2\pi \int_{b-a}^{b+a} \sqrt{a^2 - (y-b)^2} \, y \, dy$. Let $u = y - b$,
$y = u + b$, $du = dy$. Then $V = 2\pi \int_{-a}^{a} \sqrt{a^2 - u^2} (u + b) \, du = 2\pi \left(\int_{-a}^{a} \sqrt{a^2 - u^2} \, u \, dy + b \right.$
$\left. \int_{-a}^{a} \sqrt{a^2 - u^2} \, du \right)$. The first integral is 0, since the integrand is an odd function (see
Question 187). The second integral is the area of a semicircle of radius a (see Question
187) and is therefore equal to $\frac{1}{2} \pi a^2$. Hence, $V = 2\pi b \cdot \frac{1}{2} \pi a^2 = \pi^2 ba^2$, which, doubled,
yields the answer $2\pi^2 ba^2$.

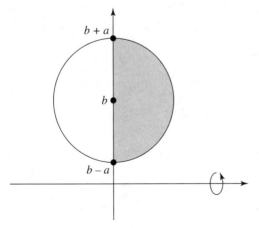

Figure A22.6

199. **(A)** Let the center of the circular base be the origin, and the fixed diameter the x-axis (Figure A22.7). The circle has the equation $x^2 + y^2 = r^2$. Then the base of the triangle is $2\sqrt{r^2 - x^2}$, the altitude is $\sqrt{r^2 - x^2}$, and the area A of the triangle is $\frac{1}{2}(2\sqrt{r^2 - x^2})(\sqrt{r^2 - x^2}) = r^2 - x^2$. Hence, by the cross-section formula,

$$V = \int_{-r}^{r} A\,dx = \int_{-r}^{r}(r^2 - x^2)\,dx = \left(r^2 x - \frac{1}{3}x^3\right)\Big|_{-r}^{r} = \left(r^3 - \frac{1}{3}r^3\right) - \left(-r^3 + \frac{1}{3}r^3\right) = \frac{4}{3}r^3.$$

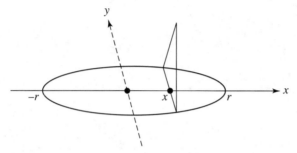

Figure A22.7

(B) Let the x-axis be the intersection of the two planes, with the origin on the tree's axis. Then a typical cross-section is a right triangle with base $\sqrt{r^2 - x^2}$ and height $h = \sqrt{r^2 - x^2}\tan 30° = \frac{1}{\sqrt{3}}\sqrt{r^2 - x^2}$. So the area A is $\frac{1}{2}\sqrt{r^2 - x^2}\cdot\frac{1}{\sqrt{3}}\sqrt{r^2 - x^2} = \frac{1}{2\sqrt{3}}(r^2 - x^2)$. By symmetry, we can compute the volume for $x \geq 0$ and then double the result. The cross-section formula yields the volume

$$V = 2\int_{0}^{r}\frac{1}{2\sqrt{3}}(r^2 - x^2)\,dx = \frac{1}{\sqrt{3}}\left(r^2 x - \frac{1}{3}x^3\right)\Big|_{0}^{r} = \frac{1}{\sqrt{3}}\left(r^3 - \frac{1}{3}r^3\right) = \frac{1}{\sqrt{3}}\cdot\frac{2}{3}r^3 = \frac{2\sqrt{3}}{9}r^3.$$

(C) Locate the x-axis perpendicular to the base, with the origin at the center of the base (Figure A22.8). By similar right triangles, $\frac{d}{e} = \frac{h-x}{h}$ and $\frac{A(x)}{r^2} = \left(\frac{d}{e}\right)^2$. So $A(x) = r^2\left(\frac{h-x}{h}\right)^2$ and, by the cross-section formula,

$$V = \int_{0}^{h} A(x)\,dx = \frac{r^2}{h^2}\int_{0}^{h}(h-x)^2\,dx = \frac{r^2}{h^2}\left(-\frac{1}{3}\right)(h-x)^3\Big|_{0}^{h} = -\frac{r^2}{3h^2}(0 - h^3) = \frac{1}{3}r^2 h.$$

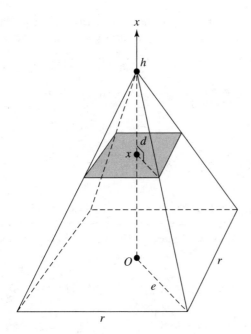

Figure A22.8

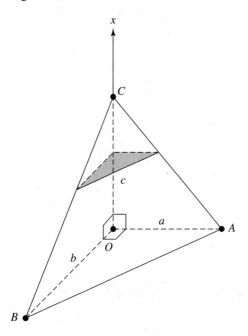

Figure A22.9

(D) Let the origin be the intersection of the edges, and let the x-axis lie along the edge of length c (Figure A22.9). A typical cross-section is a right triangle with legs of lengths d and e, parallel respectively to the edges of lengths a and b. By similar triangles, $\dfrac{d}{a} = \dfrac{c-x}{c}$

and $\dfrac{e}{b} = \dfrac{c-x}{c}$. So the area $A(x) = \dfrac{1}{2}\left[\dfrac{a(c-x)}{c}\right]\left[\dfrac{b(c-x)}{c}\right] = \dfrac{ab}{2c^2}(c-x)^2$. By the

cross-section formula,

$$V = \frac{ab}{2c^2}\int_0^c (c-x)^2 \ dx = \frac{ab}{2c^2}\left(-\frac{1}{3}\right)(c-x)^3 \Big]_0^c = -\frac{ab}{6c^2}(0 - c^3) = \frac{abc}{6}$$

200. Solving $y = x^2 - 4x + 6$ and $y = x + 2$, we obtain $x^2 - 5x + 4 = 0$, $x = 4$ or $x = 1$. So the curves meet at $(4, 6)$ and $(1, 3)$. Note that $y = x^2 - 4x + 6 = (x - 2)^2 + 2$. Hence, the latter curve is a parabola with vertex $(2, 2)$ (see Figure A22.10). We use the circular ring formula:

$$V = \pi \int_1^4 \{(x+2)^2 - [(x-2)^2 + 2]^2\} \ dx = \pi \int_1^4 [(x+2)^2 - (x-2)^4 - 4(x-2)^2 - 4]$$

$$dx = \pi\left(\frac{1}{3}(x+2)^3 - \frac{1}{5}(x-2)^5 - \frac{4}{3}(x-2)^3 - 4x\right)\Bigg]_1^4$$

$$= \pi\left[\left(72 - \frac{32}{5} - \frac{32}{3} - 16\right) - \left(9 + \frac{1}{5} + \frac{4}{3} - 4\right)\right] = 162\pi/5.$$

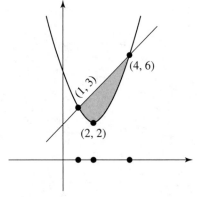

Figure A22.10

201. The disk formula applies: $V = \pi \int_1^b \left(\dfrac{1}{x}\right)^2 dx = \pi \int_1^b x^{-2} \ dx = \pi\left(-\dfrac{1}{x}\right)\Bigg]_1^b =$

$\pi\left[-\dfrac{1}{b} - (-1)\right] = \pi\left(1 - \dfrac{1}{b}\right)$. Note that this approaches π as $b \to +\infty$.

202. (A) We double the value obtained from the disk formula applied to the part of the region in the first quadrant (see Figure A22.11):

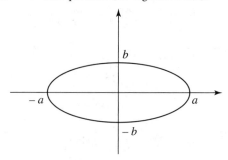

Figure A22.11

$$V = 2 \cdot \pi \int_0^a y^2\, dx = 2\pi \int_0^a b^2\left(1 - \frac{x^2}{a^2}\right) dx = 2\pi b^2\left(x - \frac{1}{3a^2}x^3\right)\Big|_0^a = 2\pi b^2\left(a - \frac{a}{3}\right) = \frac{4}{3}\pi ab^2$$

(B) Interchange a and b in **(A)**: $V = \dfrac{4}{3}\pi ba^2$.

203. The equation of the line is $y = \dfrac{1}{b}[(r_2 - r_1)x + r_1 b]$. By the disk formula,

$$V = \pi \int_0^b y^2\, dx = \frac{\pi}{b^2}\int_0^b [(r_2 - r_1)x + r_1 b]^2\, dx = \frac{\pi}{b^2}\int_0^b [(r_2 - r_1)^2 x^2 + 2r_1 b(r_2 - r_1)x + r_1^2 b^2]\, dx$$

$$= \frac{\pi}{b^2}\left(\frac{1}{3}(r_2 - r_1)^2 x^3 + r_1 b(r_2 - r_1)x^2 + r_1^2 b^2 x\right)\Big|_0^b = \frac{\pi}{b^2}\left[\frac{1}{3}(r_2 - r_1)^2 b^3 + r_1(r_2 - r_1)b^3 + r_1^2 b^3\right]$$

$$= \pi b\left[\frac{1}{3}(r_2 - r_1)^2 + r_1(r_2 - r_1) + r_1^2\right] = \frac{1}{3}\pi b(r_2^2 + r_1 r_2 + r_1^2).$$

Chapter 23: The Natural Logarithm

204. (A) $\ln = \displaystyle\int_1^x \frac{1}{t}\, dt$ for $x > 0$. Hence (Question 183(A)), $D_x(\ln x) = D_x\left(\displaystyle\int_1^x \frac{1}{t}\, dt\right) = \dfrac{1}{x}$.

(B) Case 1. $x > 0$. Then $D_x(\ln |x| + C) = D_x(\ln x) = \dfrac{1}{x}$. **Case 2.** $x < 0$. Then

$$D_x(\ln |x| + C) = D_x[\ln(-x)] = \frac{1}{-x} \cdot D_x(-x) = -\frac{1}{x} \cdot (-1) = \frac{1}{x}.$$

205. (A) By the chain rule, $D_x[\ln(4x - 1)] = \dfrac{1}{4x - 1} \cdot D_x(4x - 1) = \dfrac{4}{4x - 1}$.

(B) By the chain rule, $D_x[\ln(\ln x)] = \dfrac{1}{\ln x} \cdot D_x(\ln x) = \dfrac{1}{\ln x} \cdot \dfrac{1}{x} = \dfrac{1}{x \ln x}$.

(C) By the chain rule,

$$D_x\left[\ln\left(\frac{x-1}{x+1}\right)\right] = \frac{1}{(x-1)/(x+1)} \cdot D_x\left(\frac{x-1}{x+1}\right) = \frac{x+1}{x-1} \cdot \frac{(x+1)-(x-1)}{(x+1)^2}$$

$$= \frac{1}{(x-1)} \cdot \frac{2}{(x+1)} = \frac{2}{(x-1)(x+1)}.$$

206. **(A)** $\int \frac{1}{3x} dx = \frac{1}{3}\int \frac{1}{x} dx = \frac{1}{3}\ln|x| + C.$

(B) Let $u=7x-2$, $du=7\,dx$. Then $\int \frac{1}{7x-2} dx = \frac{1}{7}\int \frac{1}{u} du = \frac{1}{7}\ln|u| + C = \frac{1}{7}\ln|7x-2| + C.$

(C) Let $u = \ln x$, $du = \frac{1}{x} dx$. Then $\int \frac{1}{x\ln x} dx = \int \frac{1}{u} du = \ln|u| + C = \ln(|\ln x|) + C.$

[Compare Question 205(B).]

(D) $\int \frac{\ln x}{x} dx = \int (\ln x)\left(\frac{1}{x}\right) dx = \frac{1}{2}(\ln x)^2 + C.$

207. **(A)** Let $u = g(x)$, $du = g'(x)\,dx$. Then

$$\int \frac{g'(x)}{g(x)} dx = \int \frac{1}{u} du = \ln|u| + C = \ln|g(x)| + C.$$

(B) Use Question 207(A): $\int \frac{x}{3x^2+1} dx = \frac{1}{6}\int \frac{6x}{3x^2+1} dx = \frac{1}{6}\ln|3x^2+1| + C.$

(C) Use Question 207(A): $\int \tan x\, dx = \int \frac{\sin x}{\cos x}dx = -\int \frac{-\sin x}{\cos x} dx = -\ln|\cos x| + C.$

Since $-\ln|\cos x| = \ln(|\cos x|^{-1}) = \ln(|\sec x|)$, the answer can be written as $\ln|\sec x| + C.$

208. $\ln y = \ln x^3 + \ln(4-x^2)^{1/2} = 3\ln x + \frac{1}{2}\ln(4-x^2).$ By implicit differentiation,

$$\frac{1}{y}y' = 3\cdot\frac{1}{x} + \frac{1}{2}\cdot\frac{1}{4-x^2}\cdot(-2x) = \frac{3}{x} - \frac{x}{4-x^2} = \frac{12-3x^2-x^2}{x(4-x^2)} = \frac{12-4x^2}{x(4-x^2)} = \frac{4(3-x^2)}{x(4-x^2)}.$$

Hence, $y' = \frac{4(3-x^2)}{x(4-x^2)}\cdot y = \frac{4(3-x^2)}{x(4-x^2)}\cdot x^3(4-x^2)^{1/2} = \frac{4x^2(3-x^2)}{\sqrt{4-x^2}}.$

209. **(A)** $\ln x\,10 = \ln(2\cdot 5) = \ln 2 + \ln 5.$

(B) $\ln\frac{1}{2} = \ln 2^{-1} = -\ln 2.$

(C) $\ln\frac{1}{5} = \ln 5^{-1} = -\ln 5.$

(D) $\ln 25 = \ln 5^2 = 2 \ln 5.$

(E) $\ln \sqrt{2} = \ln 2^{1/2} = \frac{1}{2} \ln 2.$

(F) $\ln \sqrt[3]{5} = \ln 5^{1/3} = \frac{1}{3} \ln 5.$

(G) $\ln \frac{1}{20} = \ln (20)^{-1} = -\ln 20 = -\ln(4 \cdot 5) = -(\ln 4 + \ln 5) = -(\ln 2^2 + \ln 5) =$
$-(2 \ln 2 + \ln 5).$

(H) $\ln 2^{12} = 12 \ln 2.$

210. (A) Case 1. $x \geq 1$. By looking at areas in Figure A23.1, we see that
$1 - \frac{1}{x} = \frac{1}{x}(x-1) \leq \ln x \leq x - 1.$ **Case 2.** $0 < x < 1$. Then $1/x > 1$. So by Case 1, $1 - x \leq$
$\ln (1/x) \leq 1/x - 1.$ Thus, $1 - x \leq -\ln x \leq 1/x - 1$, and multiplying by -1, we obtain $x - 1$
$\geq \ln x \geq 1 - 1/x.$

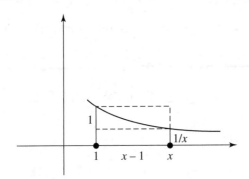

Figure A23.1

(B) By Question 210(A), $\ln x \leq x - 1 < x$. Substituting $\sqrt{x}$ for x, $\ln \sqrt{x} < \sqrt{x}$, $\ln x^{1/2}$
$< \sqrt{x}, \frac{1}{2} \ln x < \sqrt{x}, \frac{\ln x}{x} < \frac{2\sqrt{x}}{x} = \frac{2}{\sqrt{x}}.$

(C) $\lim\limits_{x \to +\infty} \frac{2}{\sqrt{x}} = 0.$ Hence, by Question 210(B), $\lim\limits_{x \to +\infty} \frac{\ln x}{x} = 0.$

(D) Let $y = 1/x$. As $x \to 0^+$, $y \to +\infty$. By Question 210(C), $\lim\limits_{y \to +\infty} \frac{\ln y}{y} = 0.$ But
$\frac{\ln y}{y} = \frac{\ln(1/x)}{1/x} = x (-\ln x) = -x \ln x.$ Hence, $\lim\limits_{x \to 0^+} x \ln x = 0.$

(E) $x - \ln x = x \left(1 - \frac{\ln x}{x}\right).$ By Question 210 (E), $\lim\limits_{x \to +\infty} \frac{\ln x}{x} = 0.$ Hence,
$\lim\limits_{x \to +\infty} (x - \ln x) = +\infty.$

211. $\Delta x = \dfrac{1}{10}$. For $\displaystyle\int_1^2 \dfrac{1}{x}\,dx$, The trapezoidal rule yields $\dfrac{1}{20}\left[1+\dfrac{1}{2}+2\left(\dfrac{10}{11}+\dfrac{10}{12}+\cdots+\dfrac{10}{19}\right)\right]=$

$\dfrac{3}{40}+\left(\dfrac{1}{11}+\dfrac{1}{12}+\cdots+\dfrac{1}{19}\right) \approx 0.0750 + (0.0909 + 0.0833 + \cdots + 0.0526) = 0.0750 +$

$0.6187 = 0.6937.$ (The actual value, correct to four decimal places, is 0.6931.)

212. Case 1. $a < b$. By the mean-value theorem, $\dfrac{\ln b - \ln a}{b-a} = \dfrac{1}{c}$ for some c in (a, b). Since $c > a \geq 1, \dfrac{1}{c} < 1$.

Hence, $\left|\dfrac{\ln b - \ln a}{b-a}\right| < 1$ and, therefore, $|\ln b - \ln a| < |b - a|$. **Case 2.** $b < a$. By Case 1, $|\ln a - \ln b| < |a - b|$. But $|\ln a - \ln b| = |\ln b - \ln a|$ and $|a - b| = |b - a|$.

213. In $\ln v = \displaystyle\int_1^v \dfrac{1}{t}\,dt$, make the change of variable $w = ut$ (u fixed). Then $dw = u\,dt$ and the limits of integration $t = 1$ and $t = v$ go over into $w = u$ and $w = uv$, respectively. Hence,

$$\ln v = \int_u^{uv} \dfrac{u}{w}\dfrac{1}{u}\,dw = \int_u^{uv} \dfrac{1}{w}\,dw = \int_u^{uv} \dfrac{1}{t}\,dt.$$

So $\ln u + \ln v = \displaystyle\int_1^u \dfrac{1}{t}\,dt + \int_u^{uv} \dfrac{1}{t}\,dt = \int_1^{uv} \dfrac{1}{t}\,dt = \ln uv.$

Chapter 24: Exponential Functions

214. (A) $e^{-\ln x} = e^{\ln(1/x)} = 1/x.$

(B) In $e^{-x} = -x$ by virtue of the identity $\ln e^u = u.$

(C) $(e^2)^{\ln x} = (e^{\ln x})^2 = x^2.$ Here, we have used the laws $(e^u)^v = e^{uv}$ and $e^{\ln u} = u.$

215. (A) By the chain rule, $D_x(e^{-x}) = e^{-x} \cdot D_x(-x) = e^{-x} \cdot (-1) = -e^{-x}.$ Here, we have used the fact that $D_u(e^u) = e^u.$

(B) By the chain rule, $D_x(e^{1/x}) = e^{1/x} \cdot D_x(1/x) = e^{1/x} \cdot (-1/x^2) = -e^{1/x}/x^2.$

(C) By the chain rule, $D_x(e^{\cos x}) = e^{\cos x} \cdot D_x(\cos x) = e^{\cos x} \cdot (-\sin x) = -e^{\cos x}\sin x.$

(D) $D_x(x^\pi) = D_x(e^{\pi \ln x}) = e^{\pi \ln x} \cdot D_x(\pi \ln x) = e^{\pi \ln x} \cdot \pi \cdot \dfrac{1}{x} = \pi \dfrac{x^\pi}{x} = \pi x^{\pi-1}$. (In like manner, $D_x(x^r) = rx^{r-1}$ for any real number r.)

(E) $D_x(\pi^x) = D_x(e^{x \ln \pi}) = e^{x \ln \pi} \cdot D_x(x \ln \pi) = e^{x \ln \pi} \cdot \ln \pi = \ln \pi \cdot \pi^x$.

(F) $D_x(\ln e^{2x}) = D_x(2x) = 2$.

(G) $D_x(e^x - e^{-x}) = D_x(e^x) - D_x(e^{-x}) = e^x - (-e^{-x}) = e^x + e^{-x}$. Here, $D_x(e^{-x}) = -e^{-x}$ is taken from Question 215(A).

216. (A) Let $u = 3x$, $du = 3\,dx$. Then $\displaystyle\int e^{3x}\,dx = \dfrac{1}{3}\int e^u\,du = \dfrac{1}{3}e^u + c = \dfrac{1}{3}e^{3x} + C$.

(B) Let $u = -x$, $du = -dx$. Then $\displaystyle\int e^{-x}\,dx = -\int e^u\,du = -e^u + c = -e^{-x} + C$.

(C) $\displaystyle\int e^{\cos x} \sin x\,dx = -e^{\cos x} + C$, by Question 215(C).

(D) $a^x = e^{x \ln a}$. So, let $u = (\ln a)x$, $du = (\ln a)\,dx$. Then

$$\int a^x\,dx - \int e^{x \ln a}\,dx = \frac{1}{\ln a}\int e^u\,du = \frac{1}{\ln a} \cdot e^u + C = \frac{1}{\ln a}e^{x \ln a} + C - \frac{1}{\ln a}a^x + C.$$

217. $\ln y = \ln x \cdot \ln x = (\ln x)^2$. So $\dfrac{1}{y}y' = 2(\ln x) \cdot \dfrac{1}{x}$, $y' = \dfrac{2 \ln x}{x}x^{\ln x} = 2(\ln x)x^{\ln x - 1}$.

218. (A) $\ln 2 = \ln (e^{3x}) = 3x$, $x = \dfrac{1}{3}\ln 2$.

(B) $-1 = 3 \ln x$, $\ln x = -\dfrac{1}{3}$, $e^{\ln x} = e^{-1/3}$, $x = e^{-1/3}$.

(C) Multiply by e^x: $e^{2x} - 2 = e^x$, $e^{2x} - e^x - 2 = 0$, $(e^x - 2)(e^x + 1) = 0$. Since $e^x > 0$, $e^x + 1 \neq 0$. Hence, $e^x - 2 = 0$, $e^x = 2$, $x = \ln 2$.

(D) $e = e^{\ln (\ln x)} = \ln x$, since $e^{\ln u} = u$. Hence, $e^e = e^{\ln x} = x$.

(E) $x - 1 = 1$, since $\ln u = 0$ has the unique solution 1. Hence, $x = 2$.

219. (A) The area $A = \displaystyle\int_0^1 e^x\,dx = e^x\big]_0^1 = e^1 - e^0 = e - 1$.

(B) By the disk formula, $V = \pi \displaystyle\int_0^1 (e^x)^2\,dx = \pi \int_0^1 e^{2x}\,dx = \pi \cdot \dfrac{1}{2}e^{2x}\bigg]_0^1 = \dfrac{\pi}{2}(e^2 - e^0) = \dfrac{\pi}{2}(e^2 - 1)$.

220. Since e^u is an increasing function of u, the maximum and minimum values of y correspond to the maximum and minimum values of the exponent sin x,—that is, 1 and −1. Hence, the absolute maximum is e (when $x = \pi/2$), and the absolute minimum is $e^{-1} = 1/e$ (when $x = -\pi/2$).

221. (A) $y' = e^{-x^2} \cdot (-2x) = -2xe^{-x^2}$. Hence, $x = 0$ is the only critical number $y'' = -2[e^{-x^2} + x \cdot (-2xe^{-x^2})] = -2e^{-x^2}(1 - 2x^2)$. By the second-derivative test, there is a relative (and, therefore, absolute) maximum at $(0, 1)$. As $x \to \pm\infty$, $e^{x^2} \to +\infty$, and, therefore, $y \to 0$. Thus, the x-axis is a horizontal asymptote on the right and left. The graph is symmetric with respect to the y-axis since e^{-x^2} is an even function. There are inflection points where $y'' = 0$,—that is, at $x = \pm\sqrt{2}/2$. Thus, the graph has the bell-shaped appearance indicated in Figure A24.1.

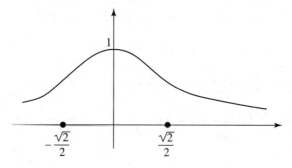

Figure A24.1

(B) See Figure A24.2. The function is defined only for $x > 0$. $y' = x \cdot \dfrac{1}{x} + \ln x = 1 + \ln x$. $y'' = 1/x$. Setting $y' = 0$, $\ln x = -1$, $x = e^{\ln x} = e^{-1} = 1/e$. This is the only critical number, and, by the second-derivative test, there is a relative (and, therefore, an absolute) minimum at $(1/e, -1/e)$. As $x \to +\infty$, $y \to +\infty$. As $x \to 0^+$, $y \to 0$, by Question 210(D).

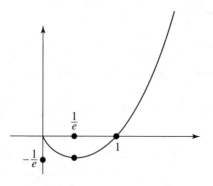

Figure A24.2

(C) $y' = \dfrac{1 - \ln x}{x^2}$ and $y'' = \dfrac{-x - 2x(1 - \ln x)}{x^4} = \dfrac{(2 \ln x - 3)}{x^3}$. The only critical

number occurs when $\ln x = 1$, $x = e$. By the second-derivative test, there is a relative (and, therefore, an absolute) maximum at $(e, 1/e)$. As $x \to +\infty$, $y \to 0$, by Question 210(C). As $x \to 0^+$, $y \to -\infty$. Hence, the positive x-axis is a horizontal asymptote, and the negative y-axis is a vertical asymptote. There is an inflection point where $2 \ln x - 3 = 0$,—that is,

$\ln x = \dfrac{3}{2}$, $x = e^{3/2}$. See Figure A24.3.

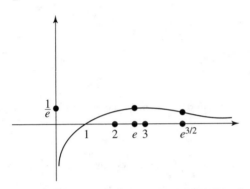

Figure A24.3

(D) The graph, Figure A24.4, is obtained by reflecting the graph of $y = e^x$ in the y-axis.

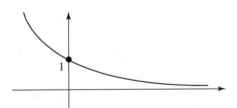

Figure A24.4.

222. (A) $D_x(\log_a x) = D_x\left(\dfrac{\ln x}{\ln a}\right) = \dfrac{1}{\ln a} D_x(\ln x) = \dfrac{1}{\ln a} \cdot \dfrac{1}{x} = \dfrac{1}{x \ln a}$.

(B) $a^{\log_a x} = a^{\ln x / \ln a} = e^{(\ln a)(\ln x / \ln a)} = e^{\ln x} = x$.

(C) $\log_a a^x = \dfrac{\ln a^x}{\ln a} = \dfrac{x \ln a}{\ln a} = x$.

(D) $\log_e x = \dfrac{\ln x}{\ln e} = \dfrac{\ln x}{1} = \ln x.$

(E) $\log_a uv = \dfrac{\ln uv}{\ln a} = \dfrac{\ln u + \ln v}{\ln a} = \dfrac{\ln u}{\ln a} + \dfrac{\ln v}{\ln a} = \log_a u + \log_a v.$

(F) By Question 222 (E), $\log_u \dfrac{u}{v} + \log_u v = \log\left(\dfrac{u}{v} \cdot v\right) = \log u.$ Subtract $\log_u v$ from both sides.

(G) $\log_a u^r = \dfrac{\ln u^r}{\ln a} = \dfrac{r \ln u}{\ln a} = r \cdot \dfrac{\ln u}{\ln a} = r \log_a u.$

(H) $\dfrac{\log_a x}{\log_a e} = \dfrac{\ln x / \ln a}{\ln e / \ln a} = \dfrac{\ln x}{\ln a} \cdot \dfrac{\ln a}{1} = \ln x.$

223. We know that one nonvanishing solution is e^x, so make the substitution $f(x) = e^x g(x)$: $e^x g' + e^x g = e^x g$, $e^x g' = 0$, $g' = 0$, $g = C$.

224. Let $y = \left(1 + \dfrac{x}{u}\right)^u$. Then $\ln y = u \ln\left(1 + \dfrac{x}{u}\right) = u[\ln(u + x) - \ln u] = u \cdot x \cdot \dfrac{1}{u^*}$ where u^* is between u and $u + x$. (In the last step, we used the mean-value theorem.) Either $u < u^* < u + x$ or $u + x < u^* < u$. Then either $1 < u^*/u < 1 + x/u$ or $1 + x/u < u^*/u < 1$. In either case, $u^*/u \to 1$ as $u \to +\infty$. Hence, $\ln y \to x$ as $u \to +\infty$. Therefore, $y = e^{\ln y} \to e^x$ as $u \to +\infty$.

225. $\dfrac{x^n}{e^x} = \dfrac{e^{n \ln x}}{e^x} = \dfrac{1}{e^{x - n \ln x}} = \dfrac{1}{e^{x[1 - n(\ln x/x)]}}$. But $\ln x / x \to 0$ as $x \to +\infty$. Hence, since $e^x \to +\infty$, $x^n / e^x \to 0$.

226. Let $y = x^{\sin x}$. $\ln y = \sin x \cdot \ln x = \dfrac{\sin x}{x} \cdot (x \ln x)$. Since $\dfrac{\sin x}{x} \to 1$ and $x \ln x \to 0$ as $x \to 0^+$, $\ln y \to 0$ as $x \to 0^+$. Hence, $y = e^{\ln y} \to e^0 = 1$.

227. Since $\cos x \to 1$ and $\sin x \to 0$ as $x \to 0$, $(\sin x)^{\cos x} \to 0^1 = 0$.

228. Set $x = 1$ in the formula of Question 224.

229. See Figure A24.5. $y' = x^2 e^x + 2x e^x = x e^x(x + 2)$. $y'' = x e^x + (x + 2)(x e^x + e^x) = e^x(x^2 + 4x + 2)$. The critical numbers are $x = 0$ and $x = -2$. The second-derivative test shows that there is a relative minimum at $(0, 0)$ and a relative maximum at $(-2, 4e^{-2})$. As $x \to +\infty$, $y \to +\infty$. As $x \to -\infty$, $y \to 0$ (by Question 225). There are inflection points where $x^2 + 4x + 2 = 0$,—that is, at $x = -2 \pm \sqrt{2}$.

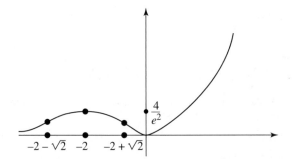

Figure A24.5

Question 230 concerns the hyperbolic sine and cosine functions $\sinh x = \dfrac{1}{2}(e^x - e^{-x})$ and $\cosh x = \dfrac{1}{2}(e^x + e^{-x})$.

230. (A) $D_x(\sinh x) = D_x\left[\dfrac{1}{2}(e^x - e^{-x})\right] = \dfrac{1}{2}(e^x + e^{-x}) = \cosh x.$

$D_x(\cosh x) = D_x\left[\dfrac{1}{2}(e^x + e^{-x})\right] = \dfrac{1}{2}(e^x - e^{-x}) = \sinh x.$

(B) By Question 230 (A), $D_x^2 (\sinh x) = D_x(\cosh x) = \sinh x$ and $D_x^2 (\cosh x) = D_x(\sinh x) = \cosh x.$

Chapter 25: L'Hôpital's Rule

231. First let us state the *zero-over-zero case*. Under certain simple conditions, if $\lim\limits_{x \to b} f(x) = \lim\limits_{x \to b} g(x) = 0$ and $\lim\limits_{x \to b} \dfrac{f'(x)}{g'(x)} = L$, then $\lim\limits_{x \to b} \dfrac{f(x)}{g(x)} = L$. Here, $x \to b$ can be replaced by $x \to b^+$, $x \to b^-$, $x \to +\infty$, or $x \to -\infty$. The conditions are that f and g are differentiate in an open interval around b and that g' is not zero in that interval, except possibly at b. (In the case of one-sided limits, the interval can have b as an endpoint. In the case of $x \to \pm\infty$, the conditions on f and g hold for sufficiently large, or sufficiently small, values of x.) The second case is the *infinity-over-infinity case*. If $\lim\limits_{x \to b} f(x) = \lim\limits_{x \to b} g(x) = \pm\infty$ and $\lim\limits_{x \to b} \dfrac{f'(x)}{g'(x)} = L$, then $\lim\limits_{x \to b} \dfrac{f(x)}{g(x)} = L$. Here, again $x \to b$ can be replaced by $x \to b^+$, $x \to b^-$, $x \to +\infty$, or $x \to -\infty$. The conditions on f and g are the same as in the first case.

232. $\lim\limits_{x \to 0} \dfrac{\sin x}{x} = \lim\limits_{x \to 0} \dfrac{D_x(\sin x)}{D_x(x)} = \lim\limits_{x \to 0} \dfrac{\cos x}{1} = \dfrac{1}{1} = 1.$

233. $\lim\limits_{x\to 0}\dfrac{1-\cos x}{x}=\lim\limits_{x\to 0}\dfrac{\sin x}{1}=\dfrac{0}{1}=0.$

234. $\lim\limits_{x\to +\infty}\dfrac{5x^3-4x+3}{2x^2-1}=\lim\limits_{x\to +\infty}\dfrac{15x^2-4}{4x}=\lim\limits_{x\to +\infty}\dfrac{30x}{4}=+\infty.$ Here, we have applied L'Hôpital's rule twice in succession. In subsequent questions, successive use of L'Hôpital's rule will be made without explicit mention.

235. Here we have the difference of two functions that both approach ∞. However, $\dfrac{1}{x}-\dfrac{1}{\sin x}=\dfrac{\sin x-x}{x\sin x}$, to which L'Hôpital's rule is applicable. $\lim\limits_{x\to 0}\dfrac{\sin x-x}{x\sin x}=$ $\lim\limits_{x\to 0}\dfrac{\cos x-1}{x\cos x+\sin x}=\lim\limits_{x\to 0}\dfrac{-\sin x}{-x\sin x+2\cos x}=\dfrac{0}{0+2}=0.$

236. $\lim\limits_{x\to 0}\dfrac{\tan x}{x}=\lim\limits_{x\to 0}\dfrac{\sec^2 x}{1}=\dfrac{1}{1}=1.$

237. $\lim\limits_{x\to 0}\dfrac{3^x-2^x}{x}=\lim\limits_{x\to 0}\dfrac{\ln 3\cdot 3^x-\ln 2\cdot 2^x}{1}=\ln 3-\ln 2.$

238. Let $y=x^{\sin x}$. Then $\ln y=\sin x\cdot\ln x=\dfrac{\ln x}{\csc x}$, to which L'Hôpital's rule applies. $\lim\limits_{x\to 0^+}\dfrac{\ln x}{\csc x}=\lim\limits_{x\to 0^+}\dfrac{1/x}{-\csc x\cot x}=-\lim\limits_{x\to 0^+}\dfrac{\sin x}{x}\cdot\dfrac{1}{\cos x}\cdot\sin x=-1\cdot 1\cdot 0=0$ Thus, $\lim\limits_{x\to 0^+}\ln y=0.$ Hence, $\lim\limits_{x\to 0^+}y=\lim\limits_{x\to 0^+}e^{\ln y}=e^0=1.$

239. $\lim\limits_{x\to 0}\dfrac{e^{3x}-1}{\tan x}=\lim\limits_{x\to 0}\dfrac{3e^{3x}}{\sec^2 x}=\dfrac{3\cdot 1}{1}=3.$

240. $\lim\limits_{x\to 0}\dfrac{\tan x-\sin x}{x^3}=\lim\limits_{x\to 0}\dfrac{\sec^2 x-\cos x}{3x^2}=\lim\limits_{x\to 0}\dfrac{2\sec^2 x\tan x+\sin x}{6x}=$ $\lim\limits_{x\to 0}\dfrac{2\sec^4 x+4\tan^2 x\sec^2 x+\cos x}{6}=\dfrac{3}{6}=\dfrac{1}{2}.$

Chapter 26: Exponential Growth and Decay

241. (A) $D_t\left(\dfrac{y}{e^{Kt}}\right)=\dfrac{e^{Kt}\cdot D_t y-y(Ke^{Kt})}{e^{2Kt}}=\dfrac{e^{Kt}(D_t y-Ky)}{e^{2Kt}}=0.$ Hence, y/e^{Kt} is a constant $C,y=Ce^{Kt}.$ When $t=0,y_0=Ce^0=C.$ Thus, $y=y_0e^{Kt}.$

(B) Let y be the number of bacteria. Then $y = y_0 e^{Kt}$. By the given information, $2y_0 = y_0 e^{3K}$, $2 = e^{3K}$, $\ln 2 = \ln e^{3K} = 3K$, $K = (\ln 2)/3$. When $t = 9$, $y = y_0 e^{9K} = y_0 e^{3\ln 2} = y_0 (e^{\ln 2})^3 = y_0 \cdot 2^3 = 8y_0$. Thus, the initial number has been multiplied by 8.

(C) Let y be the number of grams present at time t. Then $y = y_0 e^{Kt}$. The given information tells us that $50 = 200 e^K$, $e^K = \dfrac{1}{4}$, $K = \ln \dfrac{1}{4} = -\ln 4$. When $t = 3$, $y = 200 e^{3K} =$

$$200(e^K)^3 = 200\left(\frac{1}{4}\right)^3 = \frac{200}{64} = 3.125 \text{ grams.}$$

(D) $y = y_0 e^{Kt}$. When $t = 1$, $y = (1 + r/100)y_0$. Hence, $(1 + r/100)y_0 = y_0 e^K$, $1 + r/100 = e^K$. So $K = \ln(1 + r/100)$ and $r = 100(e^K - 1)$.

242. In the notation of Question 241(D), $r = 2$, $K = \ln(1.02) \approx 0.0198$ (by a table of logarithms). Hence, after 10 years, $y = y_0 e^{Kt} = y_0 e^{(0.0198)10} = y_0 e^{0.198} \approx (1.219)y_0$ (using a table for the exponential function). Hence, over 10 years, there will be an increase of about 21.9 percent.

243. (A) After the first period of interest ($\frac{1}{n}$ th of a year), the amount will be $y_0(1 + r/100n)$; after the second period, $y_0(1 + r/100n)^2$, etc. The interval of k years contains kn periods of interest, and, therefore, the amount present after k years will be $y_0(1 + r/100n)^{kn}$.

(B) By Question 243 (A), $y = y_0(1 + r/100n)^{kn}$ if the money is compounded n times per year. If we let n approach infinity, we get $\lim_{n\to\infty} y_0(1+r/100n)^{kn} = y_0 \lim_{n\to+\infty}(1+r/100n)^{nk}$ $= y_0[\lim_{b\to+\infty}(1+r/100n)^n]^k = y_0(e^{r/100})^k = y_0 e^{0.01rk}$. (Here we have used Question 224.) Thus, the money grows exponentially, with growth constant $K = 0.01r$.

(C) By Question 243 (A), the amount present after 1 year will be

$$y_0\left(1 + \frac{8}{400}\right)^4 = y_0(1.02)^4 \approx 1.0824 y_0.$$ Thus, the equivalent yearly rate is 8.24 percent.

(D) $2y_0 = y_0 e^{0.5t}$, by Question 243 (B). So $2 = e^{0.05t}$, $0.05t = \ln 2$, $t = 20\ln 2 \approx 20(0.6931) = 13.862$. Thus, the money will double in a little less than 13 years and 315 days.

244. (A) $y = y_0 e^{Kt}$. By definition, $\frac{1}{2}y_0 = y_0 e^{KT}$. So $\frac{1}{2} = e^{KT}$, $KT = \ln\frac{1}{2} = -\ln 2$.

(B) Let y be the number of grams of radium t years after the radium was created. Then $y = y_0 e^{Kt}$, where $1690\,K = -\ln 2$, by Question 244(A). If at the present time t, $y = \frac{1}{10}y_0$, then $\frac{1}{10}y_0 = y_0 e^{Kt}$, $\frac{1}{10} = e^{Kt}$, $Kt = \ln\frac{1}{10} = -\ln 10$. Hence, $-(\ln 2/1690)t = -\ln 10$, $t = 1690\ln 10/\ln 2 \approx 5614.477$. Thus, the radium was created about 5,614 years ago.

(C) The amount of carbon is $y = y_0 e^{Kt}$. We know that $5750\,K = -\ln 2$. Since $y_0 = 1$ and $t = 3000$, $y = e^{3000K} = e^{-\frac{3000}{5750}\ln 2} \approx e^{-0.3616} \approx 0.69657$ (from a table for e^{-x}). Thus, about 0.7 grams will remain.

(D) Let y_0 be the original amount, and let T be the half-life. Then $0.8y_0$ remains when $t = 1$. Thus, $0.8y_0 = y_0 e^K$, $0.8 = e^K$, $K = \ln 0.8 \approx -0.2231$ (from a table of logarithms). But $KT = \ln 2$. So $0.2231\,T \approx 0.6931$, $T \approx 3.1067$ years.

245. Since $D_t y = Ky$, $y = y_0 e^{Kt} = 8e^{Kt}$. The given facts tell us that $7 = 8e^K$, $e^K = \dfrac{7}{8}$. When $t = 2$, $y = 8e^{2K} = 8(e^K)^2 = 8\left(\dfrac{7}{8}\right)^2 = 6.125$ degrees.

246. Let y be the number of pounds of salt in the mixture at time t. Since the concentration of salt at any given time is $y/400$ pounds per gallon, and 20 gallons flow out per minute, the rate at which y is diminishing is $20 \cdot y/400 = 0.05y$ pounds per minute. Hence, $D_t y = -0.05y$, and, thus, y is decaying exponentially with a decay constant of -0.05. Hence, $y = 100e^{-0.05t}$. So, after 30 minutes, $y = 100e^{-1.5} \approx 100(0.2231) = 22.31$ pounds.

Chapter 27: Inverse Trigonometric Functions

247. By definition, as x varies from -1 to 1, y varies from $-\pi/2$ to $\pi/2$. The graph of $y = \sin^{-1} x$ is obtained from the graph of $y = \sin x$ (Figure A27.1 (a)) by reflection in the line $y = x$. See Figure A27.1(b).

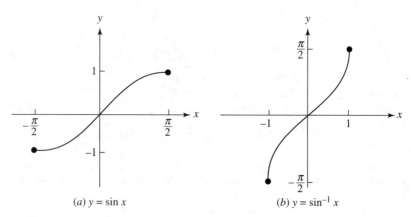

(a) $y = \sin x$ (b) $y = \sin^{-1} x$

Figure A27.1

248. Let $y = \sin^{-1} x$. Then $\sin y = x$. By implicit differentiation, $\cos y \cdot D_x y = 1$, $D_x y = 1/\cos y$. But $\cos y = \pm\sqrt{1 - \sin^2 y} = \pm\sqrt{1 - x^2}$. Since, by definition, $-\pi/2 \le y \le \pi/2$, $\cos y \ge 0$, and therefore, $\cos y = \sqrt{1 - x^2}$ and $D_x y = 1/\sqrt{1 - x^2}$.

249. As x varies from $-\infty$ to $+\infty$, $\tan^{-1} x$ varies from $-\pi/2$ to $\pi/2$. The graph of $y = \tan^{-1} x$ is obtained from that of $y = \tan x$ (Figure A27.2(a)) by reflection in the line $y = x$. See Figure A27.2(b).

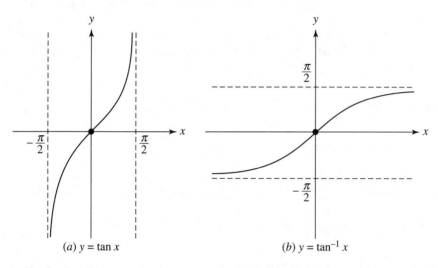

$(a)\ y = \tan x$ $(b)\ y = \tan^{-1} x$

Figure A27.2

250. Let $y = \tan^{-1} x$. Then $\tan y = x$. By implicit differentiation, $\sec^2 y \cdot D_x y = 1$, $D_x y = 1/\sec^2 y = 1/(1 + \tan^2 y) = 1/(1 + x^2)$.

251. **(A)** $\cos^{-1}(-\sqrt{3}/2)$ is the angle θ between 0 and π for which $\cos\theta = -\sqrt{3}/2$. It is seen from Figure A27.3 that θ is the supplement of $\pi/6$, that is, $\theta = 5\pi/6$.

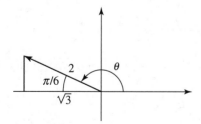

Figure A27.3

(B) $\sin^{-1}(\sqrt{2}/2)$ is the angle θ between $-\pi/2$ and $\pi/2$ for which $\sin\theta = -\sqrt{2}/2$. Clearly, $\theta = \pi/4$.

(C) $\sin^{-1}(-\sqrt{2}/2)$ is the angle θ between $-\pi/2$ and $\pi/2$ for which $\sin\theta = -\sqrt{2}/2$. Clearly, $\theta = -\pi/4$.

(D) $\tan^{-1} 1$ is the angle θ between $-\pi/2$ and $\pi/2$ for which $\tan\theta = 1$, that is—$\theta = \pi/4$.

(E) $\pi/6$ is the angle θ between $-\pi/2$ and $\pi/2$ for which $\tan\theta = (\sqrt{3}/3)$. So $\tan^{-1}(\sqrt{3}/3) = \pi/6$.

252. (A) Let $\theta = \cos^{-1}\dfrac{4}{5}$. Since $\dfrac{4}{5} > 0$, $0 < \theta < \pi/2$ and $\sin\theta$ must be positive.

$$\sin\theta = \sqrt{1 - \cos^2\theta} = \sqrt{\dfrac{9}{25}} = \dfrac{3}{5}.$$

(B) Let $\theta_1 = \sin^{-1}\dfrac{3}{5}$ and $\theta_2 = \sec^{-1} 3$. Since $\dfrac{3}{5}$ and 3 are positive, θ_1 and θ_2 are in the first

quadrant. Then $\cos\left(\sin^{-1}\dfrac{3}{5} + \sec^{-1} 3\right) = \cos(\theta_1 + \theta_2) = \cos\theta_1 \cos\theta_2 - \sin\theta_1 \sin\theta_2 = \dfrac{4}{5} \cdot \dfrac{1}{3} - \dfrac{3}{5}(2\sqrt{2}/3) = \dfrac{4}{15} - 6\sqrt{2}/15 = (4 - 6\sqrt{2})/15.$

(C) $\sin\pi = 0$. Hence, $\sin^{-1}(\sin\pi) = \sin^{-1} 0 = 0$. Note that $\sin^{-1}(\sin x)$ is not necessarily equal to x.

253. (A) Let $x = 2u$, $dx = 2du$. Then $\displaystyle\int \dfrac{dx}{4+x^2} = \dfrac{1}{2}\int \dfrac{du}{1+u^2} = \dfrac{1}{2}\tan^{-1} u + C = \dfrac{1}{2}\tan^{-1}\dfrac{x}{2} + C.$
This is a special case of the formula $\displaystyle\int \dfrac{dx}{a^2+x^2} = \dfrac{1}{a}\tan^{-1}\dfrac{x}{a} + C$ for $a > 0$.

(B) Let $x = 5u$, $dx = 5du$. Then $\displaystyle\int \dfrac{dx}{\sqrt{25-x^2}} = \int \dfrac{5du}{\sqrt{25-25u^2}} = \int \dfrac{du}{\sqrt{1-u^2}} = \sin^{-1} u +$
$C = \sin^{-1}\dfrac{x}{5} + C.$ This is a special case of the formula $\displaystyle\int \dfrac{dx}{\sqrt{a^2-x^2}} = \sin^{-1}\dfrac{x}{a} + C$ for $a > 0$.

254. From Figure A27.4, $\theta = \tan^{-1} 4/x - \tan^{-1} 2/x$. So

$$D_x\theta = \dfrac{1}{1+(4/x)^2} \cdot \dfrac{-4}{x^2} - \dfrac{1}{1+(2/x)^2} \cdot \dfrac{-2}{x^2} = \dfrac{-4}{x^2+16} + \dfrac{2}{x^2+4}$$

$$= \dfrac{-4x^2 - 16 + 2x^2 + 32}{(x^2+16)(x^2+4)} = \dfrac{2(8-x^2)}{(x^2+16)(x^2+4)}$$

Thus, the only positive critical number is $x = \sqrt{8} = 2\sqrt{2}$, which, by the first-derivative test, yields a relative (and, therefore, an absolute) maximum.

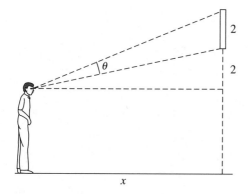

Figure A27.4

Chapter 28: Integration by Parts

255. We use integration by parts: $\int u\,dv = uv - \int v\,du$. In this case, let $u = x^2$, $dv = e^{-x}\,dx$. Then $du = 2x\,dx$, $v = -e^{-x}$. Hence, $\int x^2 e^{-x}\,dx = -x^2 e^{-x} + 2\int xe^{-x}\,dx$. (To calculate the latter, we use another integration by parts: $u = x$, $dv = e^{-x}\,dx$; $du = dx$, $v = -e^{-x}$. Then $\int xe^{-x}\,dx = -xe^{-x} + \int e^{-x}\,dx = -xe^{-x} - e^{-x} = -e^{-x}.(x+1)$.) Hence, $\int x^2 e^{-x}\,dx = -x^2 e^{-x} + 2[-e^{-x}(x+1)] + C = -e^{-x}(x^2 + 2x + 2) + C$.

256. Let $u = \sin x$, $dv = e^x\,dx$, $du = \cos x\,dx$, $v = e^x$. Then

$$\int e^x \sin x\,dx = e^x \sin x - \int e^x \cos x\,dx. \qquad (1)$$

We use integration by parts again for the latter integral: let $u = \cos x$, $dv = e^x\,dx$, $du = -\sin x\,dx$, $v = e^x$. Then $\int e^x \cos x\,dx = e^x \cos x + \int e^x \sin x\,dx$. Substituting in (1), $\int e^x \sin x\,dx = e^x \sin x - (e^x \cos x + \int e^x \sin x\,dx) = e^x \sin x - e^x \cos x - \int e^x \sin x\,dx$. Thus, $2\int e^x \sin x\,dx = e^x(\sin x - \cos x) + C$, $\int e^x \sin x\,dx = \frac{1}{2}e^x(\sin x - \cos x) + C_1$.

257. Let $u = \sin^{-1} x$, $dv = dx$, $du = (1/\sqrt{1-x^2})\,dx$, $v = x$. Then $\int \sin^{-1} x\,dx = x\sin^{-1} x - \int (x/\sqrt{1-x^2})\,dx = x\sin^{-1} x + \frac{1}{2}\int (1-x^2)^{-1/2}(-2x)\,dx = x\sin^{-1} x + \frac{1}{2} \cdot 2(1-x^2)^{1/2} + C = x\sin^{-1} x + \sqrt{1-x^2} + C$.

258. Let $u = x$, $dv = \sin x\,dx$, $du = dx$, $v = -\cos x$. Then $\int x \sin x\,dx = -x\cos x + \int \cos x\,dx = -x\cos x + \sin x + C$.

259. Let $u = \sin x$, $dv = \sin x\, dx$, $du = \cos x\, dx$, $v = -\cos x$. Then $\int \sin^2 x\, dx = -\sin x \cos x +$

$\int \cos^2 x\, dx = -\sin x \cos x + \int (1 - \sin^2 x)\, dx = -\sin x \cos x + x - \int \sin^2 x\, dx$. So $2\int \sin^2 x\, dx =$

$x - \sin x \cos x + C$, $\int \sin^2 x\, dx = \dfrac{1}{2}(x - \sin x \cos x) + C_1$.

260. Let $u = x$, $dv = e^{3x}\, dx$, $du = dx$, $v = \dfrac{1}{3}e^{3x}$. Then $\int xe^{3x}\, dx = \dfrac{1}{3}xe^{3x} - \dfrac{1}{3}\int e^{3x}\, dx =$

$\dfrac{1}{3}xe^x - \dfrac{1}{3}\cdot\dfrac{1}{3}e^{3x} + C = \dfrac{1}{9}e^{3x}(3x - 1) + C$.

261. Let $u = \ln x$, $dv = x^n\, dx$, $du = \dfrac{1}{x}\, dx$, $v = \dfrac{x^{n+1}}{n+1}$. Then $\int x^n \ln x\, dx = \dfrac{x^{n+1}}{n+1}\ln x -$

$\dfrac{1}{n+1}\int x^n\, dx = \dfrac{x^{n+1}}{n+1}\ln x - \dfrac{1}{n+1}\dfrac{x^{n+1}}{n+1} + C = \dfrac{x^{n+1}}{(n+1)^2}[(n+1)\ln x - 1] + C$.

Chapter 29: Trigonometric Integrands and Substitutions

262. Let $u = \cos x$, $du = -\sin x\, dx$. Then $\int \sin x \cos^2 x\, dx = -\int u^2\, du = -\dfrac{1}{3}u^3 + C = -\dfrac{1}{3}\cos^3 x + C$.

263. Since the power of $\cos x$ is odd, let $u = \sin x$, $du = \cos x\, dx$. Then

$\int \sin^4 x \cos^5 x\, dx = \int \sin^4 x(1 - \sin^2 x)^2 \cos x\, dx = \int u^4(1 - u^2)^2\, du = \int u^4(1 - 2u^2 + u^4)\, du =$

$\int (u^4 - 2u^6 + u^8)\, du = \dfrac{1}{5}u^5 - \dfrac{2}{7}u^7 + \dfrac{1}{9}u^9 + C = u^5\left(\dfrac{1}{5} - \dfrac{2}{7}u^2 + \dfrac{1}{9}u^4\right) + C = \sin^5 x$

$\left(\dfrac{1}{5} - \dfrac{2}{7}\sin^2 x + \dfrac{1}{9}\sin^4 x\right) + C$.

264. Use the formula $\sin Ax \cos Bx = \dfrac{1}{2}[\sin(A + B)x + \sin(A - B)x]$. Then

$\int \sin \pi x \cos 3\pi x\, dx = \dfrac{1}{2}\int [\sin 4\pi x + \sin(-2\pi x)]\, dx = \dfrac{1}{2}\int (\sin 4\pi x - \sin 2\pi x)\, dx =$

$\dfrac{1}{2}\left(-\dfrac{\cos 4\pi x}{4\pi} + \dfrac{\cos 2\pi x}{2\pi}\right) + C = \dfrac{1}{8\pi}(2\cos 2\pi x - \cos 4\pi x) + C$.

265. Recall $\sin Ax \sin Bx = \dfrac{1}{2}[\cos(A - B)x - \cos(A + B)x]$. So $\int \sin 5x \sin 7x\, dx =$

$\dfrac{1}{2}\int [\cos(-2x) - \cos 12x]\, dx = \dfrac{1}{2}\int (\cos 2x - \cos 12x)\, dx = \dfrac{1}{2}\left(\dfrac{\sin 2x}{2} - \dfrac{\sin 12x}{12}\right) + C =$

$\dfrac{1}{24}(6\sin 2x - \sin 12x) + C$.

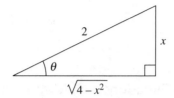

Figure A29.1

266. Since $\sqrt{4-x^2}$ is present, we let $x = 2\sin\theta$, $dx = 2\cos\theta\, d\theta$. Then (Figure A29.1),

$\sqrt{4-x^2} = 2\cos\theta$. So $\displaystyle\int \frac{x^2}{\sqrt{4-x^2}}\, dx = \int \frac{4\sin^2\theta}{2\cos\theta} 2\cos\theta\, d\theta = 4\int \sin^2\theta\, d\theta =$

$4\displaystyle\int \frac{1-\cos 2\theta}{2}\, d\theta = 2\left(\theta - \frac{\sin 2\theta}{2}\right) + C = 2(\theta - \sin\theta\cos\theta) + C =$

$2\left(\sin^{-1}\dfrac{x}{2} - \dfrac{x}{2}\cdot\dfrac{\sqrt{4-x^2}}{2}\right) + C = 2\sin^{-1}\dfrac{x}{2} - \dfrac{x\sqrt{4-x^2}}{2} + C.$

267. Since $\sqrt{1+x^2}$ is present, we let $x = \tan\theta$, $dx = \sec^2\theta\, d\theta$. Then (Figure A29.2),

$\sqrt{1+x^2} = \sec\theta$. So $\displaystyle\int \frac{\sqrt{1+x^2}}{x}\, dx = \int \frac{\sec\theta}{\tan\theta}\sec^2\theta\, d\theta = \int \frac{\sec\theta}{\tan\theta}(1+\tan^2\theta)\, d\theta = \int(\csc\theta +$

$\sec\theta\tan\theta)\, d\theta = \ln|\csc\theta - \cot\theta| + \sec\theta + C = \ln\left|\dfrac{\sqrt{1+x^2}-1}{x}\right| + \sqrt{1+x^2} + C.$

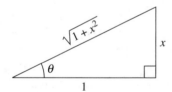

Figure A29.2

268. Since $\sqrt{x^2-9}$ is present, let $x = 3\sec\theta$, $dx = 3\sec\theta\tan\theta\, d\theta$, and (Figure A29.3)

$\sqrt{x^2-9} = 3\tan\theta$. Then $\displaystyle\int \frac{dx}{x^2\sqrt{x^2-9}} = \int \frac{3\sec\theta\tan\theta\, d\theta}{9\sec^2\theta\cdot 3\tan\theta} = \frac{1}{9}\int \cos\theta\, d\theta = \frac{1}{9}\sin\theta + C =$

$\dfrac{1}{9}\dfrac{\sqrt{x^2-9}}{x} + C.$

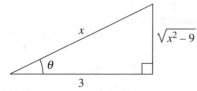

Figure A29.3

269. $y' = \dfrac{1}{\cos x}(-\sin x) = -\tan x$, $1 + (y')^2 = \sec^2 x$. So $L = \displaystyle\int_0^{\pi/3} \sec x \, dx = \ln|\sec x +$
$\tan x \, |]_0^{\pi/3} = \ln|2 + \sqrt{3}| - \ln 1 = \ln(2 + \sqrt{3})$.

Chapter 30: Integration of Rational Functions: The Method of Partial Fractions

270. $\dfrac{1}{x^2 - 9} = \dfrac{1}{(x-3)(x+3)} = \dfrac{A}{x-3} + \dfrac{B}{x+3}$. Clear the denominators by multiplying
both sides by $(x-3)(x+3)$: $1 = A(x+3) + B(x-3)$. Let $x = 3$. Then $1 = 6A$, $A = \dfrac{1}{6}$. Let
$x = -3$. Then $1 = -6B$, $B = -\dfrac{1}{6}$. So $1/(x^2 - 9) = \dfrac{1}{6}[1/(x-3)] - \dfrac{1}{6}[1/(x+3)]$. Hence,
$\displaystyle\int \dfrac{dx}{x^2 - 9} = \dfrac{1}{6}\ln|x-3| - \dfrac{1}{6}\ln|x+3| + C = \dfrac{1}{6}\ln|(x-3)/|(x+3)| + C$.

271. $\dfrac{x-5}{x^2(x+1)} = \dfrac{A}{x} + \dfrac{B}{x^2} + \dfrac{C}{x+1}$. Multiply both sides by $x^2(x+1)$, obtaining
$x - 5 = Ax(x+1) + B(x+1) + Cx^2$. Let $x = 0$. Then $-5 = B$. Let $x = -1$. Then
$-6 = C$. To find A, compare coefficients of x^2 on both sides of the equation: $0 =$
$A + C$, $A = -C = 6$. Thus, $\dfrac{x-5}{x^2(x+1)} = \dfrac{6}{x} - \dfrac{5}{x^2} - \dfrac{6}{x+1}$, and $\displaystyle\int \dfrac{x-5}{x^2(x+1)} dx = 6\ln|x| +$
$\dfrac{5}{x} - 6\ln|x+1| + C_1 = 6\ln\left|\dfrac{x}{x+1}\right| + \dfrac{5}{x} + C_1$.

272. $\dfrac{1}{x(x^2 + 5)} = \dfrac{A}{x} + \dfrac{Bx + C}{x^2 + 5}$. So $1 = A(x^2 + 5) + Bx^2 + Cx$. Let $x = 0$. Then $1 = 5A$,
$A = \dfrac{1}{5}$. Equate coefficients of x^2: $0 = A + B$, $B = -A = -\dfrac{1}{5}$. Equate coefficients of x: $0 =$
C. Hence, $\dfrac{1}{x(x^2 + 5)} = \dfrac{1}{5}\dfrac{1}{x} - \dfrac{1}{5}\dfrac{x}{x^2 + 5}$, and $\displaystyle\int \dfrac{dx}{x(x^2 + 5)} = \dfrac{1}{5}\left(\ln|x| - \dfrac{1}{2}\ln|x^2 + 5|\right) + C_1 =$
$\dfrac{1}{5}\ln\left|\dfrac{x}{\sqrt{x^2 + 5}}\right| + C_1$.

273. Neither $x^2 + 1$ nor $x^2 + 4$ factor. Then $\dfrac{1}{(x^2 + 1)(x^2 + 4)} = \dfrac{Ax + B}{x^2 + 1} + \dfrac{Cx + D}{x^2 + 4}$. Hence, $1 =$
$(Ax + B)(x^2 + 4) + (Cx + D)(x^2 + 1)$. Equate coefficients of x^3: (*) $0 = A + C$. Equate coefficients
of x: $0 = 4A + C$. Subtracting (*) from this equation, we get $3A = 0$, $A = 0$, $C = 0$. Equate coefficients of x^2: (**) $0 = B + D$. Equate constant coefficients: $1 = 4B + D$. Subtracting (**) from
this equation, we get $3B = 1$, $B = \dfrac{1}{3}$, $D = -\dfrac{1}{3}$. Thus, $\dfrac{1}{(x^2 + 1)(x^2 + 4)} = \dfrac{1}{3}\dfrac{1}{x^2 + 1} - \dfrac{1}{3}\dfrac{1}{x^2 + 4}$.
Hence, $\displaystyle\int \dfrac{dx}{(x^2 + 1)(x^2 + 4)} = \dfrac{1}{3}\tan^{-1}x - \dfrac{1}{3}\dfrac{1}{2}\tan^{-1}(x/2) + C_1 = \dfrac{1}{3}\tan^{-1}x - \dfrac{1}{6}\tan^{-1}(x/2) + C_1$.

274. $\dfrac{1}{x(x^2+1)^2} = \dfrac{A}{x} + \dfrac{Bx+C}{x^2+1} + \dfrac{Dx+E}{(x^2+1)^2}$. Then $1 = A(x^2+1)^2 + x(x^2+1)(Bx+C) + x(Dx$

$+ E)$. Let $x=0$. Then $1 = A$. Equate coefficients of x^4: $0 = A + B$, $B = -A = -1$.
Equate coefficients of x^3: $0 = C$. Equate coefficients of x^2: $0 = 2A + B + D$,
$D = -2A - B = -1$. Equate coefficients of x: $0 = C + E$, $E = -C = 0$. Thus

$$\dfrac{1}{x(x^2+1)^2} = \dfrac{1}{x} - \dfrac{1}{x^2+1} - \dfrac{x}{(x^2+1)^2}.$$ Hence,

$$\int \dfrac{dx}{x(x^2+1)^2} = \ln|x| - \tan^{-1}x - \dfrac{1}{2}\dfrac{1}{x^2+1} + C_1.$$

275. Let $u = 1 + e^x$, $du = e^x\,dx$. Then $\int \dfrac{dx}{1+e^x} = \int \dfrac{du}{u(u-1)}$. Let $\dfrac{1}{u(u-1)} = \dfrac{A}{u} + \dfrac{B}{u-1}$.

Then $1 = A(u-1) + Bu$. Let $u = 0$. Then $1 = -A$, $A = -1$. Let $u = 1$. Then $1 = B$. So

$\dfrac{1}{u(u-1)} = -\dfrac{1}{u} + \dfrac{1}{u-1}$, and $\int \dfrac{du}{u(u-1)} = -\ln|u| + \ln|u-1| + C = -\ln(1+e^x) + \ln e^x + C =$

$-\ln(1+e^x) + x + C.$

276. $\dfrac{x^2+3}{(x-1)^3(x+1)} = \dfrac{A}{x+1} + \dfrac{B}{x-1} + \dfrac{C}{(x-1)^2} + \dfrac{D}{(x-1)^3}$. Then $x^2 + 3 = A(x-1)^3 +$

$B(x+1)(x-1)^2 + C(x+1)(x-1) + D(x+1)$. Let $x = -1$. Then $4 = -8A$, $A = -\dfrac{1}{2}$.

Let $x = 1$. Then $4 = 2D$, $D = 2$. Equate coefficients of x^3: $0 = A + B$, $B = -A = \dfrac{1}{2}$.

Equate constant coefficients: $3 = -A + B - C + D$, $C = -A + B + D - 3 = 0$. Thus,

$\dfrac{x^2+3}{(x-1)^3(x+1)} = -\dfrac{1}{2}\dfrac{1}{x+1} + \dfrac{1}{2}\dfrac{1}{x-1} + \dfrac{2}{(x-1)^3}$, and $\int \dfrac{(x^2+3)\,dx}{(x-1)^3(x+1)} = -\dfrac{1}{2}\ln|x+1| +$

$\dfrac{1}{2}\ln|x-1| - \dfrac{1}{(x-1)^2} + C_1 = \dfrac{1}{2}\ln\left|\dfrac{x-1}{x+1}\right| - \dfrac{1}{(x-1)^2} + C_1.$

Chapter 31: Integrals for Surface Area, Work, Centroids

277. $S = 2\pi \displaystyle\int y\,ds = 2\pi \int_a^b y\sqrt{1+\left(\dfrac{dy}{dx}\right)^2}\,dx = 2\pi \int_{f(a)}^{f(b)} y\sqrt{1+\left(\dfrac{dx}{dy}\right)^2}\,dy.$

(For revolution about the y-axis, change the factor y to x in either integrand.)

278. Revolve the upper semicircle $y = \sqrt{r^2 - x^2}$ about the x-axis. Since $x^2 + y^2 = r^2$,
$2x + 2yy' = 0$, $y' = -x/y$, $(y')^2 = x^2/y^2$, $1 + (y')^2 = 1 + x^2/y^2 = (y^2 + x^2)/y^2 = r^2/y^2$. Hence, the
surface area $S = 2\pi \displaystyle\int_{-r}^r y \cdot \dfrac{r}{y}\,dx = 2\pi \int_{-r}^r r\,dx = 2\pi rx]_{-r}^r = 4\pi r^2.$

279. (A) $y' = 3x^2$, so $S = 2\pi \int_0^1 x^3 \sqrt{1+9x^4}\, dx = 2\pi \cdot \frac{1}{36}\left(\frac{2}{3}\right)(1+9x^4)^{3/2}\Big]_0^1$

$$= \frac{\pi}{27}[(10)^{3/2} - 1] = \frac{\pi}{27}(10\sqrt{10} - 1).$$

(B) Use $S = 2\pi \int_1^2 x\sqrt{1+(y')^2}\, dx.$ $y' = x^3 - \frac{1}{4x^3}, (y')^2 = x^6 - \frac{1}{2} + \frac{1}{16x^6}.$ Then

$1+(y')^2 = x^6 + \frac{1}{2} + \frac{1}{16x^6} = \left(x^3 + \frac{1}{4x^3}\right)^2.$ So $S = 2\pi \int_1^2 x\left(x^3 + \frac{1}{4x^3}\right) dx =$

$\pi \int_1^2 \left(x^4 + \frac{1}{4x^2}\right) dx = 2\pi \left(\frac{1}{5}x^5 - \frac{1}{4x}\right)\Big]_1^2 = 2\pi\left[\left(\frac{32}{5} - \frac{1}{8}\right) - \left(\frac{1}{5} - \frac{1}{4}\right)\right] = \frac{253\pi}{20}.$

280. As is shown in Figure A31.1, the cone is obtained by revolving about the x-axis the

region in the first quadrant under the line $y = \frac{r}{h}(h-x).$ $y' = -\frac{r}{h}, 1+(y')^2 = \frac{r^2+h^2}{h^2}.$

Hence, $S = 2\pi \int_0^h \frac{r}{h}(h-x)\cdot\frac{\sqrt{r^2+h^2}}{h}\, dx = \frac{2\pi r\sqrt{r^2+h^2}}{h^2}\left(hx - \frac{1}{2}x^2\right)\Big]_0^h = \frac{2\pi r\sqrt{r^2+h^2}}{h^2}$

$\left(h^2 - \frac{1}{2}h^2\right) = \pi r\sqrt{r^2+h^2}.$

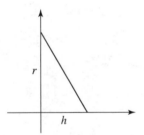

Figure A31.1

281. We use Hooke's law: The spring pulls back with a restoring force of $F = kx$ pounds, where the spring is stretched x inches beyond its natural length, and k is a constant. Then, $12 = \frac{1}{2}k, k = 24.$ $F = 24x$, and the work $W = \int_0^8 F\, dx = \int_0^8 24x\, dx = 12x^2\Big]_0^8 = 12(64) = 768$ in · pounds = 64 feet · pounds.

282. The area $A = \int_0^1 x^2 \, dx = \frac{1}{3} x^3 \Big]_0^1 = \frac{1}{3}$. The moment about the y-axis is

$M_y = \int_0^1 x \cdot x^2 \, dx = \frac{1}{4} x^4 \Big]_0^1 = \frac{1}{4}$. Hence, the x-coordinate of the centroid is $\bar{x} = M_y/A =$

$\frac{1}{4} \Big/ \frac{1}{3} = \frac{3}{4}$. The moment about the x-axis is $M_x = \int_0^1 y(1-\sqrt{y}) \, dy = \frac{1}{2} y^2 - \frac{2}{5} y^{5/2} \Big]_0^1 =$

$\frac{1}{2} - \frac{2}{5} = \frac{1}{10}$. Hence, the y-coordinate of the centroid is $\bar{y} = M_x/A = \left(\frac{1}{10}\right) \Big/ \left(\frac{1}{3}\right) = \frac{3}{10}$.

Thus, the centroid is $\left(\frac{3}{4}, \frac{3}{10}\right)$.

283. By symmetry, $\bar{x} = 0$. (In general, the centroid lies on any line of symmetry of the

region.) The area $A = \frac{\pi a^2}{2}$. The moment about the x-axis $M_x = 2 \int_0^a y \sqrt{a^2 - y^2} \, dy =$

$-\frac{2}{3} (a^2 - y^2)^{3/2} \Big]_0^a = \frac{2}{3} (a^2)^{3/2} = \frac{2}{3} a^3$. Thus, $\bar{y} = \left(\frac{2}{3} a^3\right) \Big/ (\pi a^2/2) = \frac{4a}{3\pi}$. Thus, the centroid

is $\left(0, \frac{4a}{3\pi}\right)$.

Chapter 32: Improper Integrals

284. This is equivalent to determining whether the improper integral $\int_1^\infty (1/x) \, dx$ is

convergent. $\int_1^\infty (1/x) \, dx = \lim_{v \to +\infty} \int_1^v (1/x) \, dx = \lim_{v \to +\infty} \ln v \Big]_1^v = \lim_{v \to +\infty} \ln v = +\infty$. Thus, the integral

diverges and the area is infinite.

285. (A) $\int_1^\infty \frac{1}{x^2} \, dx = \lim_{v \to +\infty} \int_1^v \frac{1}{x^2} \, dx = \lim_{v \to +\infty} -\frac{1}{x} \Big]_1^v = \lim_{v \to +\infty} \left(-\frac{1}{v} + 1\right) = 1$. Thus, the integral

converges.

(B) By Question 284, we know that the integral is divergent when $p = 1$.

$\int_1^\infty \frac{1}{x^p} \, dx = \lim_{v \to +\infty} \int_1^v \frac{1}{x^p} \, dx = \lim_{v \to +\infty} \left(-\frac{1}{p-1} \cdot \frac{1}{x^{p-1}}\right) \Big]_1^v = \lim_{v \to +\infty} \left[-\frac{1}{p-1} \left(\frac{1}{v^{p-1}} - 1\right)\right]$.

The last limit is $1/(p-1)$ if $p > 1$, and $+\infty$ if $p < 1$. Thus, the integral converges if and only if $p > 1$.

286. (A) First we evaluate $\int [(\ln x)/x^p]\, dx$ by integration by parts. Let $u = \ln x$, $dv = (1/x^p)\, dx$, $du = (1/x)\, dx$, $v = \dfrac{1}{1-p}\dfrac{1}{x^{p-1}}$. Thus, $\int \dfrac{\ln x}{x^p}\, dx = \dfrac{1}{1-p}\dfrac{\ln x}{x^{p-1}} - \int \dfrac{1}{1-p}\dfrac{1}{x^p}\, dx = \dfrac{1}{1-p}\dfrac{\ln x}{x^{p-1}} - \dfrac{1}{(1-p)^2}\dfrac{1}{x^{p-1}}$. Hence,

$$\int_1^\infty \frac{\ln x}{x^p}\, dx = \lim_{v \to +\infty} \int_1^v \frac{\ln x}{x^p}\, dx = \lim_{v \to +\infty} \left(\frac{1}{1-p}\frac{\ln x}{x^{p-1}} - \frac{1}{(1-p)^2}\frac{1}{x^{p-1}} \right)\Bigg]_1^v$$

$$= \lim_{v \to +\infty} \left[\frac{1}{1-p}\frac{\ln v}{v^{p-1}} - \frac{1}{(1-p)^2}\frac{1}{v^{p-1}} \right] - \left[-\frac{1}{(1-p)^2} \right] = \frac{1}{(1-p)^2}.$$

(In the last step, we used L'Hôpital's rule to evaluate $\displaystyle\lim_{v \to +\infty} \frac{\ln v}{v^{p-1}} = \lim_{v \to +\infty} \frac{1/v}{(p-1)v^{p-2}} = \lim_{v \to +\infty} \frac{1}{p-1} \times \frac{1}{v^{p-1}} = 0$.)

Thus, the integral converges for all $p > 1$.

(B) $\dfrac{\ln x}{x^p} \geq \dfrac{1}{x^p}$ for $x \geq e$. Hence, $\int_e^v \dfrac{\ln x}{x^p}\, dx \geq \int_e^v \dfrac{1}{x^p}\, dx \to +\infty$ by Question 285(B). Hence, $\int_1^\infty \dfrac{\ln x}{x^p}\, dx$ is divergent for $p \leq 1$.

287. By integration by parts, we find $\int xe^{-x}\, dx = -e^{-x}(x+1)$. Hence, $\int_a^\infty xe^{-x}\, dx = \lim_{v \to +\infty} (-e^{-x}(x+1))]_a^v = \lim_{v \to +\infty} [(-e^{-v}(v+1) + e^{-a}(a+1)] = e^{-a}(a+1)$. (In the last step, we used L'Hôpital's rule to evaluate $\lim_{v \to +\infty} (v+1)/e^v = \lim_{v \to +\infty} (1/e^v) = 0$.)

288. (A) By successive applications of L'Hôpital's rule, we see that $\lim_{x \to +\infty} (\ln x)^p/x = 0$. Hence, $(\ln x)^p/x < 1$ for sufficiently large x. Thus, for some x_0, if $x \geq x_0$, $(\ln x)^p < x$, $1/(\ln x)^p > 1/x$. So $\int_{x_0}^v \dfrac{dx}{(\ln x)^p} > \int_{x_0}^v \dfrac{dx}{x} \to +\infty$. Hence, the integral must be divergent for arbitrary $p \geq 1$.

(B) $\int_a^v g(x)\, dx = \int_a^{x_0} g(x)\, dx + \int_{x_0}^v g(x)\, dx \geq \int_a^{x_0} g(x)\, dx + \int_{x_0}^v f(x)\, dx \to +\infty$.

289. For $x \geq e$, $(\ln x)^p \leq \ln x$, and, therefore, $1/(\ln x)^p \geq 1/\ln x$. Now apply Questions 288(A) and (B).

290. $\int_0^v \dfrac{dx}{x^2 + a^2} = \dfrac{1}{\sqrt{a}} \tan^{-1} \dfrac{x}{a} \Big]_0^v = \dfrac{1}{\sqrt{a}} \tan^{-1} \dfrac{v}{a}$. But $\lim_{v \to +\infty} \tan^{-1} \dfrac{v}{a} = \dfrac{\pi}{2}$. Hence,

$$\int_0^\infty \frac{dx}{x^2 + a^2} = \frac{\pi}{2\sqrt{a}}.$$

291. $\int_0^\infty e^{-x}\,dx = \lim_{v\to+\infty}\int_0^v e^{-x}\,dx = \lim_{v\to+\infty}(-e^{-x})]_0^v = \lim_{v\to+\infty}(1-e^{-v}) = 1-0 = 1.$

292. (A) $\int_0^1 \frac{1}{x}\,dx = \lim_{u\to0^+}\int_u^1 \frac{1}{x}\,dx = \lim_{u\to0^+}(\ln 1 - \ln u) = +\infty.$ Thus, the integral diverges.

(B) $\int_0^1 \frac{1}{\sqrt{x}}\,dx = \lim_{u\to0^+}\int_u^1 \frac{1}{\sqrt{x}}\,dx = \lim_{u\to0^+}2\sqrt{x}\,]_u^1 = \lim_{u\to0^+}2(1-\sqrt{u}) = 2.$

(C) $\int_0^1 \frac{1}{x^2}\,dx = \lim_{u\to0^+}\int_u^1 \frac{1}{x^2}\,dx = \lim_{u\to0^+}\left(-\frac{1}{x}\right)\Big]_u^1 = \lim_{u\to0^+}\left(-1+\frac{1}{u}\right) = +\infty.$ Thus, the integral

diverges.

(D) $\int_0^1 \frac{1}{x^k}\,dx = \lim_{u\to0^+}\int_u^1 \frac{1}{x^k}\,dx = \lim_{u\to0^+}\frac{1}{-k+1}x^{-k+1}\Big]_u^1 = \lim_{u\to0^+}\frac{1}{1-k}\left(1-\frac{1}{u^{k-1}}\right).$ If $k > 1$,

this limit is $+\infty$, whereas, if $k < 1$, the limit is $1/(1-k)$.

293. There is a discontinuity at $x = 2$. So $\int_1^3 \frac{dx}{x-2} = \lim_{v\to2^-}\int_1^v \frac{dx}{x-2} + \lim_{w\to2^+}\int_w^3 \frac{dx}{x-2} =$

$\lim_{v\to2^-}\ln|x-2|]_1^v + \lim_{w\to2^+}\ln|x-2|]_w^3 \lim_{v\to2^-}\ln|v-2| + \lim_{w\to2^+}-\ln|w-2|.$ Neither limit exists.

Therefore, the integral diverges.

294. There is a discontinuity at $x = 0$. So $\int_{-1}^8 \frac{1}{x^{1/3}}\,dx = \int_{-1}^0 \frac{dx}{x^{1/3}} + \int_0^8 \frac{dx}{x^{1/3}}.$ For the

first integral, $\int_{-1}^0 \frac{dx}{x^{1/3}} = \lim_{u\to0^-}\frac{3}{2}x^{2/3}\Big]_{-1}^u = \lim_{u\to0^-}\frac{3}{2}(u^{2/3}-1) = -\frac{3}{2}.$ Also, $\int_0^8 \frac{dx}{x^{1/3}} = \lim_{v\to0^+}\frac{3}{2}x^{2/3}\Big]_v^8 =$

$\lim_{v\to0^+}\frac{3}{2}(4-v^{2/3}) = 6.$ Thus, the value is $-\frac{3}{2}+6 = \frac{9}{2}.$

295. By integration by parts, $\int \ln x\,dx = x(\ln x - 1).$ Thus, $\int_0^1 \ln x\,dx = \lim_{v\to0^+}x(\ln x - 1)]_v^1 =$

$\lim_{v\to0^+}[-1-v(\ln v - 1)] = -1-0 = -1.$ (The limit $\lim_{v\to0^+}v(\ln v - 1) = 0$ is obtained by

L'Hôpital's rule.)

Chapter 33: Planar Vectors

296. The vector $\overrightarrow{AB} = (3-1, 7-(-2)) = (2, 9).$ In general the vector $\overrightarrow{P_1P_2}$ from $P_1(x_1, y_1)$

to $P_2(x_2, y_2)$ is $(x_2 - x_1, y_2 - y_1).$

297. $\mathbf{A} + \mathbf{C} = 5\mathbf{i} + 3\mathbf{j}.$ Therefore, $|\mathbf{A} + \mathbf{C}| = \sqrt{(5)^2 + (3)^2} = \sqrt{34}.$ If θ is the angle made by

$\mathbf{A} + \mathbf{C}$ with the positive x-axis, $\tan\theta = \frac{3}{5}.$ From a table of tangents, $\theta \approx 30° 58'.$

298. $\mathbf{A} = \mathbf{A}_1 + \mathbf{A}_2$, $\mathbf{A}_1 = c\mathbf{B}$, $\mathbf{A}_2 \cdot \mathbf{B} = 0$. So $\mathbf{A}_2 = \mathbf{A} - \mathbf{A}_1 = \mathbf{A} - c\mathbf{B}$, $0 = \mathbf{A}_2 \cdot \mathbf{B} = (\mathbf{A} - c\mathbf{B}) \cdot \mathbf{B} = \mathbf{A} \cdot \mathbf{B} - c|\mathbf{B}|^2$. Hence, $c = (\mathbf{A} \cdot \mathbf{B})/|\mathbf{B}|^2$. Therefore, $\mathbf{A}_1 = \dfrac{\mathbf{A} \cdot \mathbf{B}}{|\mathbf{B}|^2}\mathbf{B}$, and $\mathbf{A}_2 = \mathbf{A} - c\mathbf{B} = \mathbf{A} - \dfrac{\mathbf{A} \cdot \mathbf{B}}{|\mathbf{B}|^2}\mathbf{B}$. Here, $(\mathbf{A} \cdot \mathbf{B})/|\mathbf{B}|$ is the *scalar projection* of $\mathbf{A}$ on $\mathbf{B}$, and $\left(\dfrac{\mathbf{A} \cdot \mathbf{B}}{|\mathbf{B}|}\right)\dfrac{\mathbf{B}}{|\mathbf{B}|} = \mathbf{A}_1$ is the *vector projection* of $\mathbf{A}$ on $\mathbf{B}$.

299. At any convenient point on the line, say $A(4, 0)$, construct the vector $\mathbf{B} = (3, 4)$, which is perpendicular to the line. The required distance d is the magnitude of the scalar projection of $\overrightarrow{AP}$ on $\mathbf{B}$:

$$\dfrac{|\overrightarrow{AP} \cdot \mathbf{B}|}{|\mathbf{B}|} = \dfrac{|(-2, 3) \cdot (3, 4)|}{\sqrt{3^2 + 4^2}} = \dfrac{6}{5} \text{ [by Question 298]}$$

300. Take the point $A(-c/a, 0)$ on the line. The vector $\mathbf{B} = (a, b)$ is perpendicular to the line. As in Question 299,

$$d = \dfrac{|\overrightarrow{AP} \cdot \mathbf{B}|}{|\mathbf{B}|} = \dfrac{|(x_1 + c/a, y_1 - 0) \cdot (a, b)|}{\sqrt{a^2 + b^2}} = \dfrac{|ax_1 + by_1 + c|}{\sqrt{a^2 + b^2}}$$

This derivation assumes $a \neq 0$. If $a = 0$, a similar derivation can be given, taking A to be $(0, -c/b)$.

301. In general, the vector of length r obtained by a counterclockwise rotation θ from the positive axis is given by $r(\cos\theta\,\mathbf{i} + \sin\theta\,\mathbf{j})$. In this case, we have $2\left(-\dfrac{\sqrt{3}}{2}\mathbf{i} + \dfrac{1}{2}\mathbf{j}\right) = -\sqrt{3}\mathbf{i} + \mathbf{j}$.

302. Let $\mathbf{A} = (3, 1)$ and $\mathbf{B} = (1, 5)$. Then, by the parallelogram law, $\overrightarrow{OP} = \mathbf{A} + \mathbf{B} = (3, 1) + (1, 5) = (4, 6)$. Hence, P has coordinates $(4, 6)$.

303. In general, given a vector (a, b), a perpendicular vector is $(b, -a)$, since $(a, b) \cdot (b, -a) = ab - ab = 0$. In this case, take $(5, -2)$.

Chapter 34: Parametric Equations, Vector Functions, Curvilinear Motion

304. Note that $x^2 + y^2 = a^2\cos^2\theta + a^2\sin^2\theta = a^2(\cos^2\theta + \sin^2\theta) = a^2$. Thus, we have a circle of radius a with center at the origin. As shown in Figure A34.1, the parameter θ can be thought of as the angle between the positive x-axis and the vector from the origin to the curve.

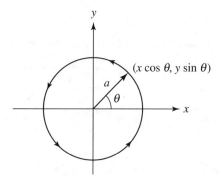

Figure A34.1

(B) $\dfrac{x^2}{4} + \dfrac{y^2}{9} = 1$. Hence, the curve is an ellipse with semimajor axis of length 3 along the y-axis and semiminor axis of length 2 along the x-axis (Figure A34.2)

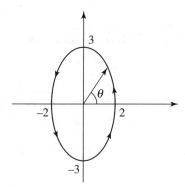

Figure A34.2

(C) $y = t^2 = x^2$. Hence, the curve is a parabola with vertex at the origin and the y-axis as its axis of symmetry (Figure A34.3).

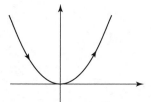

Figure A34.3

305. Recall that the arc length $s = \int_a^b \sqrt{(dx/du)^2 + (dy/du)^2}\, du$, where u is the parameter. $dx/dt = e^t(-\sin t) + e^t(\cos t) = e^t(\cos t - \sin t)$, $(dx/dt)^2 = e^t(\cos^2 t - 2\sin t \cos t + \sin^2 t) = e^{2t}(1 - 2\sin t \cos t)$. $dy/dt = e^t \cos t + e^t \sin t = e^t(\cos t + \sin t)$, $(dy/dt)^2 = e^{2t}(\cos^2 t + 2\sin t \cos t + \sin^2 t) = e^{2t}(1 + 2\sin t \cos t)$. So,

$$s = \int_0^\pi \sqrt{e^{2t}(1 - 2\sin t \cos t) + e^{2t}(1 + \sin t \cos t)}\, dt = \int_0^\pi \sqrt{2}\, e^t\, dt = \sqrt{2}\, e^t\big]_0^\pi = \sqrt{2}(e^\pi - 1).$$

306. $F'(u) = \lim\limits_{\Delta u \to 0} \dfrac{F(u + \Delta u) - F(u)}{\Delta u} = \lim\limits_{\Delta u \to 0} \dfrac{(f(u + \Delta u),\, g(u + \Delta u)) - (f(u),\, g(u))}{\Delta u}$

$= \lim\limits_{\Delta u \to 0} \dfrac{(f(u + \Delta u) - f(u),\, g(u + \Delta u) - g(u))}{\Delta u}$

$= \lim\limits_{\Delta u \to 0} \left(\dfrac{f(u + \Delta u) - f(u)}{\Delta u},\, \dfrac{g(u + \Delta u) - g(u)}{\Delta u} \right).$

This last limit is, by the definition, equal to

$$\left(\lim\limits_{\Delta u \to 0} \dfrac{f(u + \Delta u) - f(u)}{\Delta u},\, \lim\limits_{\Delta u \to 0} \dfrac{g(u + \Delta u) - g(u)}{\Delta u} \right) = (f'(u),\, g'(u)).$$

307. Refer to Figure A34.4. Let $\overrightarrow{OP} = R(u)$ and $\overrightarrow{OQ} = R(u + \Delta u)$. Then $\overrightarrow{PQ} = R(u + \Delta u) - R(u)$ and $\dfrac{1}{\Delta u}\overrightarrow{PQ} = \dfrac{R(u + \Delta u) - R(u)}{\Delta u}$. As $\Delta u \to 0$, Q approaches P, and the direction of $\overrightarrow{PQ}$ (which is the direction of $\overrightarrow{PQ}/\Delta u$) approaches the direction of $\boldsymbol{R}'(u)$, which is thus a tangent vector at P.

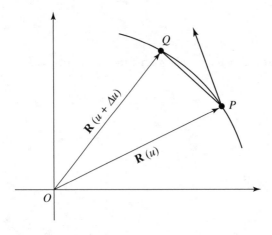

Figure A34.4

308. By Question 307, we already know that $R'(t)$ has the direction of the tangent vector along the curve. By Question 306, $\mathbf{R}'(t) = (dx/dt, dy/dt)$, since $\mathbf{R}(t) = (x(t), y(t))$. Hence, $|\mathbf{R}'(t)| = \sqrt{(dx/dt)^2 + (dy/dt)^2} = ds/dt$, where s is the arc length along the curve (measured from some fixed point on the curve). But ds/dt is the speed. (The "speed" is how fast the end of the position vector $\mathbf{R}(t)$ is moving, which is the rate of change of its position s along the curve.)

309.
$$\frac{h(u + \Delta u) - h(u)}{\Delta u} = \frac{\mathbf{F}(u + \Delta u) \cdot \mathbf{G}(u + \Delta u) - \mathbf{F}(u) \cdot \mathbf{G}(u)}{\Delta u}$$

$$= \frac{[\mathbf{F}(u + \Delta u) - \mathbf{F}(u)] \cdot \mathbf{G}(u + \Delta u) + \mathbf{F}(u) \cdot [\mathbf{G}(u + \Delta u) - \mathbf{G}(u)]}{\Delta u}$$

$$= \frac{\mathbf{F}(u + \Delta u) - \mathbf{F}(u)}{\Delta u} \cdot \mathbf{G}(u + \Delta u) + \mathbf{F}(u) \cdot \frac{\mathbf{G}(u + \Delta u) - \mathbf{G}(u)}{\Delta u}$$

$$\rightarrow \mathbf{F}'(u) \cdot \mathbf{G}(u) + \mathbf{F}(u) \cdot \mathbf{G}'(u) \text{ as } \Delta u \rightarrow 0.$$

310. $\mathbf{R}(t) \cdot \mathbf{R}(t) = |\mathbf{R}(t)|^2 = c^2$. So $\frac{d}{dt}[\mathbf{R}(t) \cdot \mathbf{R}(t)] = 0$. But, by Question 309 $\frac{d}{dt}[\mathbf{R}(t) \cdot \mathbf{R}(t)] = \mathbf{R}(t) \cdot \mathbf{R}'(t) + \mathbf{R}'(t) \cdot \mathbf{R}(t) = 2\mathbf{R}(t) \cdot \mathbf{R}'(t)$. Hence, $\mathbf{R}(t) \cdot \mathbf{R}'(t) = 0$.

311. Let $\mathbf{F}(u) = (f(u), g(u))$. Then $\mathbf{F}(h(u)) = (f(h(u)), g(h(u)))$. Hence, by Question 306 and the regular chain rule, $\frac{d}{du}[\mathbf{F}(h(u))] = \left(\frac{d}{du} f(h(u)), \frac{d}{du} g(h(u)) \right) = (f'(h(u))h'(u), g'(h(u))h'(u)) = h'(u)(f'(h(u)), g'(h(u))) = h'(u)\mathbf{F}'(h(u))$.

312. The position vector $\mathbf{R}(t)$ satisfies $|\mathbf{R}(t)| = r$ and $|\mathbf{R}'(t)| = v$. Let θ be the angle from the positive x-axis to $\mathbf{R}(t)$, and let s be the corresponding arc length on the circle. Then $s = r\theta$, and, since the object moves with constant speed v, $s = vt$. Hence, $\theta = vt/r$. We can write $\mathbf{R}(t) = r(\cos \theta, \sin \theta)$. By the chain rule, $\mathbf{R}'(t) = r(-\sin \theta, \cos \theta) \frac{d\theta}{dt} = r(-\sin\theta, \cos\theta)\frac{v}{r} = v(-\sin\theta, \cos\theta)$. Again by the chain rule, $\mathbf{R}''(t) = v(-\cos\theta - \sin\theta)\frac{d\theta}{dt} = -v(\cos\theta, \sin\theta)\frac{v}{r} = -\frac{v^2}{r^2}(r\cos\theta, r\sin\theta) = -\frac{v^2}{r^2}\mathbf{R}(t)$. Hence, the acceleration vector $\mathbf{R}''(t)$ points in the opposite direction to $\mathbf{R}(t)$,—that is, toward the center of the circle, and $|\mathbf{R}''(t)| = \frac{v^2}{r^2}|\mathbf{R}(t)| = \frac{v^2}{r^2} \cdot r = v^2/r$.

313. (A) Since $\mathbf{T}$ is a unit vector in the same direction as the velocity vector, $\mathbf{T} = (\cos \phi, \sin \phi)$. Hence, $d\mathbf{T}/d\phi = (-\sin \phi, \cos \phi)$ and $|d\mathbf{T}/d\phi| = 1$.

(B) As in Question 313(A), let ϕ denote the angle between the velocity vector $\mathbf{R}'(t)$ and the positive x-axis. The curvature κ is defined as $d\phi/ds$, where s is the arc length. The curvature measures how fast the tangent vector turns as a point moves along the curve. The radius of curvature is defined as $\rho = |1/\kappa|$.

(C) If (x_0, y_0) is the center of the circle, then $\mathbf{R}(t) = (x_0 + a\cos t, y_0 + a\sin t)$ traces out the circle, where t is the angle from the positive x-axis to $\mathbf{R}(t) - (x_0, y_0)$. Then $\mathbf{R}'(t) = a(-\sin t, \cos t)$, and $ds/dt = a$. The angle ϕ made by the positive x-axis with $\mathbf{R}'(t)$ is

$$\tan^{-1}\left(\frac{a\cos t}{-a\sin t}\right) = \tan^{-1}(-\cot t), \text{ or that angle} + \pi. \text{ Hence,}$$

$$\frac{d\phi}{ds} - \frac{1}{1+\cot^2 t}(\csc^2 t) \cdot \frac{dt}{ds} = \frac{dt}{ds} = \frac{1}{a}.$$

So $\kappa = 1/a$, and by definition, the radius of curvature is a.

(D) $\mathbf{R}'(t) = \mathbf{B}$. Since $\mathbf{R}'(t)$ is constant, ϕ is constant, and, therefore, $\kappa = d\phi/ds = 0$.

(E) Since y' is the slope of the tangent line, $\tan\phi = y'$. Hence, differentiating with respect to s, $\sec^2\phi\,(d\phi/ds) = y''/(ds/dx)$. But $\sec^2\phi = 1 + \tan^2\phi = 1 + (y')^2$, and $ds/dx = [1 + (y')^2]^{1/2}$. Thus,

$$\kappa = \frac{d\phi}{ds} = \frac{y''/[1+(y')^2]}{[1+(y')^2]^{1/2}} = \frac{y''}{[1+(y')^2]^{3/2}}.$$

Chapter 35: Polar Coordinates

314. **(A)** $x = r\cos\theta$, $y = r\sin\theta$; or, inversely, $r^2 = x^2 + y^2$, $\tan\theta = y/x$. See Figure A35.1. Note that, because $\cos(\theta + \pi) = -\cos\theta$ and $\sin(\theta + \pi) = -\sin\theta$, (r, θ) and $(-r, \theta + \pi)$ represent the same point (x, y).

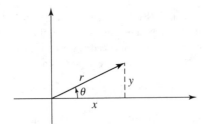

Figure A35.1

(B) $(1, 2\pi n)$ for all integers n, and $(-1, (2n + 1)\pi)$ for all integers n.

315. **(A)** $x^2 + y^2 = r^2 = 4$. Thus, the graph is the circle of radius 2 with center at the pole.

(B) The graph is the line through the pole making an angle of $\pi/4$ radians with the polar axis (Figure A35.2). Note that we obtain the points on that line below the x-axis because r can assume negative values.

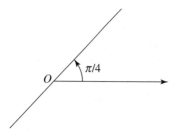

Figure A35.2

(C) This is simply the line through the polar axis, or the *x*-axis in rectangular coordinates.

316. $\theta = \pi/2$ yields the line perpendicular to the polar axis and going through the pole, which is the *y*-axis.

317. Multiplying both sides by *r*, we obtain $r^2 = 2r \sin\theta$, $x^2 + y^2 = 2y$, $x^2 + y^2 - 2y = 0$, $x^2 + (y - 1)^2 = 1$.

Thus, the graph is the circle with center at (0, 1) and radius 1.

318. $r\cos\theta = 3$, $r = 3\sec\theta$.

319. (A) See Figure A35.3. At $\theta = 0$, $r = 2$. As θ increases to $\pi/2$, *r* decreases to 1. As θ increases to π, *r* decreases to 0. Then, as θ increases to $3\pi/2$, *r* increases to 1, and finally, as θ increases to 2π, *r* increases to 2. After $\theta = 2\pi$, the curve repeats itself. The graph is called a cardioid.

θ	0	$\pi/2$	π	$3\pi/2$	2π
r	2	1	0	1	2

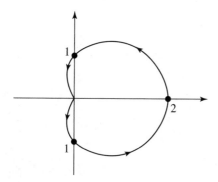

Figure A35.3

(B) See Figure A35.4. As θ goes from 0 to $\pi/2$, r decreases from 3 to 1. As θ increases further to $2\pi/3$, r decreases to 0. As θ goes on to π, r decreases to −1, and then, as θ moves up to $4\pi/3$, r goes back up to 0. As θ moves on to $3\pi/2$, r goes up to 1, and, finally, as θ increases to 2π, r grows to 3. This kind of graph is called a limaçon.

θ	0	$\pi/2$	$2\pi/3$	π	$4\pi/3$	$3\pi/2$	2π
r	3	1	0	1	0	1	3

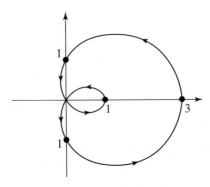

Figure A35.4

(C) The construction of the graph, Figure A35.5, is indicated in the table of values. Note that some values of θ yield two values of r, and some yield none at all (when $\cos 2\theta$ is negative). The graph repeats from $\theta = \pi$ to $\theta = 2\pi$. The graph is called a lemniscate.

θ	0	$\pi/4$	$\cdots$	$3\pi/4$	π
r	±1	0	$\cdots$	0	±1

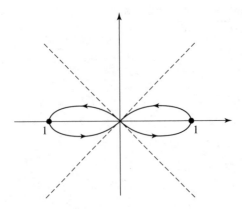

Figure A35.5

(D) The accompanying table of values yields Figure A35.6. The graph is called a four-leaved rose.

θ	0	$\pi/4$	$\pi/2$	$3\pi/4$	π	$5\pi/4$	$3\pi/2$	$7\pi/4$	2π
r	0	1	0	−1	0	1	0	−1	0

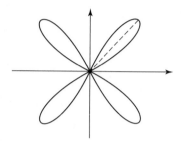

Figure A35.6

320. (A) It is convenient to use increments in θ of $\pi/6$ to construct Figure A35.7. Note that the graph repeats itself after $\theta = \pi$. The result is a three-leaved rose.

θ	0	$\pi/6$	$\pi/3$	$\pi/2$	$2\pi/3$	$5\pi/6$	π
r	0	1	0	−1	0	1	0

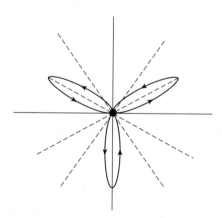

Figure A35.7

(B) Figure A35.8 shows an eight-leaved rose. Use increments of $\pi/8$ in θ.

θ	0	$\pi/8$	$\pi/4$	$3\pi/8$	$\pi/2$	$5\pi/8$	$3\pi/4$	$7\pi/8$	π	$9\pi/8$	$5\pi/4$	$11\pi/8$
r	0	1	0	−1	0	1	0	−1	0	1	0	−1

θ	$3\pi/2$	$13\pi/8$	$7\pi/4$	$15\pi/8$	2π
r	0	1	0	−1	0

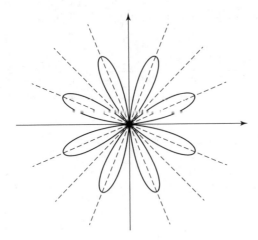

Figure A35.8

321. If we try to solve the equations simultaneously, we obtain $2 \sin^2 \theta = -2$, $\sin^2 \theta = -1$, which is never satisfied. However, there are, in fact, infinitely many points of intersection because the curves are identical. Assume (r, θ) satisfies $r = 1 + \sin^2 \theta$. The point (r, θ) is identical with the point $(-1 - \sin^2 \theta, \theta + \pi)$, which satisfies the equation $r = -1 - \sin^2 \theta$ (because $\sin^2(\theta + \pi) = \sin^2 \theta$).

322. As was shown in Question 319(A), the curve is traced out for $\theta = 0$ to $\theta = 2\pi$. The general formula for the area is $\frac{1}{2} \int_{\theta_1}^{\theta_2} r^2 \, d\theta$. In this case, we have

$$A = \frac{1}{2} \int_0^{2\pi} (1 + \cos\theta)^2 \, d\theta = \frac{1}{2} \int_0^{2\pi} (1 + 2\cos\theta + \cos^2\theta) \, d\theta$$

$$= \frac{1}{2} \int_0^{2\pi} \left[1 + 2\cos\theta + \frac{1}{2}(1 + \cos 2\theta) \right] d\theta$$

$$= \frac{1}{2} \left(\theta + 2\sin\theta + \frac{1}{2}\left(\theta + \frac{1}{2}\sin 2\theta \right) \right) \Bigg]_0^{2\pi} = \frac{1}{2}(3\pi) = \frac{3\pi}{2}.$$

323. **(A)** The general arc length formula is $\int_{\theta_1}^{\theta_2} \sqrt{r^2 + (dr/d\theta)^2} \, d\theta$. In this case, $dr/d\theta = 1$, and we have $L = \int_0^1 \sqrt{\theta^2 + 1} \, d\theta$. Letting $\theta = \tan u$, $d\theta = \sec^2 u \, du$, we obtain $\int_0^{\pi/4} \sec^3 u \, du = \frac{1}{2} \left[(\sec u \tan u + \ln|\sec u + \tan u|) \right]_0^{\pi/4} = \frac{1}{2}[\sqrt{2} + \ln(\sqrt{2}+1)]$.

(B) $dr/d\theta = e^\theta$. Hence, $L = \int_0^{\ln 2} \sqrt{e^{2\theta} + e^{2\theta}} \, d\theta = \int_0^{\ln 2} \sqrt{2} e^\theta \, d\theta = \sqrt{2} \, e^\theta]_0^{\ln 2} = \sqrt{2}(2-1) = \sqrt{2}$.

Chapter 36: Infinite Sequences

324. $a_n = \dfrac{n}{n+1}$. $\displaystyle\lim_{n \to +\infty} \dfrac{n}{n+1} = \lim_{n \to +\infty} \left(1 - \dfrac{1}{n+1} \right) = 1$.

325. $a_n = \left(\dfrac{n+1}{n}\right)^n$. $\lim\limits_{n\to+\infty} a_n = \lim\limits_{n\to+\infty}\left(1+\dfrac{1}{n}\right)^n = e$, since $\lim\limits_{x\to+\infty}\left(1+\dfrac{1}{x}\right)^x = e$.

326. $a_n = \ln\dfrac{n+1}{n}$. $\lim\limits_{n\to+\infty} \ln\left(1+\dfrac{1}{n}\right) = \ln 1 = 0$. Note that this depends on the continuity of $\ln x$ at $x=1$.

327. $a_n = \dfrac{2^n}{n!}$. For $n>4$, $\dfrac{2}{1}\cdot\dfrac{2}{2}\cdot\dfrac{2}{3}\cdot\dfrac{2}{4}\cdot\dfrac{2}{5}\cdots < \dfrac{2}{n}\cdot\dfrac{2}{1}\cdot\dfrac{2}{2}\cdot\dfrac{2}{3}\cdot\dfrac{2}{4}\cdot\dfrac{1}{2}\cdot\dfrac{1}{2}\cdots = \dfrac{1}{2}\cdot\dfrac{2}{3}\cdot\dfrac{1}{2^{n-4}}$.

Since $\lim\limits_{n\to+\infty}\dfrac{2}{3}\cdot\dfrac{1}{2^{n-4}} = 0$, $\lim\limits_{n\to+\infty} a_n = 0$.

328. $a_n = \sqrt[n]{n} = n^{1/n} = e^{(\ln n)/n} \to e^0 = 1$. Here we have used the fact that $\lim\limits_{n\to+\infty}(\ln n)/n = 0$, which follows by L'Hôpital's rule.

329. In general, the same method that was used for rational functions $\left(\text{like } \dfrac{4x+5}{x^3-2x+5}\right)$ can be used here. Divide by the highest power in the denominator. $\lim\limits_{n\to+\infty}\dfrac{4n+5}{n^3-2n+3} = \lim\limits_{n\to+\infty}\dfrac{4/n^2+5/n^3}{1-2/n^2+3/n^3} = \dfrac{0}{1} = 0$.

330. $\lim\limits_{n\to+\infty}\dfrac{2n^5-3n+20}{5n^4+2} = \lim\limits_{n\to+\infty}\dfrac{2n-3/n^3+20/n^4}{5+2/n^4} = +\infty$.

331. $\sqrt{n+1}-\sqrt{n} = (\sqrt{n+1}-\sqrt{n})\dfrac{\sqrt{n+1}+\sqrt{n}}{\sqrt{n+1}+\sqrt{n}} = \dfrac{1}{\sqrt{n+1}+\sqrt{n}} \to 0$.

332. $\lim\limits_{n\to+\infty} 2n\sin\dfrac{\pi}{n} = 2\pi\lim\limits_{n\to+\infty}\dfrac{\sin(\pi/n)}{\pi/n} = 2\pi\lim\limits_{\theta\to 0^+}\dfrac{\sin\theta}{\theta} = 2\pi\cdot 1 = 2\pi$.

333. $a_{n+1} = \dfrac{2(n+1)}{3(n+1)+1} = \dfrac{2n+2}{3n+4}$. Then $a_n < a_{n+1} \Leftrightarrow \dfrac{2n}{3n+1} < \dfrac{2n+2}{3n+4} \Leftrightarrow 6n^2+8n < 6n^2+8n+2$. The last inequality is obvious.

334. (A) $a_{n+1} = \dfrac{1\cdot 3\cdot 5\cdots(2n+1)}{2\cdot 4\cdot 6\cdots(2n+2)}$. Then, $\dfrac{a_{n+1}}{a_n} = \dfrac{2n+1}{2n+2} < 1$. So $a_{n+1} < a_n$ and the sequence is decreasing.

(B) Since the sequence is decreasing and bounded below by 0, it must converge. (In general, any bounded monotonic sequence converges.)

Chapter 37: Infinite Series

335. Let $S = \sum\limits_{n=0}^{\infty} a_n$. Then $a_n = \sum\limits_{k=1}^{n} a_k - \sum\limits_{k=1}^{n-1} a_k \to S - S = 0$.

336. (A) $1 > \dfrac{1}{2}, \dfrac{1}{2} \ge \dfrac{1}{2}, \dfrac{1}{3} + \dfrac{1}{4} > \dfrac{2}{4} = \dfrac{1}{2}, \dfrac{1}{5} + \dfrac{1}{6} + \dfrac{1}{7} + \dfrac{1}{8} > \dfrac{4}{8} = \dfrac{1}{2}, \dfrac{1}{9} + \dfrac{1}{10} + \cdots + \dfrac{1}{16} >$

$\dfrac{8}{16} = \dfrac{1}{2}$, etc. Therefore, $1 + \dfrac{1}{2} + \dfrac{1}{3} + \dfrac{1}{4} + \cdots > \dfrac{1}{2} + \dfrac{1}{2} + \dfrac{1}{2} + \dfrac{1}{2} + \cdots \to +\infty$. (Alternatively, by

the integral test, $\displaystyle\int_1^\infty \dfrac{1}{x}\, dx = \lim_{u \to +\infty} \int_1^u \dfrac{1}{x}\, dx = \lim_{u \to +\infty} (\ln x]_1^u) = \lim_{u \to +\infty} \ln u = +\infty$.)

(B) No. The harmonic series $\sum 1/n$ (Question 336(A)) is a counterexample.

337. (A) $rS_n = ar + ar^2 + \cdots + ar^{n-1} + ar^n$. $S_n = a + ar + ar^2 + \cdots + ar^{n-1}$. Hence, $(r-1)$

$S_n = ar^n - a = a(r^n - 1)$. Thus, $S_n = \dfrac{a(r^n - 1)}{r - 1}$.

(B) By Question 337(A), $S_n = \dfrac{a(r^n - 1)}{r - 1}$. If $|r| < 1$, $s_n \to \dfrac{a(-1)}{r - 1} = \dfrac{a}{1 - r}$, since $r^n \to 0$;

if $|r| \ge 1$, $|S_n| \to +\infty$, since $|r|^n \to +\infty$. If $r = 1$, the series is $a + a + a + \cdots$, which diverges

since $a \ne 0$. If $r = -1$, the series is $a - a + a - a + \cdots$, which oscillates between a and 0.

(C) By Question 337(B) with $r = \dfrac{1}{2}$, $\displaystyle\sum_{n=0}^\infty \dfrac{1}{2^n} = \dfrac{1}{1 - \frac{1}{2}} = 2$.

(D) $d = 0.215 + \dfrac{62}{10^5} + \dfrac{62}{10^7} + \dfrac{62}{10^9} + \cdots$. By Question 337(B), with $r = \dfrac{1}{10^2}$, $\dfrac{62}{10^5} + \dfrac{62}{10^7} +$

$\dfrac{62}{10^9} + \cdots = \dfrac{62/10^5}{1 - 1/10^5} = \dfrac{62}{99,000}$. Hence, $d = \dfrac{215}{1000} + \dfrac{62}{99,000} = \dfrac{21,347}{99,000}$.

338. $\dfrac{1}{n(n+1)} = \dfrac{1}{n} - \dfrac{1}{n+1}$. Hence, the partial sum

$$S_n = \left(1 - \dfrac{1}{2}\right) + \left(\dfrac{1}{2} - \dfrac{1}{3}\right) + \left(\dfrac{1}{3} - \dfrac{1}{4}\right) + \cdots + \left(\dfrac{1}{n} - \dfrac{1}{n+1}\right) = 1 - \dfrac{1}{n+1} \to 1.$$

The series converges to 1. (The method used here is called "telescoping.")

339. This is a geometric series with ratio $r = -\dfrac{1}{4}$ and first term $a = 4$. Hence, it converges

to $\dfrac{4}{1 - (-\frac{1}{4})} = \dfrac{16}{5}$.

340. The series has the general term $a_n = \dfrac{2n + 3}{n + 1}$ (starting with $n = 0$), but

$\lim a_n = \lim \dfrac{2 + 3/n}{1 + 1/n} = 2 \ne 0$.

Hence, by Question 335, the series diverges.

341. $\displaystyle\sum_{n=0}^{\infty} \frac{1}{n+100}$ is the harmonic series minus the first 99 terms. However, convergence or divergence is not affected by deletion or addition of any finite number of terms. Since the harmonic series is divergent (by Question 336(A)), so is the given series.

342. When A reaches T's starting point, 100 seconds have passed and T has moved $0.01 \times 100 = 1$ feet. A covers that additional 1 feet in 0.1 second, but T has moved $0.01 \times 0.1 = 0.001$ feet farther. A needs 0.0001 second to cover that distance, but T meanwhile has moved $0.01 \times 0.0001 = 0.000001$ feet; and so on. The limit of the distance between A and T approaches 0. The time involved is $100 + 0.1 + 0.0001 + 0.0000001 + \cdots$, which is a geometric series with first term $a = 100$ and ratio $r = \dfrac{1}{1000}$. Its sum is $100 / \left(1 - \dfrac{1}{1000}\right)$. Thus, Achilles catches up with (and then passes) the tortoise in a little over 100 seconds, just as we knew he would. The seeming paradox arises from the artificial division of the event into infinitely many shorter and shorter steps.

343. $3/(5^n + 2) < 5/5^n = 1/5^{n-1}$. So this series of positive terms is term term less than the convergent geometric series $\displaystyle\sum_{n=1}^{\infty} \frac{1}{5^{n-1}}$. Hence, by the comparison test, the given series is convergent. However, we cannot directly compute the sum of the series. We can only say that the sum is less than $\displaystyle\sum_{n=1}^{\infty} \frac{1}{5^{n-1}} = \frac{1}{1-\frac{1}{5}} = \frac{5}{4}$.

344. $1/n^p \geq 1/n$ since $n^p \leq n$. Therefore, by the comparison test and the fact that $\displaystyle\sum_{n=1}^{\infty} \frac{1}{n}$ is divergent, $\displaystyle\sum_{n=1}^{\infty} \frac{1}{n^p}$ is divergent.

345. For $n \geq 1$, $1/n! = 1/(1 \cdot 2 \cdot \cdots \cdot n) \leq 1/(1 \cdot 2 \cdot 2 \cdot \cdots \cdot 2) = 1/2^{n-1}$. Hence, $\displaystyle\sum_{n=0}^{\infty} \frac{1}{n!}$ is convergent, by comparison with the convergent series $\displaystyle\sum_{n=0}^{\infty} \frac{1}{2^{n-1}}$. The sum $(= e)$ of the given series is $< 1 + \displaystyle\sum_{n=1}^{\infty} \frac{1}{2^{n-1}} = 1 + 2 = 3$.

346. **(A)** Let $\Sigma\, a_n$ be a series of positive terms such that there is a continuous, decreasing function $f(x)$ for which $f(n) = a_n$ for all positive integers $n \geq n_0$. Then $\Sigma\, a_n$ converges if and only if the improper integral $\displaystyle\int_{n_0}^{\infty} f(x)\,dx$ converges.

(B) Use the integral test (Question 346(A)), with $f(x) = 1/x^p$. $\displaystyle\int_1^{\infty} \frac{dx}{x^p} = \lim_{u \to +\infty}$

$\displaystyle\int_1^{u} \frac{dx}{x^p} = \lim_{u \to +\infty} \frac{1}{1-p}\, x^{p-1} \Big]_1^{u} = \lim_{u \to +\infty} \frac{1}{1-p}\left(\frac{1}{u^{p-1}} - 1\right) = \frac{1}{p-1}$. Hence, $\displaystyle\sum_{n=1}^{\infty} \frac{1}{n^p}$ converges.

(C) Use the integral test with $f(x) = \dfrac{1}{x \ln x}$.

$$\int_2^\infty \frac{1}{x \ln x}\, dx = \lim_{u \to +\infty} \int_2^u \frac{1}{x \ln x}\, dx = \lim_{u \to \infty} \ln\, (\ln x)\Big]_2^u = \lim_{u \to +\infty} [\ln\, (\ln u) - \ln\, (\ln 2)] = +\infty.$$

Hence, $\displaystyle\sum_{n=2}^\infty \frac{1}{n \ln n}$ diverges.

347. (A) Let $\Sigma\, a_n$ and $\Sigma\, b_n$ be series of positive terms.

Case I. If $\lim\limits_{n \to +\infty} a_n/b_n = L > 0$, then $\Sigma\, a_n$ converges if and only if $\Sigma\, b_n$ converges.

Case II. If $\lim\limits_{n \to +\infty} a_n/b_n = 0$ and $\Sigma\, b_n$ converges, then $\Sigma\, a_n$ converges.

Case III. If $\lim\limits_{n \to +\infty} a_n/b_n = +\infty$ and $\Sigma\, b_n$ diverges, then $\Sigma\, a_n$ diverges.

(B) Use the limit comparison test with the convergent p-series $\displaystyle\sum \frac{1}{n^{3/2}}$. Then

$$\lim_{n \to +\infty} \frac{1/\sqrt{n^3 + 3}}{1/n^{3/2}} = \lim_{n \to +\infty} \sqrt{\frac{n^3}{n^3 + 3}} = \lim_{n \to +\infty} \sqrt{\frac{1}{1 + 3/n^3}} = 1. \text{ Therefore, the given series is}$$

convergent.

(C) Intuitively, we ignore the 1 in the denominator, so we use the limit comparison test with the divergent series $\displaystyle\sum 1/n$. $\lim\limits_{n \to +\infty} \dfrac{n^3/(2n^4 + 1)}{1/n} = \lim\limits_{n \to +\infty} \dfrac{n^4}{2n^4 + 1} = \lim\limits_{n \to +\infty} \dfrac{1}{2 + 1/n^4} = \dfrac{1}{2}$.
Hence, the given series is divergent.

348. $\dfrac{1}{n^n} = \dfrac{1}{e^{n \ln n}} < \dfrac{1}{e^n}$, for $n \ge 3$. Hence, the series converges, by comparison with the convergent geometric series $\displaystyle\sum_{n=1}^\infty \dfrac{1}{e^n}$.

349. Use the integral test with $f(x) = \dfrac{\ln x}{x}$. (Note that $f(x)$ is decreasing, since $f'(x) = \dfrac{1 - \ln x}{x^2} < 0$ for $x > e$.) $\displaystyle\int_1^\infty \frac{\ln x}{x}\, dx = \lim_{u \to +\infty} \int_1^u \frac{\ln x}{x}\, dx = \lim_{u \to +\infty} \left\{ \frac{1}{2}(\ln x)^2 \Big]_1^u \right\} = \lim_{u \to +\infty} \frac{1}{2}(\ln u)^2 = +\infty.$ Therefore, the given series diverges.

350. $\displaystyle\sum_{n=1}^\infty \frac{(-1)^{n+1}}{n} = 1 - \frac{1}{2} + \frac{1}{3} - \frac{1}{4} + \cdots$ is convergent by the alternating series test (the terms are alternately positive and negative, and their magnitudes decrease to zero). But $\displaystyle\sum_{n=1}^\infty \left| \frac{(-1)^{n+1}}{n} \right| = \sum_{n=1}^\infty \frac{1}{n}$ diverges.

351. (A) Assume $a_n \neq 0$ for $n \geq n_0$.

Case I. If $\lim\limits_{n \to +\infty} |a_{n+1}/a_n| < 1$, the series is absolutely convergent.

Case II. If $\lim\limits_{n \to +\infty} |a_{n+1}/a_n| > 1$, the series is divergent.

Case III. If $\lim\limits_{n \to +\infty} |a_{n+1}/a_n| = 1$, nothing can be said about convergence or divergence.

(B) Apply the ratio test. $\lim\limits_{n \to +\infty} |a_{n+1}/a_n| = \lim\limits_{n \to +\infty} \dfrac{(n+1)^2/e^{n+1}}{n^2/e^n} = \lim\limits_{n \to +\infty} \dfrac{(n+1)^2}{n^2} \dfrac{1}{e} = \lim\limits_{n \to +\infty} \left(1 + \dfrac{1}{n}\right)^2 \cdot$
$\dfrac{1}{e} = \dfrac{1}{e} < 1.$

Hence, the series converges. (The integral test is also applicable.)

352. The error is less than the magnitude of the first term omitted. Thus, the approximation is $1 - \dfrac{1}{2} + \dfrac{1}{3} = \dfrac{5}{6}$, and the error is less than $\dfrac{1}{4}$. Hence, the actual value V satisfies $\dfrac{7}{12} < V < \dfrac{13}{12}$. (N.B. It can be shown that $V = \ln 2 \approx 0.693$.)

353. Use the ratio test. $\lim\limits_{n \to +\infty} |a_{n+1}/a_n| = \lim\limits_{n \to +\infty} \dfrac{2^{n+1}/(n+1)!}{2^n/n!} = \lim\limits_{n \to +\infty} \dfrac{2}{n+1} = 0$. Therefore, the series is absolutely convergent.

354. $\left| \dfrac{\sin(\pi/n)}{n^2} \right| \leq \dfrac{1}{n^2}$. Hence, the series is absolutely convergent by comparison with the convergent p-series $\sum\limits_{n=1}^{\infty} \dfrac{1}{n^2}$.

355. (A) Assume $\lim\limits_{n \to +\infty} \sqrt[n]{a_n} = L < 1$. Choose r so that $L < r < 1$. Then there exists an integer k such that, if $n \geq k$, $\sqrt[n]{a_n} < r$, and, therefore, $a_n < r^n$. Hence, the series $a_k + a_{k+1} + \cdots$ is convergent by comparison with the convergent geometric series $\sum\limits^{\infty} r^n$. So the given series is convergent. Assume now that $\lim\limits_{n \to +\infty} \sqrt[n]{a_n} = L > 1$. Choose r so that $L > r > 1$. Then there exists an integer k such that, if $n \geq k$, $\sqrt[n]{a_n} > r$, and, therefore, $a_n > r^n$. Thus, by comparison with the divergent geometric series $\sum\limits_{n=k}^{\infty} r^n$, the series $a_k + a_{k+1} + \cdots$ is divergent, and, therefore, the given series is divergent.

(B) Use the root test (Question 355(A)). $\lim\limits_{n \to +\infty} \sqrt[n]{a_n} = \lim\limits_{n \to +\infty} \dfrac{1}{\ln n} = 0$. Therefore, the series converges.

356. $a_n = 2^{2n-1}/(2n-1)!$. Use the ratio test. $\lim\limits_{n\to+\infty} \dfrac{a_{n+1}}{a_n} = \lim\limits_{n\to+\infty} \dfrac{2^{2n+1}/(2n+1)!}{2^{2n-1}/(2n-1)!} = \lim\limits_{n\to+\infty} \dfrac{4}{2n(2n+1)} =$ 0. Therefore, the series is absolutely convergent.

357. Use the first n_1 positive terms until the sum is > 1. Then use the first n_2 negative terms until the sum becomes < 1. Then repeat with more positive terms until the sum becomes > 1, then more negative terms until the sum becomes < 1, etc. Since the difference between the partial sums and 1 is less than the last term used, the new series $1 + \dfrac{1}{3} - \dfrac{1}{2} + \dfrac{1}{5} - \dfrac{1}{4} + \dfrac{1}{7} - \dfrac{1}{9} - \cdots$ converges to 1. (Note that the series of positive terms $1 + \dfrac{1}{3} + \dfrac{1}{5} + \cdots$ and the series of negative terms $\dfrac{1}{2} + \dfrac{1}{4} + \dfrac{1}{6} + \cdots$ are both divergent, so the described procedure always can be carried out.)

358. Let $a_n = 1/n$. Then $\Sigma\, 1/n$ is divergent, but $\lim\limits_{n\to+\infty} \left| \dfrac{a_{n+1}}{a_n} \right| = \lim\limits_{n\to+\infty} \dfrac{1/(n+1)}{1/n} = \lim\limits_{n\to+\infty} \dfrac{n}{n+1} =$ $\lim\limits_{n\to+\infty} \dfrac{1}{1 + 1/n} = 1$. On the other hand, let $a_n = 1/n^2$. Then $\Sigma\, 1/n^2$ converges, but

$$\lim_{n\to+\infty} \left| \frac{a_{n+1}}{a_n} \right| = \lim \frac{1/(n+1)^2}{1/n^2} = \lim_{n\to+\infty} \left(\frac{n}{n+1} \right)^2 = \lim_{n\to+\infty} \left(\frac{1}{1+1/n} \right)^2 = 1.$$

359. The area in question is less than the sum S of the indicated rectangles. $S = \dfrac{1}{2} +$ $\left(\dfrac{1}{2} - \dfrac{1}{3} \right) + \left(\dfrac{1}{3} - \dfrac{1}{4} \right) + \cdots = 1$. So the area is finite and < 1. On the other hand, the area is greater than the sum of the triangles (half the rectangles), which is $\dfrac{1}{2}$. Note that $\gamma = \lim\limits_{n\to+\infty} \left(\sum\limits_{k-1}^{n} \dfrac{1}{k} - \ln n \right)$. It is an unsolved problem as to whether γ is rational.

360. (A) This is a geometric series with ratio x. Therefore, it converges for $|x| < 1$. The sum is $1/(1-x)$. Thus, for $|x| < 1$, $\quad 1/(1-x) = 1 + x + x^2 + \cdots = \sum\limits_{n=0}^{\infty} x^n$.

   (B) This is a geometric series with ratio $\ln x$. It converges for $|\ln x| < 1$, $-1 < \ln x < 1$, $1/e < x < e$. The sum is $(\ln x)/(1 - \ln x)$.

Chapter 38: Power Series

361. (A) $\lim\limits_{n\to+\infty} \dfrac{|x|^{n+1}/(n+1)}{|x|^n/n} = \lim\limits_{n\to+\infty} |x| \dfrac{n}{n+1} = \lim\limits_{n\to+\infty} |x| \dfrac{1}{1+1/n} = |x|$. Therefore, the series converges absolutely for $|x| < 1$ and diverges for $|x| > 1$. When $x = 1$, we have the divergent harmonic series $\Sigma\, 1/n$. When $x = -1$, the series is $\Sigma\, (-1)^n/n$, which converges by the alternating series test. Hence, the series converges for $-1 \le x < 1$.

(B) $\lim\limits_{n \to +\infty} \dfrac{|x|^{n+1}/(n+1)^2}{|x|^n/n^2} = \lim\limits_{n \to +\infty} |x|\left(\dfrac{n}{n+1}\right)^2 = \lim\limits_{n \to +\infty} |x|\left(\dfrac{1}{1+1/n}\right)^2 = |x|.$ Thus, the

series converges absolutely for $|x| < 1$ and diverges for $|x| > 1$. When $x = 1$, we have the convergent p-series $\sum 1/n^2$. When $x = -1$, the series converges by the alternating series test. Hence, the power series converges for $-1 \le x \le 1$.

(C) $\lim\limits_{n \to +\infty} \dfrac{|x|^{n+1}/(n+1)!}{|x|^n/n!} = \lim\limits_{n \to +\infty} \dfrac{|x|}{n+1} = 0.$ Therefore, the series converges for all x.

(D) $\lim\limits_{n \to +\infty} \dfrac{(n+1)!\,|x|^{n+1}}{n!\,|x|^n} = \lim\limits_{n \to +\infty} |x|(n+1) = +\infty$ (except when $x = 0$). Thus, the series

converges only for $x = 0$.

(E) This is a geometric series with ratio $x/2$. Hence, we have convergence for $|x/2| < 1$, $|x| < 2$, and divergence for $|x| > 2$. When $x = 2$, we have $\sum 1$, which diverges. When $x = -2$, we have $\sum (-1)^n$, which is divergent. Hence, the power series converges for $-2 < x < 2$.

(F) $\lim\limits_{n \to +\infty} \dfrac{|x|^{n+1}/(n+1)2^{n+1}}{|x|^n/n2^n} = \lim\limits_{n \to +\infty} \dfrac{|x|}{2}\dfrac{n}{n+1} = \lim\limits_{n \to +\infty} \dfrac{|x|}{2}\dfrac{1}{1+1/n} = \dfrac{|x|}{2}.$ Thus, we have

convergence for $|x| < 2$, and divergence for $|x| > 2$. When $x = 2$, we obtain the divergent harmonic series. When $x = -2$, we have the convergent alternating series $\sum (-1)^n/n$. Therefore, the power series converges for $-2 \le x < 2$.

(G) $\lim\limits_{n \to +\infty} \dfrac{(n+1)\,|x|^{n+1}}{n\,|x|^n} = \lim\limits_{n \to +\infty} |x|\left(1+\dfrac{1}{n}\right) = |x|.$ So we have convergence for $|x| < 1$,

and divergence for $|x| > 1$. When $x = 1$, the divergent series $\sum n$ arises. When $x = -1$, we have the divergent series $\sum (-1)^n n$. Therefore, the series converges for $-1 < x < 1$.

362. $\lim\limits_{n \to +\infty} \dfrac{[(n+1)!]^2\,|x|^{n+1}/(2n+2)!}{(n!)^2\,|x|^n/(2n)!} = \lim\limits_{n \to +\infty} |x|\dfrac{(n+1)^2}{(2n+1)(2n+2)} = \dfrac{|x|}{4}.$ Therefore, the series

converges for $|x| < 4$ and diverges for $|x| > 4$. Hence, the radius of convergence is 4.

363. Since $\sum a_n b_n$ converges, $\lim\limits_{n \to +\infty} |a_n b^n| = 0$. Since a convergent sequence is bounded, there exists an M such that $|a_n b^n| \le M$ for all n. Let $|x/b| = r < 1$. Then $|a_n x^n| = |a_n b^n| \cdot |x^n/b^n| \le Mr^n$. Therefore, by comparison with the convergent geometric series $\sum Mr^n$, $\sum |a_n x^n|$ is convergent.

364. Assume $|x| < 1/L$. Then $L < 1/|x|$. Choose r so that $L < r < 1/|x|$. Then $|rx| < 1$. Since $\lim\limits_{n \to +\infty} \sqrt[n]{|a_n|} = L$, there exists an integer k such that, if $n \ge k$, then $\sqrt[n]{|a_n|} < r$, and, therefore, $|a_n| < r^n$. Hence, for $n \ge k$, $|a_n x^n| < r^n|x|^n = |rx|^n$. Thus, eventually, $\sum |a_n x^n|$ is term by term less than the convergent geometric series $\sum |rx|^n$ and is convergent by the comparison test.

Now, on the other hand, assume $|x| > 1/L$. Then $L > 1/|x|$. Choose r so that $L > r >$ $1/|x|$. Then $|rx| > 1$. Since $\lim_{n \to +\infty} \sqrt[n]{|a_n|} = L$, there exists an integer k such that, if $n \geq k$, then $\sqrt[n]{|a_n|} > r$, and, therefore, $|a_n| > r^n$. Hence, for $n \geq k$, $|a_n x^n| > r^n |x|^n = |rx|^n > 1$. Thus, we cannot have $\lim_{n \to +\infty} a_n x^n = 0$, and, therefore, $\Sigma a_n x^n$ cannot converge. (The theorem also holds when $L = 0$; then the series converges for all x.)

365. Use the ratio test.

$$\lim_{n \to +\infty} \frac{|m(m-1) \cdots (m-n)||x|^{n+1}/(n+1)!}{|m(m-1) \cdots (m-m+1)||x|^n/n!} = \lim_{n \to +\infty} \frac{|x|}{n+1} \cdot |m-n| = \lim_{n \to +\infty} |x| \frac{|m/n-1|}{1+1/n} = |x|.$$

Hence, the radius of convergence is 1.

366. For $|x| < r_1$, both $\Sigma a_n x^n$ and $\Sigma b_n x^n$ are convergent, and, therefore, so is $\Sigma (a_n + b_n) x^n$. Now take x so that $r_1 < |x| < r_2$. Then $\Sigma a_n x^n$ diverges and $\Sigma b_n x^n$ converges. Hence, $\Sigma (a_n + b_n) x^n$ diverges. Thus, the radius of convergence of $\Sigma (a_n + b_n) x^n$ is r_1.

367. (A) Substitute $-x$ for x in Question 361(C).

(B) Substitute x^2 for x in the series of Question 367(A).

(C) Integrate the power series of Question 367(B) term by term, and note that $\tan^{-1} 0 = 0$.

(D) *Method 1.* By Question 360(A), for $|x| < 1$, $\dfrac{1}{1-x} = 1 + x + x^2 + \cdots = \sum_{n=0}^{\infty} x^n$.

Differentiate this series term by term. Then for $|x| < 1$, $\dfrac{1}{(1-x)^2} = 1 + 2x + 3x^2 + \cdots = $
$\sum_{n=0}^{\infty} nx^{n-1} = \sum_{n=0}^{\infty} x^n(n+1)x^n$.

Method 2. $\dfrac{1}{1-x} \cdot \dfrac{1}{1-x} = \left(\sum_{n=0}^{\infty} x^n \right) \left(\sum_{m=0}^{\infty} x^m \right) = \sum_{k=0}^{\infty} \left(\sum_{n+m=k} 1 \right) x^k = \sum_{k=0}^{\infty} (k+1)x^k$.

(E) By Question 367(A), for $|x| < 1$, $\dfrac{1}{1+x} = 1 - x + x^2 - \cdots = \sum_{n=0}^{\infty} (-1)^n x^n$. Integrate term by term:

$$\ln(1+x) = x - \frac{x^2}{2} + \frac{x^3}{3} - \cdots = \sum_{n=0}^{\infty} \frac{(-1)^n}{n+1} x^{n+1} = \sum_{n=1}^{\infty} \frac{(-1)^{n+1}}{n} x^n.$$

368. (A) Let $f(x) = \sum_{n=0}^{\infty} \dfrac{x^n}{n!} = 1 + x + \dfrac{x^2}{2!} + \dfrac{x^3}{3!} + \cdots$. By Question 38.3, $f(x)$ is defined for

all x. Differentiate term by term: $f'(x) = \sum_{n=1}^{\infty} \dfrac{x^{n-1}}{(n-1)!} = \sum_{n=0}^{\infty} \dfrac{x^n}{n!} = f(x)$. Moreover,

$f(0) = 1$. Hence, by Question 223, $f(x) = e^x$.

(B) By Question 368(A), $e^x = \sum_{n=0}^{\infty} \dfrac{x^n}{n!}$. Substitute $-x$ for x: $e^{-x} = \sum_{n=0}^{\infty} \dfrac{(-1)^n}{n!} x^n = 1 - x + \dfrac{x^2}{2!} - \dfrac{x^3}{3!} + \cdots$.

(C) By Question 368(B), $e^{-x} = \sum_{n=0}^{\infty} \dfrac{(-1)^n}{n!} x^n$. Substitute $\dfrac{x^2}{2}$ for x. Then

$e^{-x^2/2} = \sum_{n=0}^{\infty} \dfrac{(-1)^n x^{2n}}{2^n \cdot n!}$.

369. By Question 368(B), $e^{-x} = 1 - x + x^2/2! - x^3/3! + \cdots$. Let $x = 1$. Then $1/e = 1 - 1 + 1/2! - 1/3! + \cdots$. Let us use the alternating series theorem here. We must

find the least n for which $1/n! < 0.0005 = \dfrac{1}{200}$, $200 < n!$, $n \geq 6$. So we can use

$1 - 1 + \dfrac{1}{2} - \dfrac{1}{6} + \dfrac{1}{24} - \dfrac{1}{120} = \dfrac{44}{120} = 0.3666\cdots$. So $1/e \approx 0.37$, correct to two decimal places.

370. (A) Substitute $-x$ for x in the series of Question 367(E): $\ln(1-x) = \sum_{n=1}^{\infty} (-1)^{n+1}$

$\dfrac{(-x)^n}{n} = \sum_{n=1}^{\infty} (-1)^{2n+1} \dfrac{x^n}{n} = -\sum_{n=1}^{\infty} \dfrac{x^n}{n}$, for $|x| < 1$.

(B) By Question 367(E) and 370(A), for $|x| < 1$, $\ln \dfrac{1+x}{1-x} = \ln(1+x) - \ln(1-x) =$

$\sum_{n-1}^{\infty} (-1)^{n+1} \dfrac{x^n}{n} + \sum_{n=1}^{\infty} \dfrac{x^n}{n} = \sum_{n=1}^{\infty} [(-1)^{n+1} + 1] \dfrac{x^n}{n} = 2 \sum_{k=0}^{\infty} \dfrac{x^{2k+1}}{2k+1}$.

(C) By Question 370(B), $\ln \dfrac{1+x}{1-x} = 2 \sum_{k=0}^{\infty} \dfrac{x^{2k+1}}{2k+1}$. When $2 = \dfrac{1+x}{1-x}$, $x = \dfrac{1}{3}$. So $\ln 2 =$

$2 \sum_{k=0}^{\infty} \dfrac{1}{2k+1} \left(\dfrac{1}{3}\right)^{2k+1} = 2 \left[\dfrac{1}{3} + \dfrac{1}{3}\left(\dfrac{1}{3}\right)^3 + \dfrac{1}{5}\left(\dfrac{1}{3}\right)^5 + \cdots \right]$. Using the first three terms, we get

$\dfrac{842}{1215} \approx 0.6930$. (The correct value to four decimal places is 0.6931.)

371. (A) Let $z = dy/dx$. Then $y'' = \dfrac{dz}{dx} = \dfrac{dz}{dy} \cdot \dfrac{dy}{dx} = \dfrac{dz}{dy} z$. Hence,

$\dfrac{dz}{dy} z = -y$, $\int z\, dz = -\int y\, dy$, $\dfrac{1}{2} z^2 = -\dfrac{1}{2} y^2 + C$, $z^2 = -y^2 + K$. Since $z = 1$ and $y = 0$ when

$x = 0$, $K = 1$. Thus, $z^2 = 1 - y^2$, $\dfrac{dy}{dx} = \pm\sqrt{1 - y^2}$, $\displaystyle\int \dfrac{dy}{\sqrt{1 - y^2}} = \pm\int dx$, $\sin^{-1} y = \pm x + C_1$.

Since $y = 0$ when $x = 0$, $C_1 = 0$. So $\sin^{-1} y = \pm x$, $y = \sin(\pm x) = \pm\sin x$. Then $y = \sin x$. (If $y = -\sin x$, then $y' = -\cos x$, and $y' = -1$ when $x = 0$.)

(B) Let $y = \displaystyle\sum_{n=0}^{\infty} (-1)^n \dfrac{x^{2n-1}}{(2n+1)!}$. When $x = 0$, $y = 0$. By differentiation, $y' = \displaystyle\sum_{n=0}^{\infty} (-1)^n \dfrac{x^{2n}}{(2n)!}$,

Hence, $y' = 1$ when $x = 0$. Further, $y'' = \displaystyle\sum_{n=1}^{\infty} (-1)^n \dfrac{x^{2n-1}}{(2n-1)!} = \sum_{n=0}^{\infty} (-1)^{n+1} \dfrac{x^{2n+1}}{(2n+1)!} =$

$-\displaystyle\sum_{n=0}^{\infty} (-1)^n \dfrac{x^{2n+1}}{(2n+1)!} = -y$. Hence, by Question 371(A), $y = \sin x$.

(C) By Question 371(B), $\sin x = \displaystyle\sum_{n=0}^{\infty} (-1)^n \dfrac{x^{2n+1}}{(2n+1)!}$. Differentiate: $\cos x = \displaystyle\sum_{n=0}^{\infty} (-1)^n \dfrac{x^{2n}}{(2n)!}$.

---

372. (A) By Question 367(E), $\ln(1+x) = \displaystyle\sum_{n=1}^{\infty} (-1)^{n+1} \dfrac{x^n}{n}$ for $|x| < 1$. By the alternating

series theorem, the series converges when $x = 1$. By Abel's theorem, $\ln 2 = \displaystyle\sum_{n=0}^{\infty} \dfrac{(-1)^{n+1}}{n}$.

(Abel's theorem reads: Let $f(x) = \displaystyle\sum_{n=0}^{\infty} a_n x^n$ for $-r < x < r$. If the series converges for $x = r$,

then $\displaystyle\lim_{x \to r^-} f(x)$ exists and is equal to $\displaystyle\sum_{n=0}^{\infty} a_n r^n$.)

(B) By Question 367(C), $\tan^{-1} x = x - \dfrac{x^3}{3} + \dfrac{x^5}{5} - \dfrac{x^7}{7} + \cdots = \displaystyle\sum_{n=0}^{\infty} (-1)^n \dfrac{x^{2n+1}}{2n+1}$, for

$|x| < 1$. The series converges for $x = 1$ by the alternating series test. Hence, by Abel's

theorem (Question 372(A)), $\dfrac{\pi}{4} = \tan^{-1} 1 = 1 - \dfrac{1}{3} + \dfrac{1}{5} - \dfrac{1}{7} + \cdots = \displaystyle\sum_{n=0}^{\infty} \dfrac{(-1)^n}{2n+1}$.

---

373. $\sin^2 x = \dfrac{1 - \cos 2x}{2}$. By Question 371(C), $\cos x = \displaystyle\sum_{n=0}^{\infty} (-1)^n \dfrac{x^{2n}}{(2n)!}$. Hence,

$\cos 2x = \displaystyle\sum_{n=0}^{\infty} (-1)^n \dfrac{2^{2n} x^{2n}}{(2n)!}$, $-\cos 2x = \displaystyle\sum_{n=0}^{\infty} (-1)^{n+1} \dfrac{2^{2n} x^{2n}}{(2n)!}$. Adding 1 eliminates the constant

term -1, yielding $1 - \cos 2x = \displaystyle\sum_{n=0}^{\infty} (-1)^{n+1} \dfrac{2^{2n} x^{2n}}{(2n)!}$. So $\sin^2 x = \dfrac{1 - \cos 2x}{2} = \displaystyle\sum_{n=1}^{\infty} (-1)^{n+1} \dfrac{2^{2n-1} x^{2n}}{(2n)!}$.

374. By Question 371(B), $\sin x = x - \dfrac{x^3}{3!} + \dfrac{x^5}{5!} - \dfrac{x^7}{7!} + \cdots = \displaystyle\sum_{n=0}^{\infty} (-1)^n \dfrac{x^{2n+1}}{(2n+1)!}$. Since this
is an alternating series, the error is less than the magnitude of the first term omitted. If we
only use x, the error is less than $|x|^3/3!$. So we need to have $|x|^3/3! < 0.0005$, $|x|^3 < 0.003$,
$|x| < 0.1441 \cdots$.

375. $e^x = 1 + x + \dfrac{x^2}{2!} + \dfrac{x^3}{3!} + \dfrac{x^4}{4!} + \dfrac{x^5}{5!} + \cdots$ and $\cos x = 1 - \dfrac{x^2}{2!} + \dfrac{x^4}{4!} - \cdots$. Hence, $e^x \cos x =$

$\left(1 + x + \dfrac{x^2}{2!} + \dfrac{x^3}{3!} + \dfrac{x^4}{4!} + \dfrac{x^5}{5!} + \cdots\right)\left(1 - \dfrac{x^2}{2!} + \dfrac{x^4}{4!} - \cdots\right) = 1 + x - \dfrac{1}{3}x^3 - \dfrac{1}{6}x^4 - \dfrac{1}{30}x^5 + \cdots$.

376. $\dfrac{1}{1-x}(a_0 + a_1 x + \cdots + a_n x^n + \cdots) = (1 + x + x^2 + \cdots + x^n + \cdots)(a_0 + a_1 x + \cdots a_n x^n + \cdots)$.
The terms of this product involving x^n are $a_0 x^n + a_1 x \cdot x^{n-1} + \cdots + a_{n-2} x^{n-2} \cdot x^2 + a_{n-1} x^{n-1} \cdot$
$x + a_n x^n$. Hence, the coefficient of x^n will be $a_0 + a_1 + \cdots + a_n$.

377. We want to find $\displaystyle\sum_{n=0}^{\infty} a_n x^n$ so that $a_0 + a_1 + \cdots + a_n = n + 1$. A simple choice is $a_i = 1$.

Thus, from $\displaystyle\sum_{n=0}^{\infty} x^n = \dfrac{1}{1-x}$ we obtain $\displaystyle\sum_{n=0}^{\infty} (n+1)x^n - \dfrac{1}{(1-x)^2}$.

378. Let $f(x) = x/2! + x^2/3! + x^3/4! + x^4/5! + \cdots$. Then $xf(x) = (x^2)/2! + x^3/3! + x^4/4! +$
$x^5/5! + \cdots = e^x - x - 1$. Hence, $f(x) = (e^x - x - 1)/x$.

379. (A) $f'(x) = m + m (m - 1) x + \cdots + \dfrac{m(m-1)\cdots(m-n+1)}{(n-1)!} x^{n-1} + \cdots$; $xf'(x) = mx +$

$m(m-1)x^2 + \cdots + \dfrac{m(m-1)\cdots(m-n+1)}{(n-1)!} x^n + \cdots$. In $(1+x)f'(x)$, the coefficient of x^n will

be $\dfrac{m(m-1)\cdots(m-n+1)(m-n)}{n!} + n\dfrac{m(m-1)\cdots(m-n+1)}{n!} = m\dfrac{m(m-1)\cdots(m-n+1)}{n!}$.

Hence, $(1 + x)f'(x) = mf(x)$.

(B) Let $g(x) = \dfrac{f(x)}{(1+x)^m}$. Then, $g'(x) = \dfrac{(1+x)^m f'(x) - mf(x)(1+x)^{m-1}}{(1+x)^{2m}} = 0$ by
Question 379(A). Hence, $g(x)$ is a constant C. But $f(x) = 1$ when $x = 0$, and, therefore,
$C = 1$. Therefore, $f(x) = (1+x)^m$.

(C) Substitute $-x$ for x and $\dfrac{1}{2}$ for m in the binomial series of Questions 379(A)
and (B).

(D) Substitute $-x$ for x and $-\dfrac{1}{2}$ for m in the binomial series of Questions 379(A) and (B). (Alternatively, take the derivative of the series in part(C).)

(E) By Question 379(D), $\dfrac{1}{\sqrt{1-t}} = 1 + \dfrac{1}{2}t + \dfrac{1 \cdot 3}{2 \cdot 4}t^2 + \dfrac{1 \cdot 3 \cdot 5}{2 \cdot 4 \cdot 6}t^3 + \cdots$. Therefore,

$$\dfrac{1}{\sqrt{1-t^2}} = 1 + \dfrac{1}{2}t^2 + \dfrac{1 \cdot 3}{2 \cdot 4}t^4 + \dfrac{1 \cdot 3 \cdot 5}{2 \cdot 4 \cdot 6}t^6 + \cdots \text{ and } \sin^{-1}x = \int_0^x \dfrac{1}{\sqrt{1-t^2}}\,dt = x + \dfrac{1}{2}\dfrac{x^3}{3} +$$

$$\dfrac{1 \cdot 3}{2 \cdot 4}\dfrac{x^5}{5} + \dfrac{1 \cdot 3 \cdot 5}{2 \cdot 4 \cdot 6}\dfrac{x^7}{7} + \cdots.$$

(F) $\sqrt[5]{33} = \sqrt[5]{32+1} = 2 \cdot \sqrt[5]{1 + \dfrac{1}{32}}$. By Question 379(B), $\left(1 + \dfrac{1}{32}\right)^{1/5} = 1 + \dfrac{1}{5}\left(\dfrac{1}{32}\right) +$

$\dfrac{\frac{1}{2}(\frac{1}{5}-1)}{2}\left(\dfrac{1}{32}\right)^2 + \cdots$. Since the series alternates in sign, the error is less than the magnitude of the first term omitted. Now, $\dfrac{\frac{1}{2}(\frac{1}{5}-1)}{2}\left(\dfrac{1}{32}\right)^2 = \dfrac{1}{12,800} < 0.0005$. Thus, it suffices to use

$1 + \dfrac{1}{5}\dfrac{1}{32} = \dfrac{161}{160} \approx 1.006$. Hence, $\sqrt[5]{33} \cong 2.012$.

380. Assume $\Sigma a_n x^n$ converges for some $|x| > 1$. Then $\lim\limits_{n \to +\infty} |a_n||x|^n = 0$. But, for infinitely many values of n, $|a_n||x|^n > 1$, contradicting $\lim\limits_{n \to +\infty} |a_n||x|^n = 0$.

Chapter 39: Taylor and Maclaurin Series

381. (A) Let $f(x) = e^x$. Then $f^{(n)}(x) = e^x$ for all $n \ge 0$. Hence, $f^{(n)}(0) = 1$ for all $n \ge 0$. Therefore, the Maclaurin series $\sum\limits_{n=0}^{\infty} \dfrac{f^{(n)}(0)}{n!}x^n = \sum\limits_{n=0}^{\infty} \dfrac{x^n}{n!}$.

(B) Let $f(x) = \sin x$. Then $f(0) = \sin 0 = 0$, $f'(0) = \cos 0 = 1$, $f''(0) = -\sin 0 = 0$, $f'''(0) = -\cos 0 = -1$, and, thereafter, the sequence of values of 0, 1, 0, −1 keeps repeating. Thus, we obtain $x - \dfrac{x^3}{3!} + \dfrac{x^5}{5!} - \dfrac{x^7}{7!} + \cdots = \sum\limits_{n=0}^{\infty}(-1)^n \dfrac{x^{2n+1}}{(2n+1)!}$.

(C) Let $f(x) = \ln(1-x)$. Then $f(0) = 0$, $f'(0) = -1$, $f''(0) = -1$, $f'''(0) = -1 \cdot 2$, $f^{(4)} = -1 \cdot 2 \cdot 3$, and, in general, $f^{(n)}(0) = -(n-1)!$ Thus, for $n \ge 1$, $f^{(n)}(0)/n! = -1/n$, and the Maclaurin series is $-x - \dfrac{x^2}{2} - \dfrac{x^3}{3} - \dfrac{x^4}{4} - \cdots$.

(D) Let $f(x) = e^{\cos x}$. Then $f'(x) = -e^{\cos x}\sin x$, $f''(x) = e^{\cos x}(\sin^2 x - \cos x)$, $f'''(x) = e^{\cos x}(\sin x)(3\cos x + 1 - \sin^2 x)$, $f^{(4)}(x) = e^{\cos x}[(-\sin^2 x)(3 + 2\cos x) + (3\cos x + 1 - \sin^2 x)$

$(\cos x - \sin^2 x)]$. Thus, $f(0) = e, f'(0) = 0, f''(0) = -e, f'''(0) = 0, f^{(4)}(0) = 4e$. Hence, the Maclaurin series is $e\left(1-\dfrac{1}{2}x^2 +\dfrac{1}{6}x^4 +\cdots\right)$.

382. (A) Let $f(x) = \sin x$. Then $f(\pi/4) = \sin(\pi/4) = \sqrt{2}/2, f'(\pi/4) = \cos(\pi/4) =$ $\sqrt{2}/2, f''(\pi/4) = -\sin(\pi/4) = -\sqrt{2}/2.$ $f'''(\pi/4) = -\cos(\pi/4) = -\sqrt{2}/2$, and, thereafter, this cycle of four values keeps repeating. Thus, the Taylor series for $\sin x$ about $\dfrac{\pi}{4}$ is

$$\dfrac{\sqrt{2}}{2}\left[1+\dfrac{x-\pi/4}{1!}-\dfrac{(x-\pi/4)^2}{2!}-\dfrac{(x-\pi/4)^3}{3!}+\dfrac{(x-\pi/4)^4}{4!}+\dfrac{(x-\pi/4)^5}{5!}-\dfrac{(x-\pi/4)^6}{6!}-\right.$$
$$\left.\dfrac{(x-\pi/4)^7}{7!}+\cdots\right].$$

(B) Let $f(x) = \dfrac{1}{x}$. Then $f'(x) = -\dfrac{1}{x^2}, f''(x) = \dfrac{2}{x^3}, f'''(x) = -\dfrac{2.3}{x^4}, f^{(4)}(x) =$ $-\dfrac{2\cdot3\cdot4}{x^5}$, and, in general, $f^{(n)}(x) = (-1)^n\dfrac{n!}{x^{n+1}}$. So $f^{(n)}(1) = (-1)^n n!$. Thus, the Taylor series is $\displaystyle\sum_{n=0}^{\infty}\dfrac{f^{(n)}(1)}{n!}(x-1)^n = \sum_{n=0}^{\infty}(-1)^n(x-1)^n = 1-(x-1)+(x-1)^2-(x-1)^3+\cdots$.

383. (A) $f(a) = a_0$. It can be shown that the power series converges uniformly on $|x-a|\le$ $\rho < r$, allowing differentiation term by term: $f'(x) = \displaystyle\sum_{n=1}^{\infty}na_n(x-a)^{n-1}, f''(x) = \sum_{n=2}^{\infty}n(n-1)a_n$ $(x-a)^{n-2}, \ldots, f^{(k)}(x) = \displaystyle\sum_{n=k}^{\infty}n(n-1)\cdots[n-(k-1)]a_n(x-a)^{n-k}$. If we let $x = a, f^{(k)}(a) = k(k-1)$ $\ldots . 1\cdot a_k = k!\cdot a_k$. Hence, $a_k = \dfrac{f^{(k)}(a)}{k!}$.

(B) By Question 367(A), we know that $\dfrac{1}{1+x} = 1-x+x^2-\cdots = \displaystyle\sum_{n=0}^{\infty}(-1)^n x^n$, for $|x| < 1$. Hence, by Question 383(A), this must be the Maclaurin series for $\dfrac{1}{1+x}$.

(C) $\cos^2 x = \dfrac{1+\cos 2x}{2}$. Now, by Question 371(C), $\cos x = \displaystyle\sum_{n=0}^{\infty}\dfrac{(-1)^n x^{2n}}{(2n)!}$, and, therefore, $\cos 2x = \displaystyle\sum_{n=0}^{\infty}\dfrac{(-1)^n 2^{2n}x^{2n}}{(2n)!}$. Since the latter series has constant term 1, 1 +

$\cos 2x = 2 + \displaystyle\sum_{n=1}^{\infty}\dfrac{(-1)^n 2^{2n}x^{2n}}{(2n)!}$, and $\dfrac{1+\cos 2x}{2} = 1+\displaystyle\sum_{n=1}^{\infty}\dfrac{(-1)^n 2^{2n-1}x^{2n}}{(2n)!}$. By Question 383(A), this is the Maclaurin series for $\cos^2 x$.

384. If $f(x)$ and its first n derivatives are continuous on an open interval containing a, then, for any x in this interval, there is a number c between a and x such that

$$f(x) = f(a) + f'(a)(x-a) + \frac{f''(a)}{2!}(x-a)^2 + \cdots + \frac{f^{(n-1)}(a)}{(n-1)!}(x-a)^{n-1} + R_n(x)$$

where $R_n(x) = \frac{f^{(n)}(c)}{n!}(x-a)^n$. If $f(x)$ has continuous derivatives of all orders then, for those x for which $\lim\limits_{n \to +\infty} R_n(x) = 0$, $f(x)$ is equal to its Taylor series.

385. We know that $e^x = \sum\limits_{n=a}^{\infty} \frac{x^n}{n!}$. Now let $x = 1$.

386. Since $e^x = 1 + x + x^2/2! + x^3/3!. + \cdots$, we are approximating $\sqrt{e}$ by

$1 + \frac{1}{2} + \frac{1}{2}\left(\frac{1}{2}\right)^2 + \frac{1}{6}\left(\frac{1}{2}\right)^3 = 1 + \frac{1}{2} + \frac{1}{8} + \frac{1}{48} \approx 1.64583$. The error $R_n(x)$ is $\frac{f^{(4)}(c)}{4!}\left(\frac{1}{2}\right)^4$ for some c between 0 and $\frac{1}{2}$. Now $f^{(4)}(x) = e^x$. The error is $e^c/384$, with $0 < c < \frac{1}{2}$. Now $e^c < e^{1/2} < 2$, since $e < 4$. Hence, the error is less than $\frac{2}{384} = \frac{1}{192} \approx 0.0052$.

387. We have $e = 1 + 1 + 1/2! + 1/3! + 1/4! + \cdots$. Since $f^{(n)}(x) = e^x$, the error $R_n(x) = e^c/n!$ for some number c such that $0 < c < 1$. Since $e^c < e < 3$, we require that $3/n! < 0.005$—that is, $600 < n!$. Hence, we can let $n = 6$. Then e is estimated by $1 + 1 + \frac{1}{2} + \frac{1}{6} + \frac{1}{24} + \frac{1}{120} = \frac{326}{120} \approx 2.72$ to two decimal places.

388. In general, $a_n = \frac{f^{(n)}(0)}{n!}$. So $f^{(33)}(0) = 33!a_{33} = 33!2^{33}$.

389. $e^x = \sum\limits_{n=0}^{\infty} \frac{x^n}{n!}$. Hence, $e^{-x^2} = \sum\limits_{n=0}^{\infty} \frac{(-1)^n x^{2n}}{n!}$, and $\int_0^1 e^{-x^2}\,dx = \sum\limits_{n=0}^{\infty} \left[\frac{(-1)^n x^{2n+1}}{(2n+1)n!}\right]_0^1 = \sum\limits_{n=0}^{\infty} \frac{(-1)^n}{(2n+1)n!}$.

Since this is an alternating series, we must find n such that $\frac{1}{(2n+1)n!} \leq 0.005$, $200 \leq (2n+1)n!$, $n \geq 4$.

Hence, we use $1 - \frac{1}{3} + \frac{1}{10} - \frac{1}{42} = \frac{26}{35} \approx 0.74$.

Chapter 40: Vectors in Space; Lines and Planes

390. **(A)** A point (x, y, z) is on $\mathscr{S}$ if and only if its distance from (a, b, c) is r—that is, if and only if $\sqrt{(x-a)^2\,(y-b)^2+(z-c)^2} = r$, or, equivalently, $(x-a)^2+(y-b)^2+(z-c)^2 = r^2$.

(B) Complete the square in x and in z: $(x+2)^2+y^2+(z-4)^2 = 5+4+16 = 25$. This is the equation of the sphere with center $(-2, 0, 4)$ and radius 5.

(C) Complete the squares: $\left(x+\dfrac{A}{2}\right)^2+\left(y+\dfrac{B}{2}\right)^2+\left(z+\dfrac{C}{2}\right)^2 = \dfrac{A^2}{4}+\dfrac{B^2}{4}+\dfrac{C^2}{4} - D$. This is a sphere if and only if the right side is positive—that is, if and only if $A^2+B^2+C^2-4D>0$. (In that case, the sphere has radius $\dfrac{1}{2}\sqrt{A^2+B^2+C^2-4D}$ and center $\left(-\dfrac{A}{2},-\dfrac{B}{2},-\dfrac{C}{2}\right)$.) When $A^2+B^2+C^2-4D=0$, the graph is a single point $\left(-\dfrac{A}{2},-\dfrac{B}{2},-\dfrac{C}{2}\right)$. When $A^2+B^2+C^2-4D<0$, there are no points on the graph at all.

391. $\overline{PR} = \sqrt{1^2+2^2+3^2} + \sqrt{14}$, $\overline{QR} = \sqrt{4^2+(-5)^2+2^2} = \sqrt{45}$, $\overline{PQ} = \sqrt{(1-4)^2+[2-(-5)]^2+(3-2)^2} = \sqrt{59}$. Thus, $\overline{PQ}^2 = \overline{PR}^2 + \overline{QR}^2$. Hence, by the valid converse of the Pythagorean theorem, $\triangle PQR$ is a right triangle with right angle at R.

392. $\overline{PQ} = \sqrt{4^2+1^2+1^2} = \sqrt{18} = 3\sqrt{2}$. $\overline{QR} = \sqrt{8^2+2^2+2^2} = \sqrt{72} = 6\sqrt{2}$. $\overline{PR} = \sqrt{12^2+3^2+3^2} = \sqrt{162} = 9\sqrt{2}$. So $\overline{PR} = \overline{PQ}+\overline{QR}$. Hence, the points are collinear. (If three points are not collinear, they form a triangle. Then the sum of two sides must be greater than the third side.) **Another method:** $Q = \dfrac{2}{3}P+\dfrac{1}{3}R$.

393. As shown in Figure A40.1, $x^2+y^2 = 1$ is a cylinder of radius 1 with the z-axis as its axis of symmetry, and $z = 2$ is a plane two units above and parallel to the xy-plane. Hence, the intersection is a circle of radius 1 with center at $(0, 0, 2)$ in the plane $z = 2$.

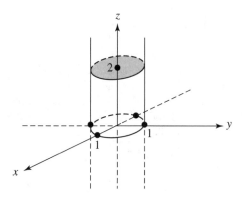

Figure A40.1

394. $|A| = \sqrt{9 + 144 + 16} = \sqrt{169} = 13$. Hence, $\cos\alpha = \dfrac{3}{13}$, $\cos\beta = \dfrac{12}{13}$, $\cos\gamma = \dfrac{4}{13}$.

395. $A \cdot B = |A||B|\cos\theta$, $1(2) + 2(-3) + 3(-1) = (\sqrt{1+4+9})(\sqrt{4+9+1})(\cos\theta)$, $-7 = 14\cos\theta$, $\cos\theta = -\dfrac{1}{2}$, $\theta = 120° = 2\pi/3$.

396. We must have $0 = A \cdot B = 3(2) + (-2)(4) + 5c$, $5c = 2$, $c = \dfrac{2}{3}$.

397. $A \times B = (a_2 b_3 - a_3 b_2, \ a_3 b_1 - a_1 b_3, \ a_1 b_2 - a_2 b_1)$. In pseudo-determinant form,

$$A \times B = \begin{bmatrix} i & j & k \\ a_1 & a_2 & a_3 \\ b_1 & b_2 & b_3 \end{bmatrix}.$$

If we expand along the first row, we obtain

$$\begin{bmatrix} a_2 & a_3 \\ b_2 & b_3 \end{bmatrix} i - \begin{bmatrix} a_1 & a_3 \\ b_1 & b_3 \end{bmatrix} j + \begin{bmatrix} a_1 & a_2 \\ b_1 & b_2 \end{bmatrix} k = (a_2 b_3 - a_3 b_2)i + (a_3 b_1 - a_1 b_3)j + (a_1 b_2 - a_2 b_1)k.$$

398. $\overrightarrow{PQ} = (1, 1, -3)$, $\overrightarrow{PR} = (-1, 3, -1)$. We can take $N = \overrightarrow{PQ} \times \overrightarrow{PR} = (1(-1) - (-3)3, (-3)(-1) - 1(-1), 1(3) - 1(-1)) = (8, 4, 4)$.

399. The volume of the parallelepiped determined by noncoplanar vectors A, B, C is $|A \cdot (B \times C)|$. Hence, in this case, the volume is $|\overrightarrow{PS} \cdot N| = (2, 4, 10) \cdot (8, 4, 4) = 16 + 16 + 40 = 72$.

400. By Question 397, the cofactors of the first row are the respective components of $B \times C$.

401. Let $A = (a_1, a_2, a_3)$ and $B = (b_1, b_2, b_3)$. Then $A \times B = (a_2 b_3 - a_3 b_2, a_3 b_1 - a_1 b_3, a_1 b_2 - a_2 b_1)$ and $B \times A = (b_2 a_3 - b_3 a_2, b_3 a_1 - b_1 a_3, b_1 a_2 - b_2 a_1) = -(A \times B)$.

402. Let $A = (a_1, a_2, a_3)$, $B = (b_1, b_2, b_3)$, $C = (c_1, c_2, c_3)$. By Questions 399 and 400, the determinant above is equal to $A \cdot (B \times C)$, which is equal in magnitude to the nonzero volume of the parallelepiped formed by A, B, C when the given points are not coplanar. If those points are coplanar, either $B \times C = 0$, and, therefore, $A \cdot (B \times C) = 0$; or $B \times C \neq 0$ and A is perpendicular to $B \times C$ (because A is in the plane of B and C), so that again $A \cdot (B \times C) = 0$.

403. (A) If R is any point on the line, then $\overline{PR} = t\,\overline{PQ}$ for some scalar t (see Figure A40.2). Hence, $\overline{OR} = \overline{OP} + \overline{PR} = \overline{OP} + t\,\overline{PQ}$. Thus, $(1, 2, -5) + t(2, 6, 1)$ is a vector function that generates the line. A parametric form is $x = 1 + 2t$, $y = 2 + 6t$, $z = -5 + t$. If we eliminate t from these equations, we obtain the rectangular equations $\dfrac{x-1}{2} = \dfrac{y-2}{6} = \dfrac{z+5}{1}$.

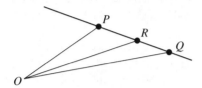

Figure A40.2

    (B) By Question 403(A), the parametric equations are $x = 1 + 2t$, $y = 2 + 6t$, $z = -5 + t$. To find the intersection with the xy-plane, set $z = 0$. Then $t = 5$, $x = 11$, $y = 32$. So the intersection point is $(11, 32, 0)$. To find the intersection with the xz-plane, set $y = 0$. Then $t = -\dfrac{1}{3}$, $x = \dfrac{1}{3}$, $z = -\dfrac{16}{3}$. So the intersection is $\left(\dfrac{1}{3}, 0, -\dfrac{16}{3}\right)$. To find the intersection with the yz-plane, set $x = 0$. Then $t = -\dfrac{1}{2}$, $y = -1$, $z = -\dfrac{11}{2}$. So the intersection is $\left(0, -1, -\dfrac{11}{2}\right)$.

404. The line is generated by the vector function $(1, 2, -6) + t(4, 1, 3)$. Parametric equations are $x = 1 + 4t$, $y = 2 + t$, $z = -6 + 3t$. A set of rectangular equations is $\dfrac{x-1}{4} = \dfrac{y-2}{1} = \dfrac{z+6}{3}$.

405. The distance from $P_0(1, 2, 1)$ to (x, y, z) is $\sqrt{(x-1)^2 + (y-2)^2 + (z-1)^2} = \sqrt{(t+2)^2 + t^2 + t^2} = \sqrt{3t^2 + 4t + 4}$. It suffices to minimize $3t^2 + 4t + 4$. Set $D_t(3t^2 + 4t + 4) = 6t + 4 = 0$. So $t = -\dfrac{2}{3}$. Hence, $P_1 = \left(\dfrac{7}{3}, \dfrac{4}{3}, \dfrac{1}{3}\right)$. Note that $\overline{P_0P_1}$ is $\left(\dfrac{4}{3}, -\dfrac{2}{3}, -\dfrac{2}{3}\right)$, and $\overline{P_0P_1} \cdot (1, 1, 1) = 0$. Hence, $\overline{P_0P_1}$ is perpendicular to the line. The distance from P_1 to the line is $\sqrt{3\left(\dfrac{4}{9}\right) - \dfrac{8}{3} + 4} = \sqrt{\dfrac{8}{3}}$.

406. For any point $P(x, y, z)$, P is in the plane if and only if $\overline{P_1P} \perp \mathbf{N}$—that is, if and only if $\overline{P_1P} \cdot \mathbf{N} = 4(x-3) + 2(y+2) - 7(z-5) = 0$, which can also be written as $4x + 2y - 7z = -27$.

407. $\mathbf{N} = \overline{PQ} \times \overline{PR}$ is normal to the plane. $\mathbf{N} = (-2, -1, -1) \times (3, 1, -5) = (6, -13, 1)$. So the equation has the form $6x - 13y + z = d$. Since R is in the plane, $6(4) - 13(4) + 0 = d$, $d = -28$. Thus, the equation is $6x - 13y + z = -28$.

408. θ is the angle between the normal vectors $(4, 4, -2)$ and $(2, 1, 1)$. So

$$\cos\theta = \frac{(4, 4, -2)\cdot(2, 1, 1)}{|(4, 4, -2)|\,|(2, 1, 1)|} = \frac{10}{6\sqrt{6}} = \frac{5\sqrt{6}}{18}$$

Of course, there is another angle between the planes: the supplement of the angle whose cosine was just found. The cosine of the other angle is $-\cos\theta = -5\sqrt{6}/18$.

409. The point $Q(0, 0, 2)$ is on the given line $\mathscr{L}$ (set $t = 0$). The vector $\overrightarrow{QP} = (1, 3, -1)$ lies in the sought plane. Since the vector $(1, 1, 1)$ is parallel to $\mathscr{L}$, the cross product $(1, 3, -1) \times (1, 1, 1) = (4, -2, -2)$ is normal to the plane. So an equation of the plane is $4x - 2y - 2z = d$. Since the point $Q(0, 0, 2)$ is in the plane, $-4 = d$. Thus, the plane has the equation $4x - 2y - 2z = -4$, or $2x - y - z = -2$.

410. (A) Let $Q(x_2, y_2, z_2)$ be any point on the given plane. Then the distance D is the magnitude of the scalar projection of $\overrightarrow{PQ} = (x_2 - x_1, y_2 - y_1, z_2 - z_1)$ on the normal vector $\mathbf{N} = (a, b, c)$ to the plane. So D is

$$\frac{|\mathbf{N}\cdot\overrightarrow{PQ}|}{|\mathbf{N}|} = \frac{|(a, b, c)\cdot(x_2 - x_1, y_2 - y_1, z_2 - z_1)|}{\sqrt{a^2 + b^2 + c^2}} = \frac{|a(x_2 - x_1) + b(y_2 - y_1) + c(z_2 - z_1)|}{\sqrt{a^2 + b^2 + c^2}}$$

$$= \frac{|ax_2 + by_2 + cz_2 - ax_1 - by_1 - cz_1|}{\sqrt{a^2 + b^2 + c^2}}.$$

Since $Q(x_2, y_2, z_2)$ is a point of the plane, $ax_2 + by_2 + cz_2 + d = 0$. Hence,

$$D = \frac{|-d - ax_1 - by_1 - cz_1|}{\sqrt{a^2 + b^2 + c^2}} = \frac{|ax_1 + by_1 + cz_1 + d|}{\sqrt{a^2 + b^2 + c^2}}.$$

(B) By the formula of Question 410(A), $D = \dfrac{|8(3) - 2(-5) + 2 - 5|}{\sqrt{(8)^2 + (2)^2 + (1)^2}} = \dfrac{31}{\sqrt{69}}$.

411. The radius vector $(1, 2, 2)$ is perpendicular to the tangent plane at $(1, 2, 2)$. Hence, the tangent plane has an equation of the form $x + 2y + 2z = d$. Since $(1, 2, 2)$ is in the plane, $1 + 2(2) + 2(2) = d$, $d = 9$. So the plane has the equation $x + 2y + 2z = 9$. When $y = 0$ and $z = 0$, $x = 9$. Hence, the point P is $(9, 0, 0)$.

412. Since the normal vectors $(1, -2, 2)$ and $(3, -1, -1)$ are not parallel, the planes are not parallel and must intersect. Their line of intersection $\mathscr{L}$ is parallel to the cross product $(1, -2, 2) \times (3, -1, -1) = (4, 7, 5)$. To find a point on $\mathscr{L}$, set $x = 0$ in the equations of the planes $-2y + 2z - 1$, $-y - z = 2$. Multiply the second equation by 2 and add: $-4y = 5$, $y = -\dfrac{5}{4}$, $z = -\dfrac{3}{4}$. So the point $\left(0, -\dfrac{5}{4}, -\dfrac{3}{4}\right)$ is on $\mathcal{L}$, and $\mathcal{L}$ has the equations $x = 4t$, $y = -\dfrac{5}{4} + 7t$, $z = -\dfrac{3}{4} + 5t$.

413. We look for a suitable constant k so that the plane $(3x - 2y + 4z - 5) + k(2x + 4y - z - 7) = 0$ contains the given point. Thus, $(3 + 2k)x + (-2 + 4k)y + (4 - k)z - (5 + 7k) = 0$ must be satisfied by $(2, 1, 2)$: $(3 + 2k)2 + (-2 + 4k) + (4 - k)2 - (5 + 7k) = 0$, $-k + 7 = 0$, $k = 7$. So the desired plane is $17x + 26y - 3z - 54 = 0$.

414. Write the equations of the line in parametric form: $x = -8 + 9t$, $y = 10 - 4t$, $z = 9 - 2t$. Substitute in the equation for the plane: $3(-8 + 9t) + 4(10 - 4t) + 5(9 - 2t) = 76$. Then $t + 61 = 76$, $t = 15$. Thus, the point P is $(127, -50, -21)$.

415. The line is parallel to the normal vector to the plane, $(6, -3, 2)$. Hence, the line has the parametric equations $x = 4 + 6t$, $y = 2 - 3t$, $z = -1 + 2t$.

Chapter 41: Functions of Several Variables

416. **(A)** See Figure A41.1. Each section parallel to one of the coordinate planes is an ellipse (or a point or nothing). The surface is bounded, $|x| \le a$, $|y| \le b$, $|z| \le c$. This surface is called an ellipsoid. When $a = b = c$, the surface is a sphere.

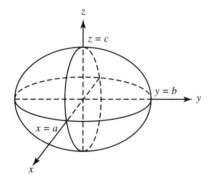

Figure A41.1

(B) See Figure A41.2. Each section $z = k$ parallel to the xy-plane cuts out an ellipse. The ellipses get bigger as $|z|$ increases. (For $z = 0$, the xy-plane, the section is the ellipse $\dfrac{x^2}{a^2} + \dfrac{y^2}{b^2} = 1$.) For sections made by planes $x = k$, we obtain hyperbolas, and, similarly for sections made by planes, $y = k$. The surface is called a hyperboloid of one sheet.

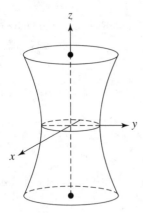

Figure A41.2

(C) See Figure A41.3. Note that $\dfrac{z^2}{c^2} = 1 + \dfrac{x^2}{a^2} + \dfrac{y^2}{b^2} \geq 1$. Hence, $|z| \geq c$. The sections by planes $z = k$, with $|k| > c$, are ellipses. When $|z| = c$, we obtain a point $(0, 0, \pm c)$. The sections determined by planes $x = k$ or $y = k$ are hyperbolas. The surface is called a hyperboloid of two sheets.

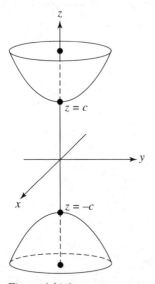

Figure A41.3

(D) See Figure A41.4. This is an elliptic cone. The horizontal cross-sections $z = c \neq 0$ are ellipses. The horizontal cross-section $z = 0$ is a point, the origin. The surface intersects the xz-plane ($y = 0$) in a pair of lines, $z = \pm\dfrac{c}{a}x$, and intersects the yz-plane ($x = 0$) in a pair of lines, $z = \pm\dfrac{c}{b}y$. The other cross-sections, determined by $x = k$ or $y = k$, are hyperbolas.

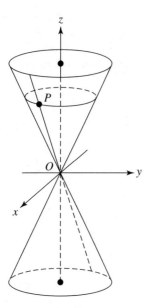

Figure A41.4

(E) See Figure A41.5. This is the graph of $z = x^2 + y^2$. Note that $z \geq 0$. When $z = 0$, $x^2 + y^2 = 0$, and, therefore, $x = y = 0$. So the intersection with the xy-plane is the origin. Sections made by planes $z = k > 0$ are circles with centers on the z-axis. Sections made by planes $x = k$ or $y = k$ are parabolas. The surface is called a circular paraboloid.

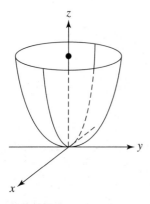

Figure A41.5

(F) This is the graph of $z = 2x + 5y - 10$, or $2x + 5y - z = 10$, a plane having (2, 5, −1) as a normal vector.

(G) See Figure A41.6. This is called a saddle surface, with the "seat" at the origin. The plane sections $z = c > 0$ are hyperbolas with the principal axis the y-axis. For $z = c < 0$, the plane sections are hyperbolas with the principal axis the x-axis. The section made by $z = 0$ is $y^2 - x^2 = 0$, $(y - x)(y + x) = 0$, the pair of lines $y = x$ and $y = -x$. The sections made by planes $x = c$ or $y = c$ are parabolas.

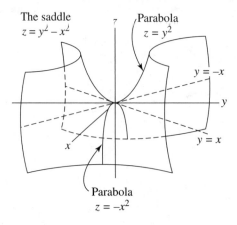

Figure A41.6

417. The plane $z = k$ cuts the ellipsoid in an ellipse:

$$\frac{x^2}{a^2} + \frac{y^2}{b^2} = 1 - \frac{k^2}{c^2} = \frac{c^2 - k^2}{c^2} \qquad \frac{x^2}{(a\sqrt{c^2 - k^2}/c)^2} + \frac{y^2}{(b\sqrt{c^2 - k^2}/c)^2} = 1$$

By Question 188, the area of this ellipse is $\pi(a\sqrt{c^2 - k^2}/c)(b\sqrt{c^2 - k^2}/c) = \pi ab(c^2 - k^2)/c^2$. Hence, by the cross-section formula for volume,

$$V = 2\int_0^c \frac{\pi ab}{c^2}(c^2 - k^2)\, dk = \frac{2\pi ab}{c^2}\left(c^2 k - \frac{1}{3}k^3\right)\Bigg]_0^c = \frac{2\pi ab}{c^2}\left(c^3 - \frac{1}{3}c^3\right) = \frac{4}{3}\pi abc.$$

418. (A) Note that, if $y = mx$ and $(x, y) \to (0, 0)$, then $\dfrac{2xy^2}{x^2 + y^2} = \dfrac{2xm^2x^2}{x^2 + m^2x^2} = \dfrac{2m^2}{1 + m^2}$
$x \to 0$. However, this is not enough to ensure that $2xy^2/(x^2 + y^2) \to 0$ *no matter how*
$(x, y) \to (0, 0)$. Take any $\varepsilon > 0$. Note that $|(x, y) - (0, 0)| = \sqrt{x^2 + y^2}$. Observe also that $|x| \le \sqrt{x^2 + y^2}$ and $y^2 \le x^2 + y^2$. So

$$\left|\frac{2xy^2}{x^2 + y^2}\right| \le \frac{2\sqrt{x^2 + y^2}(x^2 + y^2)}{x^2 + y^2} = 2\sqrt{x^2 + y^2}.$$

Hence, if we choose $\delta = \varepsilon/2$ and if $\sqrt{x^2 + y^2} < \delta$, then $|2xy^2/(x^2 + y^2)|$
$\leq 2\sqrt{x^2 + y^2} < 2\delta = \varepsilon$. Thus, $\displaystyle\lim_{(x, y)\to(0, 0)} \frac{2xy^2}{x^2 + y^2} = 0$.

(B) Let $y = mx$. Then

$$\frac{2xy^2}{x^2 + y^4} = \frac{2x(m^2x^2)}{x^2 + m^4x^4} = \frac{2m^2x}{1 + m^4x^2} \to \frac{0}{1} = 0$$

as $(x, y) \to (0, 0)$. However, if we let $x = y^2$, then $\dfrac{2xy^2}{x^2 + y^4} = \dfrac{2y^4}{y^4 + y^4} = 1$. Hence, as

$(x, y) \to (0, 0)$ along the parabola $x = y^2$, $\dfrac{2xy^2}{x^2 + y^4} \to 1$. Therefore, $\displaystyle\lim_{(x, y)\to(0, 0)} \frac{2xy^2}{x^2 + y^4}$ does

not exist.

(C) Note that

$$\left|\frac{x^3 + y^3}{x^2 + y^2}\right| \leq \frac{|x^3|}{x^2 + y^2} + \frac{|y^3|}{x^2 + y^2} = \frac{x^2}{x^2 + y^2}|x| + \frac{|y^2|}{x^2 + y^2}|y| \leq |x| + |y| \mapsto 0 \text{ as } (x, y) \to (0, 0)$$

So, $\displaystyle\lim_{(x, y)\to(0, 0)} \frac{x^3 + y^3}{x^2 + y^2} = 0$. Hence, if we define $f(0, 0) = 0$, then $f(x, y)$ will be
continuous, since it is obvious that $f(x, y)$ is continuous at all points different from the
origin.

(D) As $(x, y) \to (0, 0)$ along the line $y = mx$, $f(x, y) = \dfrac{mx^2}{(1 + m^2)x^2} = \dfrac{m}{1 + m^2}$. Hence,
$\displaystyle\lim_{(x, y)\to(0, 0)} f(x, y)$ does not exist and, therefore, $f(x, y)$ is not continuous (and cannot be
made continuous by redefining $f(0, 0)$).

419. (A) For a point with rectangular coordinates (x, y, z), corresponding cylindrical
coordinates are (r, θ, z), where $r^2 = x^2 + y^2$ and $\tan \theta = y/x$. Conversely, $x = r \cos \theta$ and
$y = r \sin \theta$. Thus, (r, θ) are "polar" coordinates corresponding to (x, y).

(B) When $k \neq 0$, this is the equation of a right circular cylinder with radius $|k|$ and
the z-axis as axis of symmetry. When $k = 0$, the graph is just the z-axis.

(C) This is a plane containing the z-axis and making an angle of k radians with the
xz-plane.

(D) $r = \sqrt{2^2 + (2\sqrt{3})^2} = \sqrt{16} = 4$, $\tan \theta = 2\sqrt{3}/2 = \sqrt{3}$, $\theta = \pi/3$. So, a set of cylindrical coordinates is $(4, \pi/3, 8)$. Other cylindrical coordinates for the same point are $(4,$
$(\pi/3) + 2\pi n, 8)$ for any integer n, as well as $(-4, (\pi/3) + (2n + 1)\pi, 8)$ for any integer n.

(E) $\tan \theta = \tan (\pi/3) = \sqrt{3}$. So $y/x = \sqrt{3}$, $y = \sqrt{3}x$, which is a plane through the z-axis.

(F) $r^2 = 2r \sin \theta$, $x^2 + y^2 = 2y$, $x^2 + (y-1)^2 = 1$. This is a right circular cylinder of radius 1 and having as axes of symmetry the lines $x = 0$, $y = 1$.

420. (A) See Figure A41.7. $x = r \cos \theta = \rho \sin \phi \cos \theta$, $y = r \sin \theta = \rho \sin \phi \sin \theta$, $z = \rho \cos \phi$. $\rho^2 = r^2 + z^2 = x^2 + y^2 + z^2$.

$$\tan \phi = \frac{r}{z} = \frac{\sqrt{x^2 + y^2}}{z} \qquad \tan \theta = \frac{y}{x} \qquad r = \rho \sin \phi$$

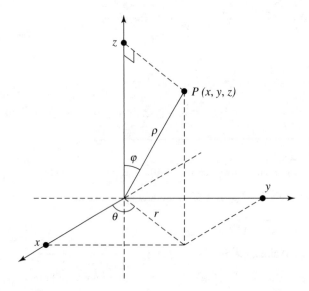

Figure A41.7

(B) $\rho = k$ represents the sphere with center at the origin and radius k.

(C) $\phi = k$ represents a one-napped cone with vertex at the origin whose generating lines make a fixed angle of k radians with the positive z-axis.

(D) $\rho^2 = 1^2 + 1^2 + (\sqrt{6})^2 = 8$. Hence, $\rho = 2\sqrt{2}$. $\tan \phi = \sqrt{1^2 + 1^2}/\sqrt{6} = \sqrt{2}/\sqrt{6} = 1/\sqrt{3}$. Therefore, $\phi = \pi/6$. $\tan \theta = \frac{1}{1} = 1$. Hence, $\theta = \pi/4$. So, the spherical coordinates are $(2\sqrt{2}, \pi/6, \pi/4)$.

(E) $x = 4 \sin \dfrac{2\pi}{3} \cos \dfrac{\pi}{3} = 4 \left(\dfrac{\sqrt{3}}{2} \right) \left(\dfrac{1}{2} \right) = \sqrt{3}. \quad y = 4 \sin \dfrac{2\pi}{3} \sin \dfrac{\pi}{3} = 4 \left(\dfrac{\sqrt{3}}{2} \right) \left(\dfrac{\sqrt{3}}{2} \right) = 3.$

$z = 4 \cos \dfrac{2\pi}{3} = 4 \left(\dfrac{1}{2} \right) = 2.$

421. $x^2 + y^2 + z^2 = \rho^2$ and $z = \rho \cos \phi$. Thus, we get $\rho^2 + 6\rho \cos \phi = 0$. Then $\rho = 0$ or $\rho + 6 \cos \phi = 0$. Since the origin is the only solution of $\rho = 0$, and the origin also lies on $\rho + 6 \cos \phi = 0$, $\rho + 6 \cos \phi = 0$ is the desired equation.

422. Since $r = \rho \sin \phi = 3$, this is the right circular cylinder with radius 3 and the z-axis as axis of symmetry.

Chapter 42: Partial Derivatives

423. First, consider y constant. Then, differentiating with respect to x, we obtain $f_x = 12x^2 - 6y^2x + 2$. If we keep x fixed and differentiate with respect to y, we get $f_y = -6x^2y + 3$.

424. Let $f(x, y) = \begin{cases} \dfrac{xy}{x^2 + y^2} & \text{if} (x, y) \neq (0, 0) \\ 0 & \text{if} (x, y) = (0, 0) \end{cases}$.

$$f_x(0,0) = \lim_{\Delta x \to 0} \frac{f(\Delta x, 0) - f(0, 0)}{\Delta x} = \lim_{\Delta x \to 0} \frac{0 - 0}{\Delta x} = 0.$$

$$f_y(0, 0) = \lim_{\Delta y \to 0} \frac{f(0, \Delta y) - f(0,0)}{\Delta y} = \lim_{\Delta y \to 0} \frac{0 - 0}{\Delta y} = 0.$$

By Question 418(D), $f(x, y)$ is discontinuous at the origin.

425. (A) If (x_0, y_0) is inside an open disk throughout which f_{xy} and f_{yx} exist, and if f_{xy} and f_{yx} are continuous at (x_0, y_0), then $f_{xy}(x_0, y_0) = f_{yx}(x_0, y_0)$. Similar conditions ensure equality for $n \geq 3$ partial differentiations, regardless of the order in which the derivatives are taken.

(B) $f_x = 6xy - 2y, f_{xy} = 6x - 2. f_y = 3x^2 - 2x + 10y, f_{yx} = 6x - 2.$

426. (A) $f_x = e^x \cos y, f_{xy} = -e^x \sin y, f_y = -e^x \sin y, f_{yx} = -e^x \sin y.$

(B) $f_x = 6x - 2y, f_{xy} = -2, f_y = -2x + 15y^2, \ f_{yx} = -2.$

(C) $f_x = 2x \cos y + y^2 \cos x, f_{xy} = -2x \sin y + 2y \cos x, f_y = -x^2 \sin y + 2y \sin x, f_{yx} = -2x \sin y + 2y \cos x.$

427. (A) $f_x = 12x^3 - 6x^2y^2, f_y = -4x^3y + 7, f_{xx} = 36x^2 - 12xy^2, f_{yy} = -4x^3,$
$f_{xy} = -12x^2y, f_{yx} = -12x^2y.$

(B) $f_x = ye^{xy}y^2 + \dfrac{1}{y} = e^{xy}y^3 + \dfrac{1}{y}$, $f_y = 2e^{xy}y + xe^{xy}y^2 - \dfrac{x}{y^2} = e^{xy}(2y+xy^2) - \dfrac{x}{y^2}$,

$f_{xx} = e^{xy}y^3(y) = e^{xy}y^4$, $f_{yy} = e^{xy}(2+2xy) + xe^{xy}(2y+xy^2) + \dfrac{2x}{y^3}$

$\qquad = e^{xy}(2+4xy+x^2y^2) + \dfrac{2x}{y^3}$,

$f_{xy} = 3e^{xy}y^2 + xe^{xy}y^3 - \dfrac{1}{y^2}$, $f_{yx} = e^{xy}(y^2) + ye^{xy}(2y+xy^2) - \dfrac{1}{y^2}$

$\qquad = 3e^{xy}y^2 + xe^{xy}y^3 - \dfrac{1}{y^2}$.

(C) $f_x = 2xy - 2z$, $f_y = x^2 + 2yz$, $f_z = y^2 - 2x$, $f_{xy} = 2x$, $f_{yx} = 2x$,

$\qquad f_{xz} = -2$, $f_{zx} = -2$, $f_{yz} = 2y$, $f_{zy} = 2y$.

428. Let $f(x,y) = \begin{cases} xy\left(\dfrac{x^2 - y^2}{x^2 + y^2}\right) & \text{if}(x,y) \neq (0,0) \\ 0 & \text{if}(x,y) = (0,0) \end{cases}$.

Then $f_x(0,y) = \lim\limits_{\Delta x \to 0} \dfrac{f(\Delta x, y) - f(0,y)}{\Delta x} = \lim\limits_{\Delta x \to 0} y\dfrac{(\Delta x)^2 - y^2}{(\Delta x)^2 + y^2} = -y$

and $f_y(x,0) = \lim\limits_{\Delta y \to 0} \dfrac{f(x,\Delta y) - f(x,0)}{\Delta y} = \lim\limits_{\Delta y \to 0} x\dfrac{x^2 - (\Delta y)^2}{x^2 + (\Delta y)^2} = x$.

Consequently, $f_{xy}(0,0) = \lim\limits_{\Delta y \to 0} \dfrac{f_x(0,\Delta y) - f_x(0,0)}{\Delta y} = \lim\limits_{\Delta y \to 0} \dfrac{-\Delta y - 0}{\Delta y} = -1$

and $f_{xy}(0,0) = \lim\limits_{\Delta x \to 0} \dfrac{f_y(\Delta x, 0) - f_y(0,0)}{\Delta x} = \lim\limits_{\Delta x \to 0} \dfrac{\Delta x - 0}{\Delta x} = 1$.

Thus, $f_{xy}(0,0) \neq f_{yx}(0,0)$. (The conditions of Question 425(A) are not met by this function.)

429. $\dfrac{\partial z}{\partial x} = ae^{ax}\sin ay$, $\dfrac{\partial^2 z}{\partial x^2} = a^2 e^{ax}\sin ay$, $\dfrac{\partial z}{\partial y} = ae^{ax}\cos ay$, $\dfrac{\partial^2 z}{\partial y^2} = -a^2 e^{ax}\sin ay$.

430. $\partial z/\partial x = e^{-t}\cos x$, $\partial^2 z/\partial x^2 = -e^{-t}\sin x$, $\partial z/\partial y = -e^{-t}\sin y$, $\partial^2 z/\partial y^2 = -e^{-t}\cos y$,

$\partial z/\partial t = -e^{-t}(\sin x + \cos y) = -e^{-t}\sin x - e^{-t}\cos y = \partial^2 z/\partial x^2 + \partial^2 z/\partial y^2$.

431. $f_x = g'(x)h(y)$, $f_{xy} = g'(x)h'(y)$. $f_y = g(x)h'(y)$, $f_{yx} = g'(x)h'(y)$.

432. **(A)** $f_x = 3(x+at)^2$, $f_{xx} = 6(x+at)$, $f_t = 3(x+at)^2(a) = 3a(x+at)^2$,

$f_{tt} = 6a(x+at)(a) = 6a^2(x+at) = a^2 f_{xx}$.

(B) $f_x = \cos(x+at)$, $f_{xx} = -\sin(x+at)$, $f_t = a\cos(x+at)$,

$f_{tt} = -a^2\sin(x+at) = a^2 f_{xx}$.

(C) $f_x = e^{x-at}$, $f_{xx} = e^{x-at}$, $f_t = -ae^{x-at}$, $f_{tt} = a^2 e^{x-at} = a^2 f_{xx}$.

433. **(A)** $\dfrac{du}{dt} = f_{x_1}\dfrac{dx_1}{dt} + \cdots + f_{x_n}\dfrac{dx_n}{dt}$.

(B) By the formula of Question 433(A),

$$\frac{du}{dt} = \frac{\partial u}{\partial x}\frac{dx}{dt} + \frac{\partial u}{\partial y}\frac{dy}{dt} + \frac{\partial u}{\partial z}\frac{dz}{dt} = 2x\cos t - 4ye^t + 3z^2(3)$$

$$= 2\sin t\cos t - 4e^t(e^t) + 9(3t)^2 = \sin 2t - 4e^{2t} + 81t^2.$$

(C) $\dfrac{\partial w}{\partial u} = \dfrac{\partial \Phi}{\partial x}\dfrac{\partial x}{\partial u} + \dfrac{\partial \Phi}{\partial y}\dfrac{\partial y}{\partial u} + \dfrac{\partial \Phi}{\partial z}\dfrac{\partial z}{\partial u}$; $\quad \dfrac{\partial w}{\partial v} = \dfrac{\partial \Phi}{\partial x}\dfrac{\partial x}{\partial v} + \dfrac{\partial \Phi}{\partial y}\dfrac{\partial y}{\partial v} + \dfrac{\partial \Phi}{\partial z}\dfrac{\partial z}{\partial v}$.

434. $V = lwh$. $\dfrac{dV}{dt} = \dfrac{\partial V}{\partial l}\dfrac{dl}{dt} + \dfrac{\partial V}{\partial w}\dfrac{dw}{dt} + \dfrac{\partial V}{\partial h}\dfrac{dh}{dt} = wh(2) + lh(-1) + lw(2)$

$= 5(3)(2) + 10(3)(-1) + 10(5)(2) = 30 - 30 + 100 = 100\text{ft}^3/\text{s}.$

435. **(A)** Differentiate $f(tx, ty) = t^n f(x, y)$ with respect to t. By the chain rule,

$f_x(tx, ty)\dfrac{\partial(tx)}{\partial t} + f_y(tx, ty)\dfrac{\partial(ty)}{\partial t} = nt^{n-1}f(x, y)$. Hence, $f_x(tx, ty)(x) + f_y(tx, ty)(y) =$

$nt^{n-1}f(x, y)$. Let $t = 1$. Then $xf_x(x, y) + yf_y(x, y) = nf(x, y)$. (A similar result holds for functions f of more than two variables.)

(B) $f(x, y)$ is homogeneous of degree 3, since $f(tx, ty) = (tx)(ty)^2 + (tx)^2(ty) - (ty)^3 = t^3(xy^2 + x^2y - y^3) = t^3 f(x, y)$. So we must show that $xf_x + yf_y = 3f$. $f_x = y^2 + 2xy$, $f_y = 2xy + x^2 - 3y^2$. Hence, $xf_x + yf_y = x(y^2 + 2xy) + y(2xy + x^2 - 3y^2) = xy^2 + 2x^2y + 2xy^2 + x^2y - 3y^3 = 3(xy^2 + x^2y - y^3) = 3f(x, y)$.

(C) $f(x, y)$ is homogeneous of degree 1, since $f(tx, ty) = \sqrt{(tx)^2 + (ty)^2} = t\sqrt{x^2 + y^2} = tf(x, y)$ for $t > 0$. We must check that $xf_x + yf_y = \sqrt{x^2 + y^2}$. But $f_x = x/\sqrt{x^2 + y^2}$ and $f_y = y/\sqrt{x^2 + y^2}$. Thus, $xf_x + yf_y = (x^2/\sqrt{x^2 + y^2}) + (y^2/\sqrt{x^2 + y^2}) = (x^2 + y^2)/\sqrt{x^2 + y^2} = \sqrt{x^2 + y^2}$.

(D) f is clearly homogeneous of degree 3. Now $f_x = 3z^2 - 2yz$, $f_y = -2xz + 2zy$, $f_z = 6xz - 2xy + y^2$. Thus,

$$x f_x + y f_y + z f_z = x(3z^2 - 2yz) + y(-2xz + 2zy) + z(6xz - 2xy + y^2)$$
$$= 3xz^2 - 2xyz - 2xyz + 2y^2z + 6xz^2 - 2xyz + y^2z = 9xz^2 - 6xyz + 3y^2z$$
$$= 3f(x, y, z).$$

436. By the chain rule, $\dfrac{dz}{dt} = \dfrac{\partial z}{\partial x}\dfrac{dx}{dt} + \dfrac{\partial z}{\partial y}\dfrac{dy}{dt} = (4x - 3y)\cos t + (-3x + 14y)(-\sin t) =$

$(4 \sin t - 3 \cos t) \cos t - (14 \cos t - 3\sin t) \sin t = 3\sin^2 t - 10 \sin t \cos t - 3 \cos^2 t.$

437. By the chain rule,

$$\frac{dz}{dt} = \frac{\partial z}{\partial x}\frac{dx}{dt} + \frac{\partial z}{\partial y}\frac{dy}{dt} = \frac{2x}{x^2 + y^2}(-e^{-t}) + \frac{2y}{x^2 + y^2}e^t = -\frac{2e^{-2t}}{e^{-2t} + e^{2t}} + \frac{2e^{2t}}{e^{-2t} + e^{2t}}$$

$$= 2\frac{e^{2t} - e^{-2t}}{e^{2t} + e^{-2t}} = 2 \tan h2t.$$

438. By the chain rule, $\dfrac{dz}{dx} = f_x\dfrac{dx}{dx} + f_y\dfrac{dy}{dx} = (4x^3 + 3y) + (3x - 2y)\cos x = (4x^3 + 3\sin x) +$

$(3x - 2\sin x)\cos x.$

439. First, think of z as a composite function of x. By the chain rule, $dz/dx = f_x + f_y(dy/dx) =$

$y^2 + 2xy + (2xy + x^2)(1/x) = y^2 + 2xy + 2y + x = (\ln x)^2 + 2(x + 1)\ln x + x.$ Next, think of z

as a composite function of y (by virtue of $x = e^y$). Then, $\dfrac{dz}{dy} = f_x\dfrac{dx}{dy} + f_y = (y^2 + 2xy)x +$

$(2xy + x^2) = x(y^2 + 2xy + 2y + x) = e^y(y^2 + 2ye^y + 2y + e^y).$

440. $S = 2\pi rh$. By the chain rule, $\dfrac{dS}{dt} = \dfrac{\partial S}{\partial r}\dfrac{dr}{dt} + \dfrac{\partial S}{\partial h}\dfrac{dh}{dt} = (2\pi h)(3) + (2\pi r)(2) = 2\pi(3h +$

$2r) = 2\pi(15 + 20) = 70\pi$ in^2/s.

441. From $x - 2y + 4 = 0$, $\dfrac{dx}{dt} - 2\dfrac{dy}{dt} = 0$. Since $dx/dt = 3$, $dy/dt = \dfrac{3}{2}$. From

$x^2 + 3xy + 3y^2 = z^2$, by the chain rule, $(2x + 3y)(dx/dt) + (3x + 6y)(dy/dt) = 2z(dz/dt).$
Hence,

$$(2x + 3y)(3) + (3x + 6y)\left(\frac{3}{2}\right) = 2z\frac{dz}{dt} \qquad (*)$$

When $x = 2$, the original equations become $3y^2 + 6y + 4 = z^2$ and $-2y + 6 = 0$, yielding $y = 3$, $z = \pm 7$. Thus, by (*), $39 + 36 = 2z(dz/dt)$, $dz/dt = \pm \dfrac{75}{14}$. Hence, the speed

$$\frac{ds}{dt} = \sqrt{\left(\frac{dx}{dt}\right)^2 + \left(\frac{dy}{dt}\right)^2 + \left(\frac{dz}{dt}\right)^2} = \sqrt{9 + \frac{9}{4} + 9\left(\frac{25}{14}\right)^2} = 3\sqrt{1 + \frac{1}{4} + \frac{625}{196}}$$

$$= 3\sqrt{\frac{870}{196}} = \frac{3}{14}\sqrt{870} \approx 6.3 \text{ units per second.}$$

442. (A) Let $w = \int_u^v f(x, y)\, dy$. By the chain rule, $\dfrac{dw}{dx} = \dfrac{\partial w}{\partial u}\dfrac{du}{dx} + \dfrac{\partial w}{\partial v}\dfrac{dv}{dx} + \dfrac{\partial w}{\partial x}$. Now,

$\partial w/\partial u = -f(x, u)$ and $\partial w/\partial u = f(x, v)$, and $\partial w/\partial x = \int_u^v \dfrac{\partial f}{\partial x}\, dy$, yielding Leibniz's formula.

$$\frac{d}{dx}\int_u^v f(x, y)\, dy = -f(x, u)\frac{du}{dx} + f(x, v)\frac{dv}{dx} + \int_u^v \frac{\partial f}{\partial x}\, dy.$$

(B) $du/dx = 1$, $dv/dx = 2x$, $\dfrac{\partial f}{\partial x} = 3x^2 y^2 + 2xy^3$, and $\int_u^v \dfrac{\partial f}{\partial x}\, dy = \int_x^{x^2} (3x^2 y^2 + 2xy^3)\, dy =$

$\left(x^2 y^3 + \dfrac{1}{2}xy^4\right)\Big]_x^{x^2} = \left(x^8 + \dfrac{1}{2}x^9\right) - \left(x^5 + \dfrac{1}{2}x^5\right)$. So $-f(x, u)\dfrac{du}{dx} + f(x, v)\dfrac{dv}{dx} + \int_u^v \dfrac{\partial f}{\partial x}\, dy =$

$-(x^3 u^2 + x^2 u^3) + (x^3 v^2 + x^2 v^3)2x + x^8 + \dfrac{1}{2}x^9 - x^5 - \dfrac{1}{2}x^5 = -2x^5 + (x^7 + x^8)(2x) + x^8 +$

$\dfrac{1}{2}x^9 - \dfrac{3}{2}x^5 = -\dfrac{7}{2}x^5 + 3x^8 + \dfrac{5}{2}x^9$. On the other hand, $\int_u^v f(x, y)\, dy = \int_x^{x^2} (x^3 y^2 + x^2 y^3)$

$dy = \left(\dfrac{1}{3}x^3 y^3 + \dfrac{1}{4}x^2 y^4\right)\Big]_x^{x^2} = \left(\dfrac{1}{3}x^9 + \dfrac{1}{4}x^{10}\right) - \left(\dfrac{1}{3}x^6 + \dfrac{1}{4}x^6\right) = \dfrac{1}{3}x^9 + \dfrac{1}{4}x^{10} - \dfrac{7}{12}x^6$.

Hence, $\dfrac{d}{dx}\int_u^v f(x, y)\, dy = 3x^8 + \dfrac{5}{2}x^9 - \dfrac{7}{2}x^5$, verifying Leibniz's formula.

443. (A) One vector in the tangent plane at (x_0, y_0, z_0) is $(1, 0, f_x)$, and another is $(0, 1, f_y)$. Hence, a normal vector is $(0, 1, f_y) \times (1, 0, f_x) = (f_x, f_y, -1)$.

(B) Assume that $F_z(x_0, y_0, z_0) \neq 0$ so that $F(x, y, z) = 0$ implicitly defines z as a function of x and y in a neighborhood of (x_0, y_0, z_0). Then, by part(A), a normal vector to the tangent plane is $\left(\dfrac{\partial z}{\partial x}, \dfrac{\partial z}{\partial y}, -1\right)$.

Differentiate $F(x, y, z) = 0$ with respect to x: $F_x + F_y \dfrac{\partial y}{\partial x} + F_z \dfrac{\partial z}{\partial x} = 0$. Hence,

$F_x + F_z \dfrac{\partial z}{\partial x} = 0$, since $\partial y/\partial x = 0$. Therefore, $\partial z/\partial x = -F_x/F_z$. Similarly, $\partial z/\partial y = -F_y/F_z$. Hence, a normal vector is $(-F_x/F_z, -F_y/F_z, -1)$. Multiplying by the scalar $-F_z$, we obtain another normal vector (F_x, F_y, F_z).

444. By Question 443(B), a normal vector to the tangent plane will be $(2x, 2y, 2z) = (1, 1, \sqrt{2})$.

Hence, an equation for the tangent plane is $\left(x - \dfrac{1}{2}\right) + \left(y - \dfrac{1}{2}\right) + \sqrt{2}[z - (1/\sqrt{2})] = 0$, or, equivalently, $x + y + \sqrt{2}z = 2$.

445. By Question 443(B), a normal vector to the tangent plane is $(yz, xz, 3z^2 + xy) = (1, 1, 4)$. Hence, the tangent plane is $(x - 1) + (y - 1) + 4(z - 1) = 0$, or, equivalently, $x + y + 4z = 6$.

446. By Question 443(B), a normal vector to the tangent plane is $\left(\dfrac{2x_0}{a^2}, \dfrac{2y_0}{b^2}, \dfrac{2z_0}{c^2}\right)$ or, better, the vector $\left(\dfrac{x_0}{a^2}, \dfrac{y_0}{b^2}, \dfrac{z_0}{c^2}\right)$. Hence, an equation of the tangent plane is

$\dfrac{x_0}{a^2}(x - x_0) + \dfrac{y_0}{b^2}(y - y_0) + \dfrac{z_0}{c^2}(z - z_0) = 0$, or equivalently, $\dfrac{x_0}{a^2}x + \dfrac{y_0}{b^2}y + \dfrac{z_0}{c^2}z = 1$.

Chapter 43: Directional Derivatives and the Gradient; Extreme Values

447. The ray in the direction u starting at the point (x_0, y_0) is $(x_0, y_0) + t\mathbf{u}$ $(t \geq 0)$. The (directional) derivative, at (x_0, y_0), of the function f in the direction $\mathbf{u}$ is the rate of

change, at (x_0, y_0), of f along that ray—that is, $\dfrac{d}{dt} f((x_0, y_0) + t\mathbf{u})$, evaluated at $t = 0$. It is

equal to $\nabla f \cdot \mathbf{u}$, the scalar projection of the gradient on $\mathbf{u}$. (Similar definitions and results apply for functions f of three or more variables.)

448. The derivative in the direction of a unit vector u is $\nabla f \cdot \mathbf{u} = |\nabla f| \cos \theta$, where θ is the angle between ∇f and $\mathbf{u}$. Since $\cos \theta$ takes on its maximum value 1 when $\theta = 0$, the maximum value of $\nabla f \cdot \mathbf{u}$ is obtained when $\mathbf{u}$ is the unit vector in the direction of ∇f. That maximum value is $|\nabla f|$. Similarly, since $\cos \theta$ takes on its minimum value -1 when $\theta = \pi$, the minimum value of $\nabla f \cdot \mathbf{u}$ is attained when $\mathbf{u}$ has the direction of $-\nabla f$. That minimum value is $-|\nabla f|$.

449. $\mathbf{u} = (\cos 45°, \sin 45°) = (\sqrt{2}/2, \sqrt{2}/2)$. $\nabla f = (4x - 3y, -3x + 10y) = (-2, 17)$ at $(1, 2)$. Hence, the derivative is $\nabla f \cdot \mathbf{u} = (-2, 17) \cdot (\sqrt{2}/2, \sqrt{2}/2) = \dfrac{\sqrt{2}}{2}(15) = \dfrac{15\sqrt{2}}{2}$.

450. The unit vector in the given direction is $\mathbf{u} = (\cos 30°, \sin 30°) = \left(\sqrt{3}/2, \dfrac{1}{2}\right)$. $\nabla f =$ $(\ln y, x/y) = (\ln 2, \dfrac{1}{2})$. So, the derivative is $\nabla f \cdot \mathbf{u} = (\ln 2, \dfrac{1}{2}) \cdot \dfrac{1}{2}(\sqrt{3}, 1) = \dfrac{1}{2}\left(\sqrt{3}\ln 2 + \dfrac{1}{2}\right)$.

451. $\nabla f = (6x, -10y, 4z) = (2, -2, 2) = 2(1, -1, 1)$. The direction in which f decreases the most rapidly is that of $-\nabla f$; thus, you should move in the direction of the vector $(-1, 1, -1)$.

452. Let $F(x_0, y_0, z_0) = k$. Then the level surface through P is $F(x, y, z) = k$. By Question 443(B), a normal vector to that surface is (F_x, F_y, F_z), which is just ∇F.

453. The appropriate direction is that of $\nabla f = (f_x, f_y, f_z) = (2(3 - x + y)(-1) + 3(4x - y + z + 2)^2(4), 2(3 - x + y) + 3(4x - y + z + 2)^2(-1), 3(4x - y + z + 2)^2) = (42, -6, 12) = 6(7, -1, 2)$.

454. We wish to show that both partial derivatives of z vanish at (x_0, y_0). The plane $y = y_0$ intersects the surface $z = f(x, y)$ in a curve $z = f(x, y_0)$ that has a relative maximum (or minimum) at $x = x_0$. Hence, $\partial z/\partial x = 0$ at (x_0, y_0). Similarly, the plane $x = x_0$ intersects the surface $z = f(x, y)$ in a curve $z = f(x_0, y)$ that has a relative maximum (or minimum) at $y = y_0$. Hence, the derivative $\partial z/\partial y = 0$ at (x_0, y_0). Similar results hold for functions f of more than two variables.

455. (A) Case 1. Assume $\Delta > 0$ at (x_0, y_0). **(i)** If $f_{xx} + f_{yy} < 0$ at (x_0, y_0), then f has a relative maximum at (x_0, y_0). **(ii)** If $f_{xx} + f_{yy} > 0$ at (x_0, y_0), then f has a relative minimum at (x_0, y_0). **Case 2.** If $\Delta < 0$, f has neither a relative maximum nor a relative minimum at (x_0, y_0). **Case 3.** If $\Delta = 0$, no conclusions can be drawn.

      (B) Each of the functions $f_1(x, y) = x^4 + y^4$, $f_2(x, y) = -(x^4 + y^4)$, and $f_3(x, y) = x^3 - y^3$ vanishes at $(0, 0)$ together with its first and second partials; hence $\Delta(0, 0) = 0$ for each function. But at $(0, 0)$, f_1 has a relative minimum, f_2 has a relative maximum, and f_3 has neither ($f_3(x, 0) = x^3$ takes on both positive and negative values in any neighborhood of the origin).

456. $f_x = 2 - 2x$, $f_y = 4 - 2y$. Setting $f_x = 0$, $f_y = 0$, we have $x = 1$, $y = 2$. Thus, $(1, 2)$ is the only critical point. $f_{xy} = 0$, $f_{xx} = -2$, and $f_{yy} = -2$. So $\Delta = f_{xx}f_{yy} - (f_{xy})^2 = 4 > 0$. Since $f_{xx} + f_{yy} = -4 < 0$, there is a relative maximum at $(1, 2)$, by Question 455(A).

457. We must minimize $S = (q - 2)^2 + (p + q - 3)^2 + (2p + q - 5)^2$. $S_q = 2(q - 2) + 2(p + q - 3) + 2(2p + q - 5) = 6q + 6p - 20$. $S_p = 2(p + q - 3) + 2(2p + q - 5)(2) = 10p + 6q - 26$. Let $S_q = 0$, $S_p = 0$. Then $3q + 3p - 10 = 0$, $5p + 3q - 13 = 0$. So $2p - 3 = 0$, $p = \dfrac{3}{2}$, $q = \dfrac{11}{6}$.

458. $f_x = 8x + 2y$, $f_y = 2x - 6y$. Set $f_x = f_y = 0$. Then $4x + y = 0$, $x - 3y = 0$. Solving, we get $x = y = 0$. Note that $f(0, 0) = 0$. Let us look at the boundary of the square (Figure A43.1). (1) On the segment L_1, $x = 0$, $0 \le y \le 1$. Then $f(0, y) = -3y^2$. The maximum is 0, and the minimum is -3 at $(0, 1)$. (2) On the segment L_2, $x = 1$, $0 \le y \le 1$. $f(1, y) = 4 + 2y - 3y^2$. $\dfrac{df}{dy}(1, y) = 2 - 6y$. Thus, $\dfrac{1}{3}$ is a critical number. We must evaluate $f(1, y)$ for $y = 0$,

$y = \dfrac{1}{3}$, and $y = 1$. $f(1, 0) = 4, f(1, \dfrac{1}{3}) = \dfrac{13}{3}, f(1, 1) = 3$. (3) On the segment L_3, $y = 0$, $0 \le$

$x \le 1$. $f(x, 0) = 4x^2$. Hence, the maximum is 4 at $(1, 0)$, and the minimum is 0 at $(0, 0)$.

(4) On the line segment L_4, $y = 1$, $0 \le x \le 1$. Then $f(x, 1) = 4x^2 + 2x - 3$. $\dfrac{df}{dx}(x, 1) = 8x +$

2. The critical number is $-\dfrac{1}{4}$, which does not lie in the interval $0 \le x \le 1$. Thus, we need

only look at $f(x, 1)$ when $x = 0$ and $x = 1$. $f(0, 1) = -3$ and $f(1, 1) = 3$. Therefore, the

absolute maximum is $\dfrac{13}{3}$ at $(1, \dfrac{1}{3})$, and the absolute minimum is -3 at $(0, 1)$.

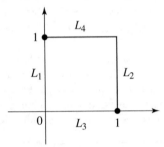

Figure A43.1

459. By the periodicity of the sine function, we may restrict attention to the square S: $-\pi \le x \le \pi, -\pi \le y \le \pi$. Since f is continuous, f will have an absolute maximum and minimum on S (and, therefore, for all x and y). These extrema will occur either on the boundary or in the interior (where they will show up as critical points). $f_x = \cos x + \cos (x + y)$, $f_y = \cos y + \cos (x + y)$. Let $f_x = f_y = 0$. Then $\cos x = -\cos (x + y) = \cos y$. Hence, either $x = y$ or $x = -y$. **Case 1:** $x = y$. Then $\cos x = -\cos (x + y) = -\cos 2x = 1 - 2 \cos^2 x$. So $2 \cos^2 x + \cos x - 1 = 0$, $(2 \cos x - 1)(\cos x + 1) = 0$, $\cos x = \dfrac{1}{2}$ or $\cos x = -1$, $x = \pm \pi/3$ or

$x = \pm\pi$. So the critical points are $(\pi/3, \pi/3)$, $(-\pi/3, -\pi/3)$, (π, π), $(-\pi, -\pi)$. The latter two are on the boundary and need not be considered separately. Note that

$$f\left(\dfrac{\pi}{3}, \dfrac{\pi}{3}\right) = \dfrac{\sqrt{3}}{2} + \dfrac{\sqrt{3}}{2} + \dfrac{\sqrt{3}}{2} = \dfrac{3\sqrt{3}}{2} \text{ and } f\left(\dfrac{-\pi}{3}, -\dfrac{\pi}{3}\right) = -\dfrac{\sqrt{3}}{2} - \dfrac{\sqrt{3}}{2} - \dfrac{\sqrt{3}}{2} = \dfrac{-3\sqrt{3}}{2}.$$

Case 2: $x = -y$. Then $\cos x = -\cos (x + y) = -\cos 0 = -1$. Hence, $x = \pm\pi$. This yields the critical numbers $(\pi, -\pi)$ and $(-\pi, \pi)$. Since these are on the boundary, they need not be treated separately. Now consider the boundary of S (Figure A43.2). (1) L_1: $f(\pi, y) = \sin \pi + \sin y + \sin (\pi + y) = \sin y - \sin y = 0$. (2) L_2: $f(-\pi, y) = f(\pi, y) = 0$. (3) L_3: $f(x, \pi) = \sin x + \sin \pi + \sin (x + \pi) = \sin x - \sin x = 0$. (4) L_4: $f(x, -\pi) = f(x, \pi) = 0$. Thus, f is 0 on the boundary. Hence, the absolute maximum is $3\sqrt{3}/2$ and the absolute minimum is $-3\sqrt{3}/2$.

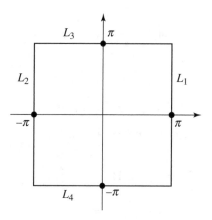

Figure A43.2

460. We must maximize $(x-2)^2 + (y-1)^2 + (z-2)^2$ subject to the constraint $g(x, y, z) = x^2 + y^2 + z^2 - 1 = 0$. $\nabla f = (2(x-2), 2(y-1), 2(z-2))$. $\nabla g = (2x, 2y, 2z)$. Let $\nabla f = \lambda \nabla g$. Then $(2(x-2), 2(y-1), 2(z-2)) = \lambda(2x, 2y, 2z)$, or $2(x-2) = 2\lambda x$, $2(y-1) = 2\lambda y$, $2(z-2) = 2\lambda z$. These are equivalent to $x(1-\lambda) = 2$, $y(1-\lambda) = 1$, $z(1-\lambda) = 2$. Hence, $1 - \lambda \neq 0$. Substitute $x = 2/(1-\lambda)$, $y = 1/(1-\lambda)$, $z = 2/(1-\lambda)$ in the constraint equation:
$$\frac{4}{(1-\lambda)^2} + \frac{1}{(1-\lambda)^2} + \frac{4}{(1-\lambda)^2} = 1, (1-\lambda)^2 = 9, 1-\lambda = \pm 3, \lambda = -2 \text{ or } \lambda = 4.$$

Case 1: $\lambda = -2$. Then $1 - \lambda = 3$, $x = \dfrac{2}{3}$, $y = \dfrac{1}{3}$, $z = \dfrac{2}{3}$, and $\sqrt{(x-2)^2 + (y-1)^2 + (z-2)^2} =$
$$\sqrt{\frac{16}{9} + \frac{4}{9} + \frac{16}{9}} = \sqrt{\frac{36}{9}} = 2.$$

Case 2: $\lambda = 4$. Then $1 - \lambda = -3$, $x = -\dfrac{2}{3}$, $y = -\dfrac{1}{3}$, $z = -\dfrac{2}{3}$, and $\sqrt{(x-2)^2 + (y-1)^2 + (z-2)^2} =$
$$\sqrt{\frac{64}{9} + \frac{16}{9} + \frac{64}{9}} = \sqrt{\frac{144}{9}} = 4. \text{ So the point on the sphere furthest from } (2, 1, 2) \text{ is}$$
$$\left(-\frac{2}{3}, -\frac{1}{3}, -\frac{2}{3}\right).$$

461. We must minimize $f(x, y, z) = x^2 + (y-1)^2 + (z-3)^2$ subject to the constraint $g(x, y, z) = y^2 + z^2 - x^2 = 0$. $\nabla f = (2x, 2(y-1), 2(z-3))$, $\nabla g = (-2x, 2y, 2z)$. Let $\nabla f = \lambda \nabla g$. Then $(2x, 2(y-1), 2(z-3)) = \lambda(-2x, 2y, 2z)$, or $2x = -2\lambda x$, $2(y-1) = 2\lambda y$, $2(z-3) = 2\lambda z$. These are equivalent to $x(\lambda+1) = 0$, $y(1-\lambda) = 1$, $z(1-\lambda) = 3$. Hence, $1 - \lambda \neq 0$. Substitute $y = 1/(1-\lambda)$, $z = 3/(1-\lambda)$ in the constraint equation:
$$x^2 = \frac{1}{(1-\lambda)^2} + \frac{9}{(1-\lambda)^2} = \frac{10}{(1-\lambda)^2}. \text{ Hence, } x \neq 0. \text{ Therefore, } x(\lambda+1) = 0 \text{ implies } \lambda+1 = 0,$$
$$\lambda = -1. \text{ Then } y = 1(1-\lambda) = \frac{1}{2}, z = 3/(1-\lambda) = \frac{3}{2}, \text{ and } x^2 = 10/(1-\lambda)^2 = \frac{10}{4} = \frac{5}{2},$$

$x = \pm\sqrt{\dfrac{5}{2}}$. Thus, $f\left(\sqrt{\dfrac{5}{2}}, \dfrac{1}{2}, \dfrac{3}{2}\right) = \dfrac{5}{2} + \dfrac{1}{4} + \dfrac{9}{4} = 5$, and $f\left(-\sqrt{\dfrac{5}{2}}, \dfrac{1}{2}, \dfrac{3}{2}\right) = 5$. Hence, the

required points are $\left(\pm\sqrt{\dfrac{5}{2}}, \dfrac{1}{2}, \dfrac{3}{2}\right)$.

Chapter 44: Multiple Integrals and Their Applications

462. (A) $\displaystyle\int_0^{\cos\theta} \rho^2 \sin\theta\, d\rho = \dfrac{1}{3}\rho^3 \sin\theta\big]_0^{\cos\theta} = \dfrac{1}{3}\cos^3\theta \sin\theta$. Hence, $I = \displaystyle\int_0^{\pi/2} \dfrac{1}{3}\cos^3\theta$

$\sin\theta\, d\theta = -\dfrac{1}{12}\cos^4\theta\big]_0^{\pi/2} = -\dfrac{1}{12}[\cos^4(\pi/2) - \cos^4 0] = -\dfrac{1}{12}(0-1) = \dfrac{1}{12}$.

(B) $\displaystyle\int e^{x^2}\, dx$ cannot be evaluated in terms of standard functions. Therefore, we change the

order of integration, using Figure A44.1. $I = \displaystyle\int_0^1\int_0^x e^{x^2}\, dy\, dx = \int_0^1 xe^{x^2}\, dx = \dfrac{1}{2}e^{x^2}\big]_0^1 = \dfrac{1}{2}(e-1)$.

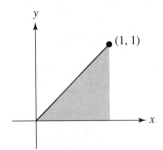

Figure A44.1

463. $\displaystyle\int_{y^4}^{y^2}\sqrt{y/x}\, dx = 2\sqrt{y}\sqrt{x}\big]_{y^4}^{y^2} = 2\sqrt{y}(y-y^2) = 2(y^{3/2} - y^{5/2})$. Therefore, $I = 2\displaystyle\int_0^1 (y^{3/2} -

y^{5/2})dy = 2\left(\dfrac{2}{5}y^{5/2} - \dfrac{2}{7}y^{7/2}\right)\Big]_0^1 = 2\left(\dfrac{2}{5} - \dfrac{2}{7}\right) = \dfrac{8}{35}$.

464. (A) The curves $y = x$ and $y = x^2$ intersect at $(0, 0)$ and $(1, 1)$, and, for $0 < x < 1$,

$y = x$ is above $y = x^2$ (see Figure A44.2). $I = \displaystyle\int_0^1\int_{x^2}^x x\, dy\, dx = \int_0^1 xy\big]_{x^2}^x dx = \int_0^1 (x^2 - x^3)\, dx =

\left(\dfrac{1}{3}x^3 - \dfrac{1}{4}x^4\right)\Big]_0^1 = \dfrac{1}{3} - \dfrac{1}{4} = \dfrac{1}{12}$.

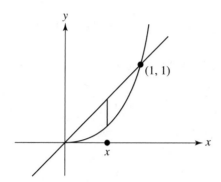

Figure A44.2

(B) The lines $y = 2x$ and $y = 5x$ intersect at the origin. For $0 < x \le 1$, the region runs from $y = 2x$ up to $y = 5x$ (Figure A44.3). Hence, $I = \int_0^1 \int_{2x}^{5x} y^2\, dy\, dx = \int_0^1 \frac{1}{3} y^3 \rceil_{2x}^{5x}\, dx = \frac{1}{3} \int_0^1 (125\, x^3 - 8x^3)\, dx = \frac{1}{3} \int_0^1 117 x^3\, dx = \frac{39}{4} x^4 \rceil_0^1 = \frac{39}{4}$.

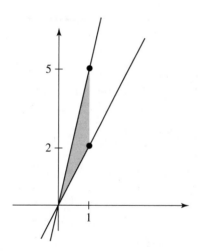

Figure A44.3

465. $V = \iint_{\mathcal{R}} (3x + 4y)\, dA = \int_0^3 \int_1^2 (3x + 4y)\, dx\, dy = \int_0^3 \left(\frac{3}{2} x^2 + 4yx \right) \Big]_1^2 dy$

$= \int_0^3 \left[(6 + 8y) - \left(\frac{3}{2} + 4y \right) \right] dy$

$= \int_0^3 \left(\frac{9}{2} + 4y \right) dy = \left(\frac{9}{2} y + 2y^2 \right) \Big]_0^3 = \frac{27}{2} + 18 = \frac{63}{2}$.

466. $V = \iint\limits_{\mathcal{R}} y^2 \, dA = \int_0^2 \int_0^4 y^2 \, dy \, dx = \int_0^2 \frac{1}{3} y^3]_0^4 \, dx = \int_0^2 \frac{64}{3} \, dx = \frac{64}{3} \cdot 2 = \frac{128}{3}.$

467. See Figure A44.4. For polar coordinates, recall that the factor r is introduced into the integrand via $dA = r \, dr \, d\theta$. By symmetry, we can restrict the integration to the first quadrant and double the result. $I = 2\int_0^{\pi/2} \int_1^{1+\cos\theta} (\sin\theta) \, r \, dr \, d\theta = 2\int_0^{\pi/2} \frac{1}{2}(\sin\theta) r^2]_1^{1+\cos\theta} \, d\theta =$
$\int_0^{\pi/2} [(1+\cos\theta)^2 \sin\theta - \sin\theta] \, d\theta = [-(1+\cos\theta)^3/3 + \cos\theta]_0^{\pi/2} = -\frac{1}{3} - \left(-\frac{8}{3} + 1\right) = \frac{4}{3}.$

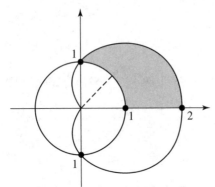

Figure A44.4

468. In cylindrical coordinates, the sphere with center $(0, 0, 0)$ is $r^2 + z^2 = a^2$. Calculate the volume in the first octant and multiply it by 8. The base is the quarter disk $0 \le r \le a, \, 0 \le \theta \le \pi/2. \, V = 8\int_0^{\pi/2} \int_0^a \sqrt{a^2 - r^2} \, r \, dr \, d\theta = 8\int_0^{\pi/2} -\frac{1}{2} \cdot \frac{2}{3} (a^2 - r^2)^{3/2}]_0^a \, d\theta =$
$8\int_0^{\pi/2} \frac{1}{3} a^3 \, d\theta = (8a^3/3)\int_0^{\pi/2} d\theta = (8a^3/3)(\pi/2) = \frac{4}{3}\pi a^3$, the standard formula.

469. Let $c = \int_0^\infty e^{-x^2} \, dx$. Then $c = \int_0^\infty e^{-y^2} \, dy$. Hence, $c^2 = \int_0^\infty e^{-x^2} \, dx \cdot \int_0^\infty e^{-y^2} \, dy = \int_0^\infty e^{-y^2}$
$\left(\int_0^\infty e^{-x^2} \, dx\right) \, dy = \int_0^\infty \int_0^\infty e^{-x^2} e^{-y^2} \, dx \, dy = \int_0^{\pi/2} \int_0^\infty e^{-(x^2+y^2)} \, dx \, dy.$ The region of integration is the entire first quadrant. Change to polar coordinates. $c^2 = \int_0^\infty \int_0^{\pi/2} e^{-r^2} r \, d\theta \, dr =$
$\int_0^\infty e^{-r^2} \cdot r\theta]_0^{\pi/2} \, dr = \frac{\pi}{2} \int_0^\infty e^{-r^2} r \, dr = (\pi/2)\left(-\frac{1}{2}\right)e^{-r^2}]_0^\infty = -(\pi/4)(\lim_{r\to+\infty} e^{-r^2} - e^0) = -(\pi/4)$
$(0 - 1) = \pi/4.$ Since $c^2 = \pi/4$, $c = \sqrt{\pi}/2$. (The rather loose reasoning in this computation can be made rigorous.)

470. In spherical coordinates a sphere of radius a is characterized by $0 \le \rho \le a$, $0 \le \theta \le 2\pi, \, 0 \le \phi \le \pi$. Recall that the volume element is given by $dV = \rho^2 \sin\phi \, d\rho \, d\theta$
$d\phi. \, V = \int_0^\pi \int_0^{2\pi} \int_0^a \rho^2 \sin\phi \, d\rho \, d\theta \, d\phi = \int_0^\pi \int_0^{2\pi} \frac{1}{3} \rho^3 \sin\phi]_0^a \, d\theta \, d\phi = \int_0^\pi \int_0^{2\pi} \frac{1}{3} a^3 \sin\phi \, d\theta d\phi =$

$$\int_0^\pi \frac{1}{3}a^3 \sin\phi \cdot \theta]_0^{2\pi} d\phi = \int_0^\pi \frac{1}{3}a^3 \sin\phi \cdot 2\pi \ d\phi = \frac{2}{3}\pi a^3 \int_0^\pi \sin\phi \ d\phi = -\frac{2}{3}\pi a^3 \cos\phi]_0^\pi = -\frac{2}{3}\pi a^3$$

$$(-1-1) = \frac{4}{3}\pi a^3.$$

471. Let the circle be $r = a$. Then $M = \iint_R r \ dA = \int_0^{2\pi}\int_0^a r \cdot r \ dr \ d\theta = \int_0^{2\pi} \frac{1}{3}r^3]_0^a \ d\theta =$

$$\int_0^{2\pi} \frac{1}{3}a^3 \ d\theta = \frac{1}{3}a^3 \cdot 2\pi = \frac{2}{3}\pi a^3.$$

472. The mass $M \int_0^a \int_0^{\sqrt{a^2-y^2}} y \ dx \ dy = \int_0^a y\sqrt{a^2 - y^2} \ dy = -\frac{1}{2}\cdot\frac{2}{3}(a^2 - y^2)^{3/2}]_0^a = -\frac{1}{3}(-a^3) =$

$\frac{1}{3}a^3$. The moment about the x-axis is

$$M_x = \iint_R y \cdot y \ dA = \int_0^{\pi/2}\int_0^a y^2 \cdot r \ dr \ d\theta = \int_0^{\pi/2}\int_0^a r^3 \sin\theta \ dr \ d\theta = \int_0^{\pi/2} \frac{1}{4}a^4 \sin^2\theta \ d\theta$$

$$= \frac{1}{4}a^4 \int_0^{\pi/2} \frac{1 - \cos 2\theta}{2} \ d\theta = \frac{1}{8}a^4 \left(\theta - \frac{1}{2}\sin 2\theta\right)\Big]_0^{\pi/2} = \frac{a^4}{8}\left(\frac{\pi}{2}\right) = \frac{\pi a^4}{16}.$$

Hence, $\bar{y} = \dfrac{M_x}{M} = \dfrac{\pi a^4/16}{a^3/3} = \dfrac{3\pi a}{16}$. The moment about the y-axis is $M_y = \int_0^a \int_0^{\sqrt{a^2-y^2}} xy$

$dx \ dy = \int_0^a \frac{1}{2}yx^2\Big]_0^{\sqrt{a^2-y^2}} dy = \frac{1}{2}\int_0^a y(a^2 - y^2) \ dy = \frac{1}{2}\left(\frac{a^2}{2}y^2 - \frac{y^4}{4}\right)\Big]_0^a = \frac{1}{2}\left(\frac{a^4}{2} - \frac{a^4}{4}\right) = \frac{a^4}{8}.$

Therefore, $\bar{x} = \dfrac{M_y}{M} = \dfrac{a^4/8}{a^3/3} = \dfrac{3a}{8}$. Hence, the center of mass is $\left(\dfrac{3a}{8}, \dfrac{3\pi a}{16}\right)$.

473. The moment of inertia with respect to the x-axis is $I_x = \int_0^8 \int_0^{6-(3/4)x} y^2 \ dy \ dx =$

$\int_0^8 \frac{1}{3}y^3\Big]_0^{6-(3/4)x} dx = \frac{9}{64}\int_0^8 (8-x)^3 \ dx = \frac{9}{64}(-1)\dfrac{(8-x)^4}{4}\Big]_0^8 = \frac{9}{64}\cdot\frac{8^4}{4} = 144.$ The moment

of inertia with respect to the y-axis is $I_y = \int_0^8 \int_0^{6-(3/4)x} x^2 \ dy \ dx = \int_0^8 x^2 \cdot \frac{3}{4}(8-x)dx =$

$\frac{3}{4}\left(\frac{8}{3}x^3 - \frac{x^4}{4}\right)\Big]_0^8 = \frac{3}{4}\cdot\frac{1}{12}(8)^4 = 256.$

474. The area $A = \int_0^6 \int_{y^{2/6}}^6 dx \ dy = \int_0^6 \left(6 - \frac{y^2}{6}\right) dy = \left(6y - \frac{1}{18}y^3\right)\Big]_0^6 = 6(6-2) = 24.$ In

Figure A44.5, the moment about the x-axis is $M_x = \int_0^6 \int_{y^{2/6}}^6 y \ dx \ dy = \int_0^6 y\left(6 - \frac{y^2}{6}\right) dy =$

$$\left(3y^2 - \frac{1}{24}y^4\right)\Bigg]_0^6 = 36\left(3-\frac{3}{2}\right) = 54. \text{ Hence, } \bar{y} = \frac{M_x}{A} = \frac{54}{24} = \frac{9}{4}. \text{ The moment about the}$$

y-axis is $M_y = \int_0^6 \int_{y^{2/6}}^6 x\,dx\,dy = \int_0^6 \frac{1}{2}x^2\Bigg]_{y^2/6}^6 dy = \frac{1}{2}\int_0^6\left(36-\frac{y^4}{36}\right)dy = \frac{1}{2}\left(36y - \frac{1}{180}y^5\right)\Bigg]_0^6 =$

$3\left(36 - \frac{36}{5}\right) - \frac{12\cdot 36}{5}$. Hence, $\bar{u} = \frac{M_y}{A} = \frac{12(36)/5}{24} = \frac{18}{5}$. So the centroid is $\left(\frac{18}{5}, \frac{9}{4}\right)$.

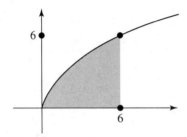

Figure A44.5

Chapter 45: Vector Functions in Space; Divergence and Curl; Line Integrals

475. (A) A tangent vector is given by the derivative $\mathbf{R}'(t) = (1, 2t, 3t^2)$. At $(1, 1, 1)$, $t = 1$. Hence, a tangent vector is $(1, 2, 3)$. Parametric equations for the tangent line are $x = 1 + u$, $y = 1 + 2u$, $z = 1 + 3u$. As a vector function, the tangent line can be represented by $(1, 1, 1) + u(1, 2, 3)$.

(B) If s is the arc length, $\frac{ds}{dt} = \sqrt{\left(\frac{dx}{dt}\right)^2 + \left(\frac{dy}{dt}\right)^2 + \left(\frac{dz}{dt}\right)^2}$ is the speed. In general, if

$\mathbf{R}(t) = (x(t), y(t), z(t))$, $\mathbf{R}'(t) = \left(\frac{dx}{dt}, \frac{dy}{dt}, \frac{dz}{dt}\right)$, and $\frac{ds}{dt} = |\mathbf{R}'(t)|$. For this particular case,

$\frac{ds}{dt} = |(1, 2t, 3t^2)| = \sqrt{1 + 4t^2 + 9t^4}$. When $t = 1$, $\frac{ds}{dt} = \sqrt{14}$.

476. A tangent vector is $\mathbf{R}'(t) = (-2\pi a \sin 2\pi t, 2\pi a \cos 2\pi t, b) = (0, 2\pi a, b)$. The tangent line is $(a, 0, b) + u(0, 2\pi a, b)$. The speed is $|\mathbf{R}'(t)| = \sqrt{4\pi^2 a^2 + b^2}$. The normal plane has the equation $(0)(x - a) + (2\pi a)(y - 0) + (b)(z - b) = 0$, or equivalently, $2\pi a y + bz = b^2$.

477. $\mathbf{R}'(t) = (-2\pi a \sin 2\pi t, 2\pi a \cos 2\pi t, b)$ has a constant z-component; thus, θ is constant.

478. The product formula $\dfrac{d}{dx}[F(t)\cdot G(t)] = F(t)\cdot G'(t) + F'(t)\cdot G(t)$ of Question 310

holds for arbitrary vector functions. So $\dfrac{d}{dt}[F(t)\cdot G(t)] = (\sin t, \cos t, t)\cdot(1, 0, 1/t) + (\cos$

$t, -\sin t, 1)\cdot(t, 1, \ln t) = \sin t + 1 + t\cos t - \sin t + \ln t = 1 + t\cos t + \ln t$.

479. $\dfrac{d}{dt}[t^2 G(t)] = t^2 G'(t) + 2t G(t)$. Hence, at $t = 3$, $\dfrac{d}{dt}[t^2 G(t)] = 9(3, -2, 5) + 6(1, 1, 2)$
$= (33, -12, 57)$.

480. $F'(t) = \lim\limits_{\Delta t \to 0}\dfrac{F(t+\Delta t) - F(t)}{\Delta t} = \lim\limits_{\Delta t \to 0}\dfrac{[G(t+\Delta t)\times H(t+\Delta t)] - [G(t)\times H(t)]}{\Delta t}$

$= \lim\limits_{\Delta t \to 0}\dfrac{\{G(t+\Delta t)\times[H(t+\Delta t) - H(t)]\} + \{[G(t+\Delta t) - G(t)]\times H(t)\}}{\Delta t}$

$= \lim\limits_{\Delta t \to 0}\left[G(t+\Delta t)\times\dfrac{H(t+\Delta t) - H(t)}{\Delta t} + \dfrac{G(t+\Delta t) - G(t)}{\Delta t}\times H(t)\right]$

$= [G(t)\times H'(t)] + [G'(t)\times H(t)]$.

481. By Question 480, $\dfrac{d}{dt}[R(t)\times R'(t)] = [R(t)\times R''(t)] + [R'(t)\times R'(t)]$. But $A\times A = 0$
for all A. Hence, the term $R'(t)\times R'(t)$ vanishes.

482. Since $G'(t)$ is perpendicular to $G(t)$, $G'(t)\cdot G(t) = 0$. Then $\dfrac{d}{dt}[|G(t)|^2] = \dfrac{d}{dt}[G(t)\cdot G(t)] =$

$G(t)\cdot G'(t) + G'(t)\cdot G(t) = 0 + 0 = 0$. Therefore $|G(t)|^2$ is constant, and hence $|G(t)|$ is
constant.

483. Let $|G(t)| = c$ for all t. Then $G(t)\cdot G(t) = |G(t)|^2 = c^2$. So $\dfrac{d}{dt}[G(t)\cdot G(t)] = 0$. Hence,
$G(t)\cdot G'(t) + G'(t)\cdot G(t) = 0$. Thus, $2G(t)\cdot G'(t) = 0$, and, therefore, $G(t)\cdot G'(t) = 0$.

484. The unit tangent vector is $T = \left[\dfrac{R'(t)}{|R'(t)|}\right] = \dfrac{(1, 2t, 3t^2)}{\sqrt{1 + 4t^2 + 9t^4}}$. The principal unit

normal vector is $N = \dfrac{T'(t)}{|T'(t)|}$. Now $T'(t) = \dfrac{d}{dt}\left[\dfrac{R'(t)}{|R'(t)|}\right] = \dfrac{1}{\sqrt{1 + 4t^2 + 9t^4}}\cdot R''(t) + \dfrac{d}{dt}$

$\left(\dfrac{1}{\sqrt{1 + 4t^2 + 9t^4}}\right)R'(t) = \dfrac{1}{\sqrt{1 + 4t^2 + 9t^4}}(0, 2, 6t) - \dfrac{4t + 18t^3}{(1 + 4t^2 + 9t^4)^{3/2}}(1, 2t, 3t^2)$. When $t = 1$,

$T'(t) = \dfrac{2(0,1,3)}{\sqrt{14}} - \dfrac{22}{14\sqrt{14}}(1, 2, 3) = \dfrac{1}{7\sqrt{14}}[14(0,1,3) - 11(1,2,3)] = \dfrac{1}{7\sqrt{14}}(-11, -8, 9)$.

Therefore, $|T'(t)| = \dfrac{1}{7\sqrt{14}}\sqrt{121 + 64 + 18} = \dfrac{\sqrt{266}}{7\sqrt{14}} = \dfrac{19}{7}$. Thus, $N = \dfrac{1}{\sqrt{266}}(-11, -8, 9)$.

485. $\mathbf{R}'(t) = (-6 \sin 2t, 6 \cos 2t, 8).\,|\mathbf{R}(t)| = \sqrt{36+64} = 10.$ Hence, $\mathbf{T} = \dfrac{1}{5}(-3 \sin 2t, 3$

$\cos 2t, 4).$ Therefore, $\mathbf{T}' = \dfrac{1}{5}(-6\cos 2t, -6\sin 2t, 0) = -\dfrac{6}{5}(\cos 2t, \sin 2t, 0),$ and $|\mathbf{T}'| =$

$\dfrac{6}{5}.$ Thus, $\mathbf{N} = \dfrac{\mathbf{T}'}{|\mathbf{T}'|} = -(\cos 2t, \sin 2t, 0)$ and $\mathbf{B} = \mathbf{T} \times \mathbf{N} = \dfrac{1}{5}(-3\sin 2t, 3\cos 2t, 4) \times$

$-(\cos 2t, \sin 2t, 0) = -\dfrac{1}{5}(-4\sin 2t, -4\cos 2t, -3) = \dfrac{1}{5}(4\sin 2t, 4\cos 2t, 3).$

486. The osculating plane is the plane determined by $\mathbf{T}$ and $\mathbf{N}$; hence, the binormal vector $\mathbf{B} = \mathbf{T} \times \mathbf{N}$ is a normal vector to the osculating plane. $\mathbf{R}'(t) = (2 - 2t, 2t, 2 + 2t).$

$|\mathbf{R}'(t)| = \sqrt{4(1-t)^2 + 4t^2 + 4(1+t)^2} = 2\sqrt{3t^2 + 2}.$ Thus, $\mathbf{T}(t) = \dfrac{1}{2\sqrt{3t^2 + 2}}(2-2t, 2t,$

$2+2t).$ Hence, $\mathbf{T}'(t) = \dfrac{1}{2\sqrt{3t^2 + 2}}(-2, 2, 2) - \dfrac{3}{2}\dfrac{t}{(3t^2 + 2)^{3/2}}(2-2t, 2t, 2+2t).$ At $t=1,$

$\mathbf{R}' = (0, 2, 4)$ and $\mathbf{T}' = \dfrac{1}{2\sqrt{5}}(-2, 2, 2) - \dfrac{3}{2}\dfrac{1}{5\sqrt{5}}(0, 2, 4) = \dfrac{1}{10\sqrt{5}}[5(-2, 2, 2) - 3(0, 2, 4)] =$

$\dfrac{1}{10\sqrt{5}}(-10, 4, -2) = \dfrac{1}{5\sqrt{5}}(-5, 2, -1).$ Since $\mathbf{T}$ is parallel to $\mathbf{R}'$ and $\mathbf{N}$ is parallel to $\mathbf{T}'$, a

normal vector to the osculating plane is given by $(0, 2, 4) \times (-5, 2, -1) = (-10, -20, 10) =$ $-10(1, 2, -1).$ Therefore, an equation of the osculating plane at $(1, 1, 3)$ is $(x-1) +$ $2(y-1) - (z-3) = 0,$ or equivalently, $x + 2y - z = 0.$

487. The osculating plane is the plane determined by $\mathbf{T}$ and $\mathbf{N}.$ Let $\mathbf{D} = \mathbf{R}' \times \mathbf{R}''.$ Now

$\mathbf{T} = \dfrac{\mathbf{R}'}{|\mathbf{R}'|}.$ Hence, $\mathbf{T}' = \dfrac{1}{|\mathbf{R}'|}\mathbf{R}'' + \dfrac{d}{dt}\left(\dfrac{1}{|\mathbf{R}'|}\right)\mathbf{R}'.$ Since $\mathbf{D} \cdot \mathbf{R}' = 0$ and $\mathbf{D} \cdot \mathbf{R}'' = 0,$ it fol-

lows that $\mathbf{D} \cdot \mathbf{T}' = 0.$ Thus, $\mathbf{D}$ is perpendicular to $\mathbf{R}'$ and to $\mathbf{T}'$ and, therefore, to $\mathbf{T}$ and to $\mathbf{N}.$ Hence, $\mathbf{D}$ is a normal vector to the osculating plane.

488. $\kappa = \left|\dfrac{d\mathbf{T}}{ds}\right|.$ First, $\mathbf{R}' = (\cos t, -\sin t, t), \dfrac{ds}{dt} = |\mathbf{R}'(t)| = \sqrt{1+t^2},$ and $\mathbf{T} = \dfrac{1}{1+t^2}(\cos t, -$

$\sin t, t).$ Hence, $\dfrac{d\mathbf{T}}{dt} = \dfrac{1}{\sqrt{1+t^2}}(-\sin t, -\cos t, 1) - \dfrac{t}{(1+t^2)^{3/2}}(\cos t, -\sin t, t).$ At $t = 0, \dfrac{ds}{dt} =$

1 and $\dfrac{d\mathbf{T}}{dt} = (0, -1, 1);$ therefore, $\dfrac{d\mathbf{T}}{ds} = \dfrac{d\mathbf{T}/dt}{ds/dt} = (0, -1, 1)$ and $\kappa = \left|\dfrac{d\mathbf{T}}{ds}\right| = \sqrt{2}.$

489. $\mathbf{R}' = |\mathbf{R}'|\mathbf{T}.$ Hence, $\mathbf{R}'' = \left[\dfrac{d}{dt}(|\mathbf{R}'|)\right]\mathbf{T} + |\mathbf{R}'|\,(\mathbf{T}').$ Note that $\mathbf{T}' = \dfrac{ds}{dt}\left(\dfrac{d\mathbf{T}}{ds}\right) =$

$|\mathbf{R}'|\kappa\mathbf{N}.$ Hence, $\mathbf{R}'' = \left[\dfrac{d}{dt}(|\mathbf{R}'|)\right]\mathbf{T} + \kappa|\mathbf{R}'|^2\,\mathbf{N}.$ Therefore, $\mathbf{R}' \times \mathbf{R}'' = |\mathbf{R}'|\mathbf{T} \times$

$\left\{\left[\dfrac{d}{dt}(|\mathbf{R}'|)\right]\mathbf{T} + \kappa|\mathbf{R}'|^2\,\mathbf{N}\right\} = |\mathbf{R}'|\left[\dfrac{d}{dt}(|\mathbf{R}'|)\right](\mathbf{T} \times \mathbf{T}) + \kappa|\mathbf{R}'|^3\,(\mathbf{T} \times \mathbf{N}) = \kappa|\mathbf{R}'|^3\,(\mathbf{T} \times \mathbf{N}).$

Since $|\mathbf{T} \times \mathbf{N}| = 1,$ it follows that $|\mathbf{R}' \times \mathbf{R}''| = \kappa|\mathbf{R}'|^3.$

490. By definition, if $\mathbf{F}(x, y, z) = (f(x, y, z), g(x, y, z), h(x, y, z))$, then div $\mathbf{F} = \dfrac{\partial f}{\partial x} + \dfrac{\partial g}{\partial y} + \dfrac{\partial h}{\partial z}$. In this case, div $\mathbf{F} = y + z + x$.

491. Curl $\mathbf{F} = \left(\dfrac{\partial h}{\partial y} - \dfrac{\partial g}{\partial z}, \dfrac{\partial f}{\partial z} - \dfrac{\partial h}{\partial x}, \dfrac{\partial g}{\partial x} - \dfrac{\partial f}{\partial y} \right)$, or more vividly,

$$\text{curl } \mathbf{F} = \nabla \times \mathbf{F} = \begin{vmatrix} \mathbf{i} & \mathbf{j} & \mathbf{k} \\ \dfrac{\partial}{\partial x} & \dfrac{\partial}{\partial y} & \dfrac{\partial}{\partial z} \\ f & g & h \end{vmatrix}$$

where $\nabla = \left(\dfrac{\partial}{\partial x}, \dfrac{\partial}{\partial y}, \dfrac{\partial}{\partial z} \right)$.

492. Curl $\mathbf{F} = \left(\dfrac{\partial(xy)}{\partial y} - \dfrac{\partial(xz)}{\partial z}, \dfrac{\partial(yz)}{\partial z} - \dfrac{\partial(xy)}{\partial x}, \dfrac{\partial(xz)}{\partial x} - \dfrac{\partial(yz)}{\partial y} \right) = (x - x, y - y, z - z)$

$= (0, 0, 0) = 0$.

493. $\nabla f = (f_x, f_y, f_z)$. Hence, div $\nabla f = \dfrac{\partial}{\partial x}(f_x) + \dfrac{\partial}{\partial y}(f_y) + \dfrac{\partial}{\partial z}(f_z) = f_{xx} + f_{yy} + f_{zz}$.

494. $\nabla f = (f_x, f_y, f_z)$. Then curl $\nabla f = (f_{zy} - f_{yz}, f_{xz} - f_{zx}, f_{yx} - f_{xy}) = (0, 0, 0) = 0$. Here, we used the equality of the mixed second partial derivatives.

495. Curl $\mathbf{F} = \left(\dfrac{\partial h}{\partial y} - \dfrac{\partial g}{\partial z}, \dfrac{\partial f}{\partial z} - \dfrac{\partial h}{\partial x}, \dfrac{\partial g}{\partial x} - \dfrac{\partial f}{\partial y} \right)$. So div curl $\mathbf{F} = \dfrac{\partial}{\partial x}\left(\dfrac{\partial h}{\partial y} - \dfrac{\partial g}{\partial z} \right) +$

$\dfrac{\partial}{\partial y}\left(\dfrac{\partial f}{\partial z} - \dfrac{\partial h}{\partial x} \right) + \dfrac{\partial}{\partial z}\left(\dfrac{\partial g}{\partial x} - \dfrac{\partial f}{\partial y} \right) = h_{yx} - g_{zx} + f_{zy} - h_{xy} + g_{xz} - f_{yz} = (h_{yx} - h_{xy}) + (g_{xz} - g_{zx}) +$

$(f_{zy} - f_{yz}) = 0 + 0 + 0 = 0$.

496. Let $\mathbf{F} = (\phi(x, y, z), \psi(x, y, z), \eta(x, y, z))$. Then div $(f\mathbf{F}) = \text{div } (f\phi, f\psi, f\eta) = f\phi_x + f_x\phi + f\psi_y + f_y\psi + f\eta_z + f_z\eta = f(\phi_x + \psi_y + \eta_z) + (f_x, f_y, f_z) \cdot (\phi, \psi, \eta) = f \text{ div } \mathbf{F} + \nabla f \cdot \mathbf{F}$.

497. $f\mathbf{F} = (f\phi, f\psi, f\eta)$. Hence, curl $(f\mathbf{F}) = ((f\eta)_y - (f\psi)_z, (f\phi)_z - (f\eta)_x, (f\psi)_x - (f\phi)_y) = (f\eta_y + f_y\eta - f\psi_z - f_z\psi, f\phi_z + f_z\phi - f\eta_x - f_x\eta, f\psi_x + f_x\psi - f\phi_y - f_y\phi) = (f\eta_y - f\psi_z, f\phi_z - f\eta_x, f\psi_x - f\phi_y) + (f_y\eta - f_z\psi, f_z\phi - f_x\eta, f_x\psi - f_y\phi) = f \text{ curl } (\phi, \psi, \eta) + (f_x, f_y, f_z) \times (\phi, \psi, \eta) = f \text{ curl } \mathbf{F} + \nabla f \times \mathbf{F}$.

498. $\mathbf{F} \times \mathbf{G} = (g\eta - h\psi, \, h\phi - f\eta, \, f\psi - g\phi)$. Hence, div $(\mathbf{F} \times \mathbf{G}) = (g\eta - h\psi)_x + (h\phi - f\eta)_y + (f\psi - g\phi)_z = g\eta_x + g_x\eta - h\psi_x - h_x\psi + h\phi_y + h_y\phi - f\eta_y - f_y\eta + f\psi_z + f_z\psi - g\phi_z - g_z\phi = \phi(h_y - g_z) + \psi(f_z - h_x) + \eta(g_x - f_y) + f(\psi_z - \eta_y) + g(\eta_x - \phi_z) + h(\phi_y - \psi_x) =$ $\mathbf{G} \cdot \text{curl } \mathbf{F} - \mathbf{F} \cdot \text{curl } \mathbf{G}$.

499. $W = \int_{\mathscr{C}} \mathbf{F} \cdot \mathbf{T} \, ds = \int_0^1 \mathbf{F} \cdot \mathbf{R}'(t) \, dt$

$$= \int_0^1 [(t^3)(1) + (t^5)(2t) + (t^4)(3t^2)] \, dt$$

$$= \frac{1}{4} + \frac{5}{7} = \frac{27}{28}.$$

500. $\displaystyle\int_{\mathscr{C}} y \, dx + x \, dy = \int_a^b \left(y \frac{dx}{dt} + x \frac{dy}{dt} \right) dt = \int_a^b \frac{d}{dx}(xy) \, dt = xy \Big]_a^b = x(b)\,y(b) - x(a)\,y(a)$.